THE BUILDINGS OF ENGLAND
FOUNDING EDITOR: NIKOLAUS PEVSNER
JOINT EDITORS: BRIDGET CHERRY
AND JUDY NAIRN

CORNWALL
NIKOLAUS PEVSNER AND ENID RADCLIFFE

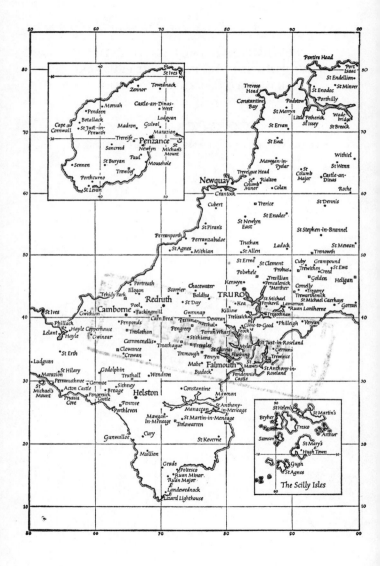

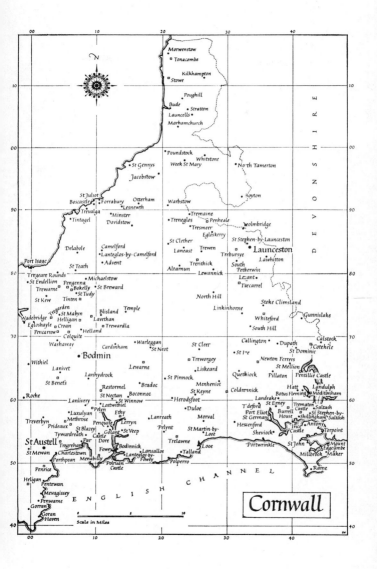

Cornwall

THE BUILDINGS OF ENGLAND

Cornwall

BY

NIKOLAUS PEVSNER

★

REVISED BY ENID RADCLIFFE

PENGUIN BOOKS

PENGUIN BOOKS

Published by the Penguin Group
Penguin Books Ltd, 80 Strand, London WC2R ORL, England
Penguin Putnam Inc., 375 Hudson Street, New York, New York 10014, USA
Penguin Books Australia Ltd, Ringwood, Victoria, Australia
Penguin Books Canada Ltd, 10 Alcorn Avenue, Toronto, Ontario, Canada M4V 3B2
Penguin Books India (P) Ltd, 11, Community Centre,
Panchsheel Park, New Delhi – 110 017, India
Penguin Books (NZ) Ltd, Cnr Rosedale and Airborne Roads, Albany, Auckland, New Zealand
Penguin Books (South Africa) (Pty) Ltd, 5 Watkins Street,
Denver Ext 4, Johannesburg 2094, South Africa

Penguin Books Ltd, Registered Offices: 80 Strand, London WC2R ORL, England

—

First published 1951
Second edition 1970
Reprinted 1977, 1983, 1990, 1996, 2000, 2001

—

ISBN 0 14 071001 9

—

Second edition copyright © Alec Clifton-Taylor,
Nikolaus Pevsner, Enid Radcliffe and
Derek Simpson, 1970
All rights reserved

—

Made and printed in Great Britain
by Butler & Tanner Ltd, Frome and London
Set in Monotype Plantin

TO LOLA
who drove the car

CONTENTS

Map References

★

The numbers printed in italic type in the margin against the place names in the gazetteer of the book indicate the position of the place in question on the index map (pages 2–3), which is divided into sections by the 10-kilometre reference lines of the National Grid. The reference given here omits the two initial letters (formerly numbers) which in a full grid reference refer to the 100-kilometre squares into which the country is divided. The first two numbers indicate the *western* boundary, and the last two the *southern* boundary, of the 10-kilometre square in which the place in question is situated. For example Gunnislake (reference 4070) will be found in the 10-kilometre square bounded by grid lines 40 (on the *west*) and 50, and 70 (on the *south*) and 80; Falmouth (reference 8030) in the square bounded by grid lines 80 (on the *west*) and 90, and 30 (on the *south*) and 40.

The map contains all those places, whether towns, villages, or isolated buildings, which are the subject of separate entries in the text.

FOREWORD

*The extracting and compiling of most of the facts on which the
following pages are based was done by Dr R. Schilling. In addition
I was greatly helped by the photographic collection of the National
Buildings Record, by Mr H. S. Goodhart-Rendel's manuscript notes
on Victorian churches which he kindly allowed me to use, and by
Sir Thomas Kendrick's manuscript notes on Victorian glass, which
he was good enough to place at my disposal. Moreover, by the
courtesy of the Ministry of Housing and Local Government, who
have a statutory duty to compile lists of buildings of architectural or
historic interest, I have had access to unpublished lists and much
other information collected by the Chief Investigator of the Ministry
and his staff. I have marked all additions from the Ministry lists by
the sign* MHLG *and put them into brackets. Similarly, information
coming from Mr Goodhart-Rendel is marked* GR, *and information
from Sir Thomas Kendrick* TK. *The abbreviation* NMR *refers to the
National Monuments Record.*

*Many rectors and vicars of churches and owners of houses had to
be pestered with letters for information on minor points, and most of
them have been sympathetic. Some have gone to much trouble in the
interests of this book.*

*The author and publisher would be grateful to any user of this
book for having any errors or omissions pointed out to them in as
much detail as possible.*

FOREWORD TO THE SECOND EDITION

Cornwall was the first volume of the whole series of The Buildings of England. *It came out in 1951. We were all beginners at the job then. I did not know about the cross-reference index of the Society of Antiquaries and a rather less systematic use was made of the lists of buildings compiled by the Ministry of Housing and Local Government. Moreover, I wrote the prehistory entries myself, totally secondhand. Now all these helps have been used for the second edition, and the prehistory has been written completely afresh by Mr Derek Simpson. There is in addition a special section on building materials supplied by Mr Alec Clifton-Taylor (to whom I am also grateful for many corrections and suggestions throughout the book). All the extensive work for the revising of and adding to the gazetteer has been done by Mrs Enid Radcliffe.*

My thanks are due to many who wrote on errors and omissions, and specially to Mr G. M. Trinick, who sent so many new entries that these have gone in all marked G M T; *to Mr Alec Clifton-Taylor, to whom I have referred in the preceding paragraph; and to Mr G. W. Copeland, Dr Athelstane Hill, Dr Royston Lambert, Mr P. Laws, Canon C. J. Meyer, and Mr H. J. Willmott. Helpful information has also been received from Mr T. Attlee, Mr W. G. V. Balchin, Mr Giles Blomfield, Mrs Margaret Budd, the Rev. C. K. Burton, Mr H. Dalton Clifford, Mr Howard Colvin, Brigadier G. Edward-Collins, Mrs E. Ettlinger, Mr Cecil Farthing, Mr H. P. R. Finberg, Mr T. W. French, Mr H. C. Gilbert, Town Architect of St Ives, Mr E. de St P. Gotch, Mr F. A. Greenhill, Mr Geoffrey Grigson, Mr R. N. Hadcock, Mr D. K. Hill, Mr H. W. Hill, Lady Mander, Mr Frank Michell, Mr A. S. B. New, Mr P. J. Oldfield, Mr D. M. Palliser, Mr E. C. Rouse, Mr T. Rundell, Mr W. Talbot, Mr Nicholas Taylor, Professor Charles Thomas, Dr Paul Thompson, Mr E. J. Whur, and Mr M. Windeatt. The County Architect, Mr Alan J. Groves, gave much assistance, as did the following librarians: Mr S. R. Fry of Bodmin, Mr A. D. Childs of Camborne and Redruth, Miss Rosalynde Beckett of Falmouth, Mr Paul Bolitho of Liskeard, Mr John H. I. Cable of Penzance, Mr P. C. Stone of St Austell, Mr J. K. Mealor of St Ives, and Mrs W. M. Becketts and her staff of the Cornwall County Library at Truro. I am also grateful to Mr John Betjeman for permission to quote Chacewater from* Collins Guide to English Parish Churches, *and also Polperro from the* Shell Guide to Cornwall *(2nd ed.) and Marazion from the first edition of the same.*

Finally, I must once more stress that mention of a house in the gazetteer does not mean that it is open to the public.

INTRODUCTION

CORNWALL possesses little of the highest aesthetic quality though much that is lovable and much that is moving. Nearly always, however, in analysing one's emotions, one will find that what is remembered is more the setting of architecture than architecture itself. While thus the county has more to reward the picturesque traveller than the architectural scholar, the archaeologist and antiquarian, on the other hand, will find more to interest him than in many more central areas.

No county except Wiltshire is as rich as Cornwall in pre-historic remains. They are described in a separate introduction (p. 25). The inscribed milestone exhibited in St Hilary church and dating from the time of Constantine takes us into the centuries of EARLY CHRISTIANITY. The subject of INSCRIBED STONES is altogether not without interest in Cornwall. There are about twenty-five of these preserved, ranging from a c6 or c7 specimen at Hayle (*see* Phillack) with a Latin Christian inscription to indubitably Saxon examples of the c10 (St Cleer; cf. the church bell at Lanhydrock with the inscription, 'Aethelstan sumpta anima sua').

SAXON invasions of Cornwall from Wessex began in the early c8. The conquest was achieved by King Egbert between 815 and 838. What he thus subdued was a Celtic Christian civilization of great spiritual power. Christianity had probably not long survived the withdrawal of the Romans. Renewed missionary work was therefore necessary, and this was done from Ireland and Wales, chiefly in the c5 and c6. Ireland was then evolving its own strictly monastic type of Christianity, influenced by Egypt and Syria more than by Rome. Such monuments as the stone cells and chapels of Glendalough or the Book of Durrow remain to testify to the vigour and the asceticism of Irish Christianity. The 'Coming of the Saints' to Cornwall is recorded for us in a whole hagiological literature, colourful and fantastic – with the stories of the great saints from Wales such as Petroc, Carantoc, Gulval, Madron, of the Welsh King Brychan and his three wives, his concubines, and his forty-nine children, all saints (for example Cleer, Morwenna, Kenya, Tudy, Nectan), with the Irish saints Breaca, Etha, Germochus, Gwithianus, Uni, and others,

with St Nun, mother of the Welsh St David and cousin of
St Cuby, and with Gunwalloe, who came from Brittany, which
had been colonized and christianized from Cornwall about 450.

Archaeological evidence of the presence of these saintly Celts
is not entirely missing. The stone cell of St Piran *in sabulo*
survives, not as telling visually as it is historically. A similar cell
was found in the dunes near St Gocianus in the C19 but has
since been recaptured by the sand, and the ground plan of one
on Tintagel rock is also known.

These tiny buildings are amongst the oldest Christian structures in England, of the same type evidently as the more
numerous and better preserved Irish chapels or cells. To conjure
up the Cornwall of King Arthur we have even less to help us,
except the grandiose scenery of Tintagel. It was Geoffrey of
Monmouth in 1147 who for the first time made the castle the
centre of Arthurian legends. Earlier versions call his favourite
seat Kelly-wic, and this has tentatively been identified with the
late Charles Henderson with Kellybury (Kelliwic) near
Egloshayle.

The inscribed stones do not help much in the resuscitation
of Celtic Cornwall, although the existence of a few with inscriptions in that curious script known as Ogam or Ogham is telling
enough (Lewannick, St Clement, St Kew). Then there are the
ubiquitous CROSSES (there are well over three hundred preserved
in churchyards, in churches, in the grounds and gardens of
private houses, and along the roads). They more than anything
else make us ever remember a civilization to which the cross
meant as much as and no more than those originally heathen,
frantic interlacings which we breathlessly and vainly try to
follow. These knots and tangles are familiar from Irish illumina-
tion and Irish crosses, and the dependence of Cornwall on
Ireland cannot be doubted. The purposes of the crosses both in
Cornwall and across the sea were probably the same: to mark
sacred sites, to commemorate the dead, guide the faithful to a
church, and simply to record boundaries. The origin of the
crosses may be in standing stones, then in inscribed stones with
commemorative inscriptions, and then in stones with inscriptions with signs of the cross or the XP monogram (e.g. Phillack,
St Just-in-Penwith). Documentary evidence is scarce and uncertain. An C8 life of St Samson tells how, on his missionary
voyage through Cornwall, he smashed an idol and replaced it
by a stone found in the neighbourhood and marked by him with
a cross. The Doniert Stone near St Cleer, no doubt the fragment

of an elaborately decorated cross, is supposed to refer to a King of Cornwall who died in 875, and King Edgar of Wessex mentions in a charter the Cristes-mace by the church of Perran-in-the-Sand (*see* St Piran's) which is probably the cross still standing close to the ruin of the chapel. Specially rich in crosses are the parishes of Lanivet, Sancreed, and Wendron. Amongst the best crosses those of Cardinham, Sancreed, and others will be found mentioned. The largest of all is at Mylor, the most elaborately decorated (with a figure of Christ crucified) at 35 Lanherne, Mawgan-in-Pydar. The wheel-cross was the most universally accepted type before the Conquest. Local variations can in several cases be distinguished by the student. The coming of the Saxons does not seem to have broken the tradition.

Saxon buildings or parts of buildings are nowhere preserved. Saxon place-names, however, are frequent in the E (Kilkhampton, Michaelstow, Otterham, Stoke Climsland). Moreover King Egbert gave to the Saxon Bishop of Sherborne three large estates in Cornwall: Pawton and Kellywic in the lands around Wadebridge, and Lawhitton (including Launceston). Finally Aethelstan established a special Cornish see at St Germans.

St Germans possesses indeed to this day (if in a fragmentary form) the most ambitious medieval church of Cornwall. It is, however, in its earliest visible parts wholly NORMAN, with the richest portal in the county, a two-tower façade, aisles, and a 21 clerestory whose windows, most oddly, were placed above the spandrels and not the apexes of the arcade, a feature taken up by a group of Cornish masons in the C14 (Lostwithiel, Fowey, Callington). In all this, and in scale, St Germans is exceptional.

Of Norman MONASTIC HOUSES in Cornwall it is impossible to speak from more than the scantiest remains. The most noteworthy were the three priories of Bodmin, Tywardreath, and Launceston, all three powerful, and no doubt extensive and ambitious in their buildings. The Norman parish church in Cornwall was as a rule a much simpler affair. Tintagel gives the 10b best idea of it: cruciform, unaisled, and with a tower over the crossing. In other cases we also find W towers (St Gennys), or towers attached to one of the transepts or above one of the transepts (Bodmin, Mawgan-in-Pydar, Blisland, Saltash, Duloe, Veryan, Lawhitton, etc., altogether about a dozen). Aisled Norman parish churches were not absent either, the most usual form of pier being apparently circular (St Germans, Morwen- 17a stow, St Breward). Some chancel aisles were built to accommodate the more numerous clergy of collegiate as against parish churches (Crantock, St Buryan). Where Norman churches were replaced during the following centuries, decorated DOORWAYS were quite often preserved (Morwenstow, Kilkhampton, Cury, St Martin-by-Looe), and FONTS, it seems, nearly always. Cornwall thus possesses Norman work in about 140 churches and about 111 fonts. Some fonts are of primeval rudeness, others surprisingly monumental and elaborately adorned with heads or busts and animals or foliage motifs in relief. Cornish fonts fall clearly into groups and will be mentioned accordingly. The following are the most remarkable: Bodmin with five shafts, heads at the corners of the square bowl, and big ornamental motifs between, Altarnun with one shaft, faces at the corners and rosettes, etc., between, Fowey with a roughly hemispherical bowl and bands of decoration with crosses, saltire, etc., on it, and Egloshayle, of Purbeck marble, table-top shape, with shallow blank arcades as its only decoration.

The plain cruciform village church with tower over the crossing was carried on after the arrival of the GOTHIC style some time in the C13. St Anthony-in-Roseland is the best example (complete with crossing tower). Early Gothic arcades are rare (Crantock, St Austell, also perhaps St Minver). If the piers at St Keverne are really as early as the C13 we possess here the first example of a type which was going to be standardized in the late Middle Ages to an unparalleled extent.

For it is true that at least three-quarters of the old churches of Cornwall belong to one of three or four set types, down to such details as the profiles of piers, the mouldings of arches, and the buttressing of towers. These standard patterns are the same in Devon as in Cornwall. They were certainly established by 1400; but where they came from, and when they were introduced, is not yet sufficiently certain.

The standard Cornish PIER has a very elementary moulding evolved probably to avoid delicate detail in a county with so intractable a building material as granite. It consists of four attached shafts in the main axes and four hollows in the diagonals (*a*). The same pier type is one of the most frequent ones in Devon too. Square piers with four attached demi-shafts (*b*) are also often to be found in Cornwall. They seem to be of earlier introduction (St Veep, Stratton) even if they were carried into the C15 (Callington). Circular piers with four attached shafts or a similar-looking form with four major and four minor shafts appear occasionally too. Finally there are a dozen or so churches

with octagonal piers, developed straight from C13 precedent.
Some of the most prominent churches, however, have their own
exceptional shapes of piers (St Ives, Launceston, St Austell chancel aisle).

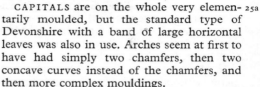

(a)

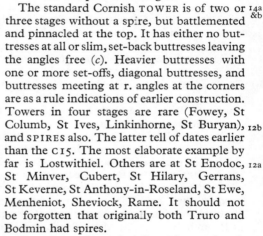

(b)

CAPITALS are on the whole very elemen- 25a
tarily moulded, but the standard type of
Devonshire with a band of large horizontal
leaves was also in use. Arches seem at first to
have had simply two chamfers, then two
concave curves instead of the chamfers, and
then more complex mouldings.

The standard Cornish TOWER is of two or 14a
three stages without a spire, but battlemented &b
and pinnacled at the top. It has either no buttresses at all or slim, set-back buttresses leaving
the angles free (c). Heavier buttresses with
one or more set-offs, diagonal buttresses, and
buttresses meeting at r. angles at the corners
are as a rule indications of earlier construction.
Towers in four stages are rare (Fowey, St
Columb, St Ives, Linkinhorne, St Buryan), 12b
and SPIRES also. The latter tell of dates earlier
than the C15. The most elaborate example by
far is Lostwithiel. Others are at St Enodoc, 12a
St Minver, Cubert, St Hilary, Gerrans,
St Keverne, St Anthony-in-Roseland, St Ewe,
Menheniot, Sheviock, Rame. It should not
be forgotten that originally both Truro and
Bodmin had spires.

To sum up, the typical Cornish C15 church
has a W tower, a nave with one or two aisles
as wide as the nave (if only one, the earlier
transept is usually preserved on the other
side), and a S porch or S and N porches. The
naves are long and run from W to E without any 19a
break in height at the beginning of the
chancel. Inside there are three wagon roofs 20
of equal height, open or ceiled. The only
division between nave and chancel is a rood
screen, often no longer in existence but generally proved by the survival of the stairway to
the rood loft. The contrast between the upright block of the
tower and the low horizontal blocks of nave and aisles is very

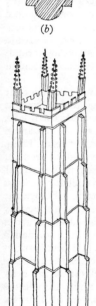

(c)

marked. It provides the most characteristic architectural motif
in Cornwall, whether the churches lie in a town or village, or on
11a their own on the hills, in exposed, windswept positions, or, also
11b on their own, in dips or close to creeks, sheltered by trees. It is a
peculiarity of Cornwall, of very ancient origin no doubt, that many
of the important towns had, until late in the Middle Ages, no
parish church inside their walls, but an older sanctuary outside,
a mile or more away. That applies for instance to Launceston,
Callington, Looe, Wadebridge.

In all these respects Cornish church architecture offers a
picture of unmistakable character and, especially for the C15 and
the early C16, of ever-recurring features. Before 1400 there was
much more variety. One small group of churches in particular is
18   worth studying. Its main representatives are Fowey and Lost-
&   withiel, and its characteristics (octagonal piers without any
12a capitals, and clerestory windows in line with the spandrels and
not the apexes of the arches) are odd and call for explanation.
Connexions with Brittany have been pointed out; priority should
probably be given to England, where piers without capitals
existed at Bristol and clerestory windows of the same peculiar
type at St Germans.

23a   To enjoy the DECORATED style of the C14 with its ogee
& b arches and its luxuriant crocketing one should go to St Germans
(s aisle), St Ives, St Michael Penkevil, Sheviock, and North Hill.

The PERPENDICULAR style meant a conscious reduction
after so much exuberance, in Cornwall as everywhere. Then,
however, after 1460, it seems, the county recovered its sense of
all-out decoration, a sense rooted in the Celtic past. The exteriors
13& of Bodmin, St Neot, St Mary Truro, and above all Launceston
24   are there to show this frenzy of ornamentation just before the
29b arrival of the Renaissance. In Cornish BENCH ENDS, a speciality
-31a most enjoyably studied at Launcells and Gorran, it even carries
29a on without any break into the Renaissance. Apart from bench
&   ends little sculpture need here be mentioned. The best work of
37
28   the early C14 is the Lostwithiel FONT, of the late C14 the carvings
36b in Catacleuse stone by the Master of St Endellion, of the early
C16 the PULPIT of Launceston. In wood the highest quality is
31b reached in the ROOD SCREENS of St Winnow, St Buryan,
&
32   St Ewe, St Levan.

PAINTING is not of high aesthetic merit, but the representations of the Warning to Sabbath-Breakers* (the tools which they

* Not Christ blessing the trades, as has been mistakenly suggested in the
past. (Information from Mr E. Clive Rouse)

use on Sundays are displayed round Christ's wounded body) are worth recording for other reasons (Breage, Lanivet, Poundstock, St Just-in-Penwith). For STAINED GLASS St Neot is of more than local importance. So much is preserved that a live impression can still be obtained of what light the coloured glass of the late Middle Ages gave to a church interior. Lesser examples of stained glass are at St Kew and St Winnow. The encaustic TILES of Launcells are among the most attractive church decoration in Cornwall. They are probably Barnstaple ware. Pre-Reformation BRASSES are few, the best at Antony (1420), others at Cardinham (c.1400), Lostwithiel (1423), etc. 34 33a &b

Pre-Reformation church plate is confined to one specimen (Morval); and one originally in domestic use (Bodmin). Of later plate much belongs to the 1570s, thanks to the introduction of a new type of cup for the laity by Queen Elizabeth. I have myself examined little plate in Cornwall, and what will be found mentioned is mostly based on extracts made by Mrs K. Michaelson from the three-volume photographic and descriptive catalogue kept in the Cathedral Library at Truro and kindly placed at our disposal. In plate, as in bench ends, stained glass, and indeed everything, it can be observed that the RENAISSANCE first appeared purely as an ornamental fashion. The best example of this early stage is Prior Vivian's tomb at Bodmin. 38

Of Vivian, the last head but one of Bodmin Priory, and his life we can form an unusually vivid picture, not only from Mr Rowse's pages in *Tudor Cornwall*, but also from what survives of his manor house at Rialton. Rialton is one of the comparatively few well preserved and ambitious C15 and early C16 HOUSES in Cornwall. Cotehele of course is the best of them. At Trecarrel the hall and chapel remain, though in a sad state. Shillingham also has a small chapel. 51 48-50

Medieval MILITARY ARCHITECTURE is chiefly represented by a small group of eminently interesting round castles. Restormel is the most perfect of them, classic C13, Trematon the one with the most extensive remains. Launceston is not now architecturally impressive any longer, and at Tintagel the unforgettable effect of the castle on its two cliffs is one of setting entirely. 47 53a 48 45

The same picturesque rather than strictly architectural appeal is what makes one take to the Cornish COTTAGE, whitewashed with a grey groated roof. Anybody familiar with Cornwall has his own favourites both of the agricultural and the fishing type. Along the coast are many picturesque FISHING VILLAGES – not 7a & 10a 6b & 9 all of them mentioned in this book – but inland the most characteristic pattern is of isolated farmsteads and isolated churches, not of villages proper.

TUDOR Cornwall, re-evoked so admirably by Mr Rowse, begins in Cornish architecture with Henry VIII's fortifications, chiefly St Mawes and Pendennis, buildings of considerable architectural merit and even greater importance in the history of military architecture in England. The LATER TUDOR and the STUART generations are not specially copiously represented in 56a Cornwall. A few greater HOUSES deserve attention, chiefly Ince &b and Lanhydrock. Most probably of the early C17, Ince is a square brick building of a rare type familiar from Osterley Park and Syon House near London, and not at all locally rooted. Mount Edgcumbe belonged to the same type, but was so badly damaged in the Second World War that it can no longer be fully 54 appreciated. Lanhydrock has all the quality of a grand Jacobean & style, even if completed only in the 1650s. In its lush setting it is 55 the most rewarding of all Cornish mansions. Elizabethan on a 52 smaller scale appears at its best at Trerice. The classical style arrived late. Church MONUMENTS will be found amazingly conservative, the Elizabethan and Jacobean type with two figures kneeling opposite each other across a prayer desk being carried 39a on right into the C18 (for example St Tudy † 1659, St Martin-by-Looe, 1678, St Mellion † 1651 and † 1711). The best collection of BRASSES is that of the Arundells of Mawgan-in-Pydar. Two of them are palimpsests of Flemish C14 brasses. The SLATE 44a PLATES of Cornwall are *Volkskunst*, whether they date from the C16 or C17 or C18. They form a Cornish speciality always delightful, but so ubiquitous that justice cannot be done to them in a book such as this. Slate slabs in churchyards especially have been neglected. Their discovery must be left to the individual visitor. A paper on them by Eric Brown and Enid Everard was published in *The Architectural Review*, vol. 95, 1944.

The first CHURCH built AFTER THE REFORMATION was the Church of King Charles the Martyr at Falmouth, begun in 1662 and still Gothic in some of its external detail even if provided 19b with a grand giant order of columns inside. The dedication is characteristic; Cornwall had been one of the most Royalist counties of England, and the Royal Arms, modelled or painted, which appear in so many Cornish churches are a token of grati-tude of Charles II to those parishes which had been loyal. A letter of thanks written by Charles I in 1643 is also recorded in churches in one way or another. GEORGIAN churches are few and far between: Helston and Redruth, and then, after 1800, Penzance, are perhaps the most noteworthy. The only Georgian HOUSE in the grand manner is Antony; of granite and con- 57a sequently very sparse in its detail. Many on the other hand are 58 the minor Georgian houses in town and country. Lemon Street 59b at Truro is a perfect example of a Georgian street of unified 6a frontages, the Assembly Rooms at Truro a sign of the gracious 59a civilization in an English country town about 1770. Pretty early Gothic Revival houses can be seen at Tregenna, St Ives, and inside Trematon Castle. But the earliest sign of the coming of the Gothic taste is the conversion of some rooms on St Michael's Mount in the 1740s.

Georgian funeral MONUMENTS, though not rare, are on the whole disappointing. There is little to compare with the grand style of *Rysbrack*'s Eliot Monument at St Germans. He worked 42 more modestly at St Michael Penkevil. Other noteworthy C18 monuments are at Launceston, 1731, Egloshayle † 1735, St Ewe 41 † 1737, Probus † 1766. Of the popular sculptors of 1800 and after 43 *Wilton*, *Nollekens*, *Bacon*, *Westmacott*, *Chantrey*, are all re-presented. Monuments entirely of *Coade* stone, that terracotta-like material with which mechanical production of art begins in England, exist at St Michael Caerhays and Lawhitton.

It was only in the early NINETEENTH CENTURY that the landed aristocracy and gentry of Cornwall began to rebuild 57b HOUSES on a large scale (a move no doubt due to better com- 60 munications with London). The Earls of Falmouth rebuilt their romantic castellated mansion of Tregothnan and obtained the 61 services of *Wilkins* for it. He also built Pentillie for the Tillies, whereas Caerhayes, equally picturesque, is an early work of 62a *John Nash*. In the Grecian taste, on the other hand, is Tre-warthenick by *Henry Harrison* (of London), and Trelissick by 62b *P. F. Robinson* (of Leamington). The most remarkable C19 CHURCH is of course Truro Cathedral, designed by *J. L. Pearson* 15 in 1880, though some of *G. E. Street*'s early works in the county (Par, 1848, St Faith's House of Mercy, Lostwithiel, 1864) are perhaps aesthetically more interesting. Truro was the first cathedral for Cornwall to possess after the Cornish see of St Germans had been deserted in 1050. It is important for an under-standing of architecture in Cornwall to remember that no cathedral existed (and that no big city existed). The largest town, Camborne with Redruth, has only about 37,000 inhabitants. The whole population of the county is 356,000, spread over an area of 870,000 acres. Compare this, say, with the 530,000 acres and the population of 964,000 in, say, Nottinghamshire, and you will at once realize the resulting differences. To describe 2a LANDSCAPE is not the job of this book; but the predominantly &b, rural character of Cornwall, the rocky coasts, the wide and 3b, 6b, deep estuaries of many rivers with their creeks and lush vege- 7b tation, the sublime bleakness of the moors, the inviting leafy shade in dips and coves, all this influences siting, if not always building. Industry also, depending on the geology and geo- graphy of the countryside, has contributed to the visual scene, chiefly with the hundreds of now mostly decaying tin mines, 4 their typical chimney and engine-house pattern appearing in most landscapes, from Botallack stretching its gallery far out under the sea to the bare top of Kit Hill near Callington. A curious contrast to these picturesque ruins, often overgrown with creepers, is formed by the sheer white cones of the china- 3a clay workings creating an astronomical landscape in the area N of St Austell Bay. The deserted slate quarries on the way down to Tintagel are equally unearthly and impressive. At Delabole, on the other hand, slate quarrying is still carried on on a scale larger than anywhere else in England.* The granite and serpentine quarries of Cornwall also keep busy. Their yield is used by the builders of the districts as a matter of course. Slate hanging has been a Cornish speciality popular since the C18. Granite came in seriously in the C15 when, cut into regular blocks, it became the material for whole churches or church towers. The very elementary profiles of piers in churches also may have been adopted so universally because granite did not permit much *finesse* of moulding. Other stones in use in Cornwall are Venter- gan, Tartan Down (St Germans), Polyphant (Launceston), and Hicks Grey Mill stone (most Norman fonts) in the E, Pentewan (St Austell) in the S, Serpentine around the Lizard and Tintagel (Tintagel Green stone), and the blue Catacleuse around Padstow. Brick is rare and occurs chiefly in the SE corner. Half-timbering also is not a Cornish habit.

After this synopsis of what Cornwall has to offer to those in sympathy with architecture and art, something must now be said about the way in which in the following pages facts and comments are set out. The information imparted is based chiefly on the following books which were extracted and digested by Mrs Schilling. For churches, C. J. Cox's *County Churches in Cornwall*, 1912, E. H. Sedding's *Norman Architecture in Cornwall*, 1909,

* A separate introduction to building materials by Mr Alec Clifton-Taylor appears on pp. 29–34.

and Charles Henderson's *Cornish Church Guide*, Truro, 1925, contain gratifyingly much and are carefully done. Only on development and questions relating to Cornish in comparison with other English styles and details they are somewhat disappointing. I have, I think, personally visited all but two of the churches of Cornwall built before 1830. I cannot say the same, however, when it comes to houses of architectural merit. There printed information is scanty and haphazard, and I had to rely, before arriving on the spot, on Sedding's notes in the book mentioned above, on *Country Life*, some picture books and gazetteers of the early C19, the Ordnance Survey maps and their marking of medieval remains, Kelly's *Directory*, and the *Complete Parochial History of the County of Cornwall* (4 vols., 1867–72; by J. Polsoe).

As regards more special literature, information has chiefly been obtained from the following: for Crosses from: A. G. Langdon, *Old Cornish Crosses*, 1896; for Brasses from: E. H. W. Dunkin, *Monumental Brasses of Cornwall*, 1882; for Bridges from: C. Henderson and H. Coates, *Old Cornish Bridges and Streams*, 1928; for everything regarding the Scilly Isles from: B. H. St J. O'Neil: *Ancient Monuments of the Isles of Scilly*, 1949.

Further literature to which we have had access for the second edition includes *The Cornishman's House* by V. M. and F. J. Chesher, 1968, which deals with the development of Cornish domestic architecture up to the C18 and has been used here for medieval houses and one or two C17 ones; and *Cornish Engine Houses: A Pictorial Survey*, Truro, 1967, and *Cornish Engine Houses: A Second Pictorial Survey*, Truro, 1968, by H. G. Ordish, though engine houses etc. have not been dealt with in any great number or detail in this new edition.

However, in spite of whatever general and special literature and other facilities may have been used, the result is, I know, still very inadequate.

PREHISTORY

BY DEREK SIMPSON

As remarked on p. 15, Cornwall is one of the few counties in England which can match Wiltshire in the wealth and diversity of its prehistoric remains. Geologically part of the Highland Zone of Britain, the readily available stone for building has also ensured the survival of many structures which elsewhere in the south were constructed of wood and of which only the ground plans of pits and postholes survive. Coupled with this is the fact that many of the structures occur in areas of great natural beauty which adds to the pleasure of visiting prehistoric sites in the county. Unlike Wiltshire however there is not the same long tradition of antiquarian research, fieldwork, and excavation stretching over the past two centuries, so that any account of the prehistory is necessarily tentative until further work has been done on the many surviving sites. Nowhere is this more evident than in the complex period of the Cornish Iron Age.

The earliest traces of human activity belong to the period of the last glaciation. At Praa Sands near Penzance an occupation horizon with hearths has been located and evidence of Late Glacial settlement has also been recovered from Trevose Head, Godrevy, and Land's End. Early Post Glacial Mesolithic settlement (c. 5000–3000 B.C.) is represented by a number of sites adjacent to the coast, reflecting both the importance of fishing and the gathering of shell-fish in the economy and also the need to live close to the only natural sources of flint in the region in the form of beach pebbles. No structures have been found in association with these sites, which are simply temporary hunting camps marked by flint-working floors and hearths. The most characteristic tool from such sites is a microlithic flint blade blunted down one side and used as a barb in bone and wooden spear points.

Evidence for Early Neolithic settlement (c. 3200 B.C.) is slight. Some form of settlement appears to have existed at Carn Brea (Camborne). From this site come a series of wide-mouthed shouldered bowls and smooth profiled pots with elaborate 'trumpet' lugs which suggest a move from north-west France. This pottery was found beneath a series of Iron Age huts associated with the later fortifications. A similar Early Neolithic occupation layer may also exist at Gwithian Towans (Gwithian). The working of igneous rock for the manufacture of axe blades also begins during this early farming phase, and the products of the Cornish factories, which represent at least twelve different sources within the county, were traded as far north as Yorkshire, although the main weight of their distribution is in Cornwall and Wessex. The only other evidence for this phase is stray finds of flint tools unassociated with any form of permanent settlement.

The first surviving monuments in the county are the three henges, the Stripple Stones (Blisland), Castlewich (Callington), and Castilly (Luxulyan). The arrival of the builders of these sites can hardly have antedated the settlement of Beaker communities, introducing the rite of single grave burial beneath a round barrow or, less commonly, at the base of a standing stone (e.g. Try Farm, Gulval). Over a dozen Beakers are known from the county, the majority from stone cist graves. The one notable exception is the settlement site at Gwithian, where excavations have recovered the plan of a sub-rectangular house defined by post-holes within a light hurdlework fence. The axe factories continued to play a part in the economy of the Late Neolithic Cornwall; shaft-hole battle axes of Beaker type are known as stray finds in the county and occur in Beaker graves elsewhere in southern Britain.

Burial beneath a round barrow, frequently in a stone cist, continued as a feature of the Early and Middle Bronze Age (1650–1000 B.C.), but a diversity of tradition is now seen in the burial rites, both inhumation in the Beaker manner and cremation in an urn. The stone circles, which form a notable group of monuments in the county, must also belong to the earlier part of this period (e.g. The Nine Maidens, Zennor; The Hurlers, St Cleer) and again reflect at least partial continuity with the henge monuments. (At the Stripple Stones, Blisland for example a stone circle occurs inside the henge.) So too, on the available evidence, do the megalithic tombs, which fall into two major groups: a series of portal dolmens, large closed chambers with massive capstones set originally within circular or more rarely long mounds, concentrated in the Penwith area (e.g. Zennor Quoit; Lanyon Quoit); and the remarkable series of small undifferentiated passage graves or entrance graves in the Scilly Isles (e.g. Porth Mellan, St Mary's; Cruthers Hill, St Martin's). Few of the tombs in either group have been excavated, but the finds from the small percentage of sites both in Cornwall and Scilly which have been examined suggest a Late Neolithic or Early Bronze Age date at least for their continuing use if not for their construction. Trade in igneous rock for the manufacture of battle-axes continued (e.g. axes from barrows at Pelynt and Trevelgue), but a new and important role played by the area at this time was in the supply of tin for bronze manufacture. Cornwall now came within the cultural orbit and probably control of the rich Wessex Culture to the E, and a number of objects characteristic of the culture have been found in the county. The most remarkable are the corrugated gold Beaker from a barrow at Rillaton (Linkinhorne) which shows in its mode of manufacture links with the Aegean, and a bronze dagger of actual Mycenaean manufacture from one of the barrows in the Pelynt cemetery. Settlements of the period are few. The most important is the farm and field system at Gwithian. The fields are defined by banks and lynchets, within which the individual furrows produced in cross-ploughing and even spade-marks were still detectable.

The Late Bronze Age is represented by even fewer surviving monuments, although some Iron Age settlement sites (e.g. Bodrifty, Gulval) have produced evidence for a Late Bronze Age phase of occupation. The most striking evidence of human activity is metalworkers' hoards containing broken and worn objects, ingots, and new and unused tools and weapons. At Kenidjack Castle (St Just) just such a hoard of raw material was found in a hut belonging presumably to a metalsmith, and in a second hut at Trevisker (St Eval) a deposit of pebble tin ore, presumably from a stream working, was discovered.

There is little immediate change in the economy and settlement pattern with the arrival of the first iron-using groups (Iron Age A), probably in the C5 B.C. The newcomers lived in small oval or circular houses frequently clustering together into almost village-like communities with associated field systems. Continuity is expressed on such sites as Bodrifty, where the main Iron Age settlement appears to succeed a Bronze Age occupation. The small promontory fort at Maen Castle (Sennen) also belongs to this period, as may other of the numerous unexcavated sites of this type, although excavation does suggest a later date for the majority of the fortified sites in Cornwall. A return to the rite of inhumation burial is seen in the cemetery of stone cist graves at Harlyn Bay (St Merryn). Among the grave goods from this site are bronze brooches of Iberian type, emphasizing the Atlantic links established at this period and which were to continue throughout the rest of prehistory in the region. Such foreign contacts must in part be related to the export of Cornish tin, for which there is documentary evidence by the C2 B.C. It is from Atlantic Europe that the main body of La Tène (Iron Age B) groups settled in the South-West in the C2 and C3 B.C. The pottery suggests two sources for these newcomers. One pottery style is characterized by curvilinear and S-scroll ornament of a type more frequently found on metalwork. With this ware one can postulate a group of immigrants from Brittany. A second series of vessels with rows of S-shaped or duck-shaped stamps suggests an Iberian source (e.g. Chun Castle and Gurnards Head, Morvah). It is to these groups that one may attribute the majority of the diverse fortifications of the Iron Age in Cornwall. Some of the sites are simple clusters of huts enclosed within an earth and rubble bank (e.g. Trewardreva, Constantine) designed more to keep wild animals out of the settlement than as true forts. The curious downhill slope of the ramparts in another series of sites (e.g. Tregeare, St Kew) and the slightness of their defences suggest a prime use as cattle kraals. Truly defensive on the other hand and a reflection of the unsettled conditions of the period are the massive stone defences of a site like Chun Castle and the complex fortifications in depth of the promontory forts developed to protect the occupants against sling warfare (e.g. The Rumps, St Minver; Gurnard's Head, Morvah).

Two other categories of monument must be mentioned at the end of this brief survey – courtyard houses and fogous. The former are peculiar to Cornwall and consist of a massive stone wall in which are a series of rooms and cells opening on to a central court. The best preserved group is the eight houses arranged on either side of a 'street' at Chysauster (Gulval). The majority of such courtyard houses form the later phases of complex Iron Age settlement sites and continued to be used and perhaps even constructed in the C4 A.D. Associated with courtyard houses in some cases (e.g. Chysauster; Carn Euny, Sancreed) are fogous. These are semi-subterranean galleries, frequently curved and provided with secondary chambers, roofed and lined with stone slabs. Their precise function is uncertain, but they probably served as some form of storehouses. As with the courtyard house, the fogou is an Iron Age development, but the type continued to be used throughout the period of the Roman occupation.

BUILDING MATERIALS

BY ALEC CLIFTON-TAYLOR

In its building materials, as in so many other ways, Cornwall is of all English counties the most untypical; and this must always have been so.

To begin with, there was the dearth of wood. Until the C16 most parts of the country were well, and some parts really thickly, wooded, and in consequence wood was a natural material of building construction. Cornwall was the exception. Here oaks were never plentiful and half-timbering is virtually unknown beyond the Tamar. Cottages and farm buildings, as in Devon,

West Somerset, and Dorset, were sometimes built of cob (or 'clob', as the local people called it); the usual recipe in Cornwall was two parts of mud and chopped straw to one of shilf, the name given to the little pieces of waste slate which are abundant in this county.

Brick was a late arrival. The only example of brickwork in Cornwall earlier than 1700 is Ince Castle near Saltash, dating probably from *c.*1630. Even today, by comparison with most English counties, brick is not greatly in evidence here, at any rate away from the immediate vicinity of Plymouth. There are no important Cornish brickworks.

Cornwall therefore is pre-eminently a county of stone buildings. In the rest of England this would mean either limestone or sandstone or both; here, primarily, it does not mean either. The predominant building materials of Cornwall are granite and slate.

The only English counties which can show any old buildings of granite are Cornwall, Devon, Cumberland, and Leicestershire; and the number of Cornish buildings in granite far outnumbers those of the other three combined. It is a stone of coarse grain, ill-suited to fine detail or to any sort of decorative enrichment: the colour is usually a light silver-grey, although at one time the Cheesewring quarry (on the E side of Bodmin Moor) yielded a pink granite as well. The principal Cornish granite areas are four: Bodmin Moor; the St Austell–Par neighbourhood; the region between Falmouth, Camborne, and Helston (in which the majority of the quarries were sited); and virtually the whole of the Land's End peninsula, s w from St Ives.

In these areas granite was in use for building even in the Bronze Age; and, in the two western ones in particular, almost everything earlier than 1800 is built of it. But usually – at least until the c 17 – the granite was not quarried; the task of cutting this intensely hard stone in pre-industrial days was dauntingly difficult. So the builders used what is known as moorstone – blocks lying about on the hills and moors just as the sarsens, or 'grey wethers', lay on the heaths and downs farther E. Before the end of the Middle Ages the masons had learnt how to dress their 'presents' of moorstone sufficiently well for rough church-building. At Altarnun, on the N side of Bodmin Moor, each pier, base and capital of the c 15 church consists of a single piece of worked-over moorstone. Humbler buildings, cottages and barns, were sometimes built without mortar. These blocks of granite, sometimes very large, were also useful for bridging streams and for walls, stiles, gate-posts and horse and cattle-troughs.

Gradually the method of dressing improved; yet in the C17 the granite was as often as not still moorstone, and the courses, if not random, were seldom quite regular. For regular coursing most builders in granite had to wait until the Georgian period: a refined example, with large keystones, is the Vicarage (23 North Street) at Lostwithiel.

It was, however, not until the C19 that granite quarrying became an important Cornish industry, principally to supply the demands of the engineers – for its compact, crystalline character and generally uniform structure renders granite exceptionally resistant to smoke pollution, and impervious to water. Hence the employment, for instance, of De Lank granite from Bodmin Moor for the Eddystone Lighthouse and Pelastine granite from Penryn for Tower Bridge and several of the other Thames bridges in London.

Slate, a metamorphic stone quarried from the Devonian rocks which cover a larger area of Cornwall than the granite, has also made an important contribution to the county's visual picture, in three different ways. First, as a walling material. Slate is quarried in slabs which fracture easily, and indeed quarrying was not always required, for beneath every rock-face quantities of it, lying about as scree, were available for the gathering. Slate-stone is entirely different from granite, and by no means as monumental. The pieces are very much smaller and tend to be wedge-shaped and rather long and thin, splitting to points, so that a good deal of mortar is necessary. Although slate-stone, too, could be very roughly dressed, the material was much less intractable than granite, and more colourful; the tints are warmer. Mixed with the greys are plenty of browns and fawns. Many Cornish walls contain both granite and slate-stone, for in some places the rocks are much intermingled.

More important still was the use of Cornish slate for roofs. Nearly all Cornish roofs, as well as many gravestones of the C18 and C19, are of local slate. But by water roofing slates were quite easily transportable, and research has now established beyond doubt that from the C12 onwards roofing slates from Cornwall (and Devon) were being despatched by sea in considerable quantities to many places in Southern England farther east, and also up the Bristol Channel. The early quarries were all on or near the coast: in the neighbourhood of Fowey, around Padstow, and at Trevalga between Tintagel and Boscastle. Later many others were opened: the great quarry at Delabole, two miles west of Camelford, was certainly being worked by 1600. During the

C19 this was to become much the most important in England, and, still in operation, although on a much reduced scale, it remains one of the most unforgettable sights of Cornwall, more than 400 ft deep and about a mile round. Delabole slates, if less attractive than the best products of Cumberland and Westmorland, are nevertheless a roofing material of great virtue: fine-grained, compact and strong, quick-drying, non-porous, impervious to frost, and not very heavy. The slates were always nicely graduated, the largest being placed at the bottom and the smallest next to the ridge; and a good roof of Cornish slate always gives pleasure. It is a great pity that in some places, to counter the force of the Atlantic gales, it became a common practice to wash over the whole roof with a cement slurry. This is aesthetically disastrous.

Slate-hung walls can be seen in and near the Lake District, but they are far commoner in Devon and Cornwall. Their heyday was the Regency, although some examples certainly go back to the C18 and a few, probably, to the C17. The slates employed were basically similar to roofing slates and their principal purpose was to provide additional protection against bad weather, but here and there a little simple ornamental patterning was introduced. Sometimes these hung slates would be nailed into the mortar courses (this is easier, of course, where the walling material is brick), but usually it was necessary to face the wall with a framework of wooden battens upon which the slates would be hung, their upper ends being bedded in mortar. Towns such as Launceston, Liskeard, St Columb Major and Padstow still exhibit many examples of slate-hanging.

Cornwall's Devonian rocks have been of much less importance to the builder than the sandstones from the Culm Measures, which are of Carboniferous age. The Culm Measures, which cover a large area of Central Devon, extend to the coast of Cornwall N of a line stretching from near Launceston to Boscastle. To this stratum belong the small, hard, somewhat rubbly and often dark brownish-red sandstones characteristic of the older buildings of North Cornwall.

Finally, mention must be made of a number of less familiar kinds of stone which are of interest because in England they can hardly be seen outside Cornwall. The ones to be seen in buildings are elvan, catacleuse, polyphant, and serpentine. All are rocks of igneous character.

As a building material, the first is decidedly the most important. Elvan is the name applied in Cornwall to the local quartz-porphyry which, from the long-abandoned Tartan Down quarry at Landrake, was used as far back as the C12 for the once magnificent but now sadly decayed w doorway of the nearby priory church of St Germans. In the Elizabethan period elvan, with granite dressings, was used at Trerice. The most important of the Cornish elvans was Pentewan stone, formerly quarried on the cliff-top north of Mevagissey: this was the material brought by sea to build Antony House in 1710–21 and overland for Trewithen, near Probus, begun in 1715. Elvan is still harder to work than granite and lacks the large flakes of mica characteristic of the more familiar stone, but its fine texture renders it suitable for ashlar – the kind of masonry which the Georgians always preferred – and its colour, usually light grey with a hint of buff, can be very agreeable.

Red porphyry was at one time quarried near Lostwithiel. It was employed internally in the eighteen-forties at Place, Fowey, where the walls of the so-called 'porphyry hall' are polished, and more curious than beautiful.

Catacleuse is worked at one place only, Cataclew Point, w of Padstow (so perhaps originally Cataclew's stone?). It is, like all the so-called basic igneous rocks, of much finer grain than granite and not as hard; the colour is dark grey, spangled with dark mica. It can be seen at St Merryn, the village closest to the former quarry.

Polyphant was quarried a few miles sw of Launceston: the name of the hamlet used to be written Polyfant. Mainly composed of silicates of magnesium and iron, this is a somewhat sombre greyish-blue stone, sometimes spotted with dull reds and browns deriving from iron. It was used here and there for the mullions and tracery of church windows. The church of St Stephen-by-Saltash has polyphant of the Tudor period, and *Pearson* introduced it during the last quarter of the C19 into Truro Cathedral.

He also used serpentine, the most distinctive of these Cornish specialities. Serpentine is the principal rock of the Lizard peninsula, and can best be seen at the church of Landewednack, in the pulpit and in some of the tombstones, and in the walls too, in combination with granite. It can be dark red or grey, veined maybe or mottled with brown or black, but the usual colour is dull green, with dark markings allegedly resembling those of a serpent's skin (although the Lizard itself does not owe its name to this resemblance). As a building stone it is not reliable, for it is very prone to flaws; seemingly hard blocks often contain soft pockets or weak veins which become exposed when it is cut up. Large pieces are therefore not easy to obtain and as a rule it is unsuitable for external work. The great attraction of serpentine is that, like polyphant, it will take a good polish, a property which accounts for its high esteem today as an internal facing material in the temples of the rich.

CORNWALL

*

ACTON CASTLE
Near Perranuthnoe

Castellated mansion of the mid C18, only three bays wide, symmetrical, of granite, with tripartite windows. The two-storeyed wings are C20.

ADVENT

ST ADWENA. In a lonely spot, 1½ m. s of Camelford. Three-staged, unbuttressed tower with eight pinnacles (probably the only one in the county). The earliest part of the church is the N transept (rebuilt in the C19) with E.E. lancet windows. The nave had a s aisle of five bays added in the C15. The arcade is of standard granite design. Beyond this there was until 1870 a s transept whose C15 entrance arch, identical with that to the N transept, is still visible. The E window of the s aisle has a flamboyant centre motif in the tracery, identical with Lanteglos-by-Camelford. The wagon roofs are ceiled. The ceiled wagon roof of the s porch has a few large bosses, for example one with three T-crosses. The s door has a pretty motif of isolated stylized fleurons in jambs and voussoir. The spandrels of the four-centred door-head have tracery decoration. – FONT. Plain, circular; Norman. – PLATE. Chalice by *Jons* of Exeter, the usual 1576 date.

ALTARNUN

The village street with picturesque stone cottages climbs down a hill to a stream (the church rises large on the other side).

ST NONNA. The w tower is 109 ft high, one of the highest in Cornwall. This is however not as noticeable as, for example, at Probus, because the tower stands against a hillside. It has the usual buttresses, leaving the corners free, and the usual division into three stages. There is a NW stair-turret rising above the pinnacles. The church has N and S aisles and N and S porches. Both porches have their old wagon roofs. Both aisles have wide four-light Perp windows of the same design, a design which takes two lights together under one pointed arch and which was specially popular in this district. The same design is repeated all along the E windows. The interior has only five bays, but they are wide and airy, the piers of standard design with capitals with very multiform mouldings. Each pier, capital, and base consists of a single piece of moorstone. – FONT. A magnificent piece of Norman decoration, uncommonly large, with bearded faces at the corners and large rosettes between. – ROOD SCREEN. Running right across nave and aisles. Each section has two lights only with Perp tracery and at the base two panels of blank tracery. – BENCH ENDS. A specially interesting set, altogether seventy-nine; later than 1523. Apart from the instruments of the Passion there are large figures of St Michael, an angel with an inscription: 'Robart Daye, Maker of this Work' and the date MD... (last figures illegible), a man with a cauldron, a fool, a man playing the bagpipes, a fiddler, angels holding shields. The detail in several cases is clearly Renaissance. – ALTAR RAIL. Running right across the building. It is dated 1684, yet still completely Jacobean in the baluster shape. – No monuments of importance.

TRERITHICK. *See* p. 227.

See p. 227.

⁴⁰⁵⁰   ANTONY

The house lies in large grounds, its show side facing N, with straight avenues, or what remains of them after much successful landscaping. The village is in no way connected with the house, and the church belongs to the village.

ST JAMES. The church was rededicated in 1259. One chancel window and the SEDILIA and PISCINA prove that the E part belongs to that phase in the building history of the church. The next phase is established by the tower, two-storeyed, of slate, with diagonal buttresses, C14 windows, and the top battlements (without pinnacles) corbelled out. In the C15 aisles were added, first on the S (square piers with four demi-shafts), then on the N (standard Cornish pier profile). The S windows are straight-headed; those of the N side have Perp tracery. – PULPIT. With four carved panels of the Evangelists; c.1500, not English, perhaps Spanish. – STAINED GLASS. Chancel and s aisle c.1850–60 by *Clayton & Bell*, N aisle w end by *Kempe*. – PLATE. Sienese C14 Chalice; Flemish Chalice, 1587; Chalice, Flagons, and Patens of 1716–17, by *A. Nelme*. – MONUMENTS. Brass to Margery Arundell, 1420, the most spectacular early brass in Cornwall, large, with a thin architectural surround with ogee arch and finials. – Sir John Carew, 1692, and his son and daughter, 1703, 1705. Good decorative wall epitaph. – Mary Carew, 1731. Pretty portrait medallion against drapery and other paraphernalia, signed by *Thomas Carter* of London. – Admiral Graves, 1755 by *Joseph Wilton*: a Roman *columna rostrata* and two urns standing on a Doric entablature. On corbels; the inscription between the corbels. – Jemima Pole-Carew, 1809 by *Sir R. Westmacott*.

ANTONY HOUSE. A Carew property since the late C15. Sir 57a William Carew built the house as it now stands. It was begun in 1710 and completed in 1721 and is without doubt the best example of its date in Cornwall. It has for long been attributed to *Gibbs* (Lysons), and the composition and proportions are worthy of a better name than that of the unknown designer of Puslinch, suggested by Mr Hussey. The house itself is of Pentewan stone, with a N front of two storeys and nine bays, the central three bays stressed by a pediment. With the exception of the door surround, with no decoration whatever. The s side has a large porte-cochère, added after 1838, and two brick wings with segment-headed windows on two floors. The wings are connected by an ornamental brick wall with corner pavilions whose almost Chinese-looking little pointed roofs contribute just one note of gaiety.

The staircase has turned balusters and columnar newel-posts and is lit by the original bubble globes. Most of the furniture of the Saloon is of the time of the building of the house. The chandelier in the Tapestry Room comes from Hamilton Palace in Lanarkshire.

There is a good circular DOVECOTE, probably coeval with the present house.*

Some time after 1800 *Repton* made a Red Book for house and grounds. The LODGE at Antony Passage and that at the main gate resemble his drawings, and some of the landscaping – the way the trees are grouped, the central vista to the water – is according to his principles, but whether it was done in Repton's time or later is not known.

* Information from G. W. Copeland.

Also in the grounds are the school and church of MERI-
FIELD. The former was built by W. H. Pole-Carew shortly
after 1847,* the latter, St Philip and St James, in 1863–71. It
is by *W. White*, picturesque outside and rich inside, with
marble columns, red and white arches, and lively tracery. –
PLATE. C14 Chalice, perhaps Sienese.

ARTHUR *see* SCILLY ISLES

AYR *see* ST IVES

7040   BALDHU

ST MICHAEL. By *W. White*, c.1848. – PLATE. Bronze-gilt
German Almsdish with Adam and Eve in the centre, given
in 1847.

BERIOW BRIDGE *see* NORTH HILL

1070   BLISLAND

The village is grouped around a green (on the Saxon plan) with
old tall trees.

ST PROTUS AND ST HYACINTH, s of the green. A church on
an unusual plan, with the tower added on the N to the N
transept (cf. St Enodoc). It has a stair-turret of rectangular
plan rising above the parapet and pinnacles. There is no w
door; a strong batter to the w wall instead. The church is
essentially Norman: see the masonry of w, N, and E walls, the
N doorway, also the N transept, and probably the ground floor
of the tower (cf. the arch into the transept). The second stage
is recessed, the third more, with buttresses. This upper stage
belongs to the time when a s aisle and s porch were added, of
granite, like the tower. The s aisle is of six bays, the arcade,
very visibly leaning to the s, is of standard Cornish granite
design. A N chancel aisle opens into the N transept with a
special 'chancel arch', an unusual feature. Of other features
the E window of the chancel is an E.E. triplet of lancets. The N
chancel aisle has a four-light Perp E window. Good wagon
roofs, ceiled. – FONTS. One Norman, circular, with four times

---

* The baronetcy of Carew became extinct in 1799, and shortly after the
estate came to a distant branch line represented by Reginald Pole, who took
the name Pole-Carew.

a motif of concentric Vs, and a herringbone moulding along the top. The other octagonal, c15, with shields in quatrefoils. – ROOD SCREEN 1896 by *F. C. Eden* (who restored the church about this date). – ALTAR in the Italian Renaissance style, oddly incongruous; 1894. – PULPIT. Late c17, with carvings in the *Grinling Gibbons* style, equally surprising and incongruous. – ROYAL ARMS. 1604. – PLATE. Very nice Elizabethan Cup and Cover, goblet type, with baluster stem, richly engraved, 1592–3. – MONUMENTS. Brass to John Balsam, rector of Blisland, 1410. – Kempe family, slate with six kneeling figures, 1624.

MANOR HOUSE, at the NE corner of the green. Well preserved, with gables* and the same scrolls at their springing as to be found, for example at Trerice, with hoodmoulds over the windows, and on the N side two yet unexplained Norman windows and a Norman arch (with incised zigzag ornament) belonging to a blocked doorway.

CLAPPER BRIDGES, Bradford, 2 m. NNE. These, the larger with four openings, are amongst the best of their kind in Cornwall.

POLEYS BRIDGE, 1½ m. NW. 1848. Five rude arches of huge granite slabs.

LAVETHAN. *See* p. 99.

TREWARDLA. *See* p. 230.

TRIPPET STONES, on Blisland Manor Common, 1 m. NE of Blisland. A stone circle 108 ft in diameter with eight standing and twelve fallen stones. The site has been considerably damaged and may originally have consisted of twenty-six stones. The tallest surviving stone is 5 ft high.

STRIPPLE STONES HENGE MONUMENT, on Hawkstor Down, 3 m. NE of Blisland. This has a roughly circular bank 225 ft in diameter and an internal ditch enclosing an irregular ring of fifteen stones. The earthwork is broken by an entrance 15 ft wide on the SW. The site has been partially excavated, without significant finds.

BOCHYM *see* HELSTON

BOCONNOC   *1060*

The chief attraction is the grounds, extensive, and laid out with the generosity and the sensitivity to landscape effects which

* Mr Alec Clifton-Taylor tells me that the gable over the porch was destroyed in 1961.

the c18 possessed and we have largely lost. They are due to Thomas Pitt, Lord Camelford, friend of Horace Walpole and nephew of Sir Richard Lyttelton, to whom he erected an obelisk 123 ft high on a hill behind the house in 1771. The HOUSE itself is not specially attractive, L-shaped, with one wing built shortly after 1719 by Thomas Pitt, Governor of Madras, and the other by Lord Camelford. The only distinguishing feature is the graceful Venetian windows in the E wing. Of *Soane*, who was called in for alterations (information kindly supplied by Miss D. Stroud), nothing characteristic appears, nor of Thomas Pitt's own Gothic taste, which was responsible for the decoration of Walpole's gilt and mirrored gallery at Strawberry Hill. Mrs Thrale, used to different bulk, called Pitt 'a finical lady-like man'. Alterations to Boconnoc were made in 1883. Of the medieval house a few windows and doorways are inserted into the garden walls and outbuildings.

CHURCH (dedication unknown). Behind the house, just as at Lanherne (Mawgan-in-Pydar) and Lanhydrock. Not an important church. No tower, only a SW turret; nave, S aisle, S porch, and N chancel aisle. The arcade of the S aisle is of six standard bays, mostly rebuilt in the c19. Old roof timbers in the nave, N aisle, and porch. – FONT. The most interesting object in the church: five supports, as in the c13, but the tracery decoration clearly of the c15 and of good quality. – PULPIT. 1629, with figures at the corners. – ROOD SCREEN. Used as a N parclose screen. Only part of the base preserved. Tracery panels as at St Winnow; no floral or foliage carving. – ROYAL ARMS. Painted plaster, still with some strapwork decoration. – PLATE. Gilt Hanap, 1623–4, with scrolly openwork top; Chalice and Paten by *Jons* of Exeter, *c.*1576, as usual. – MONUMENT. Penelope Mohun, 1637, kneeling against an aedicule background.

BODINNICK

Very picturesque village street, steep down to the river Fowey.

(BODINNICK HALL PLACE. Chapel, now used as a shippen, but an interesting little building with a very good N doorway, with scrolled ends to the label. A small embattled W bellturret like a tiny tower rises from the roof, the lower stages engaged in the W wall.)*

* Information from G. W. Copeland.

BODMIN

The county town of Cornwall, and one of its most important centres in the Middle Ages. Its history begins with the coming of St Petroc in the C6 and the assumed foundation by him of a monastery at Bodmin. Later in Anglo-Saxon times the 'place and government' of Bodmin belonged to the Diocesan Bishops of St Germans, who seem to have used Bodmin as a secondary residence. Of the monastery with its famous Shrine of St Petroc nothing is left, except a few fragments of Norman work in the PRIORY GROUNDS, for example parts of capitals of cylindrical piers. Nor can one form a clear idea of the wealth of other ecclesiastical buildings, etc., for example the Hospitals of St George and St Anthony in the town, and St Lawrence outside. The parish church, now without competitor the chief building of the town (and the largest church in Cornwall), was, seven hundred years ago, clearly of secondary importance.

CHURCHES

ST PETROC. Mostly rebuilt in 1469–72, and in that renewed form probably more ambitious and impressive than the priory, which had by then long passed its glory. Building accounts survive.* The Perp building is 151 ft long, 65 ft wide, and has a tower which, before the spire was destroyed in 1699, was 150 ft high. It stands on the N of the church at the junction of nave and chancel and is Norman up to the third storey, unbuttressed, and strongly receding from floor to floor. Large quoins, small masonry, small windows. Originally it was probably attached to a N transept. The church of 1469–72 (sweepingly‡ restored in the second half of the C19)‡ has nine bays for nave and chancel with no separation of the two in plan. In elevation, however, the three chancel arcades are a little lower than those of the nave. N and S aisles are of the

---

* All except the W end, tower, and chancel was reconstructed. Four hundred and sixty people – nearly every adult in the parish – subscribed to the rebuilding, in addition to contributions from the guilds. The vicar gave a year's salary. There were gifts of building material and other goods, and those who were too poor to give anything else gave their labour. The total sum expended was £268 17s. 9½d. About twenty masons were employed; skilled men received 6d. a day. A workshop was set up at the quarries where the stone was shaped and dressed before it was sent to Bodmin. The N and S walls cost £22. Nine shillings was paid for carving capitals, nineteen shillings for ironwork. See G. H. Cook, *The English Medieval Parish Church*, London, 1954, p. 252.

‡ The MHLG gives these dates for restorations: 1814, 1867, 1888, 1930.

same width as the nave; the piers are slim and tall, of standard Cornish section, the small capitals with a little carving; the openings are wide, with depressed two-centred arches. The system and detail are so much like St Andrew's, Plymouth, that Sedding suggested they might be designed by the same masons. Of the windows much is C19 restoration, of the original roofs the chief remains are in the S chancel aisle. Outside, the church is characterized by battlements and stair-turrets. The W front is restored out of recognition. The S porch is two-storeyed, battlemented, with niches for sculpture on the upper wall. On the ground floor is a little fan-vault. – FONT. C12, the best of its type in the county. Deep bowl on stumpy shaft, slimmer shafts in the four corners with busts of angels as capitals, interlaced and undercut foliage, scroll ornament, and, lower down, symmetrical beasts with 'trees of life' between. – CRESSET. Just inside the S door, as a collecting vessel. It is octagonal, and has an eight-foiled depression in its top (cf. Mylor). – SCREENS (N and S aisles) modern, but incorporating some panels from the former rood screen and from bench ends. – BENCH ENDS. Panels re-used in choir stalls and reredos by *Sir Charles Nicholson*, 1932. – For the benches and the PULPIT contracts of 1491 exist with Matthew More, the benches to take as their model those of St Mary's, Plympton, the pulpit that of Moretonhampstead. The carving of the pulpit is good, but its base is partly made up of fragments from the choir stalls. – Fragment of the top of a LANTERN CROSS from the churchyard, now inside the church. – PLATE. The most interesting piece is a domestic Cup of *c*.1510 converted for church use in 1576 by *IW*, a Cornish maker (*see* Merther, St Dennis, St Gennys, St Issey), who added a characteristic ornamented band and a cover; gilt Hanap of 1617, by *IS*, with steeple and figure on top, $25\frac{1}{2}$ in. high, originally domestic; two similar gilt Flagons of 1619, with over-rich repoussé decoration, the earliest of tankard-shape in the county; two foreign Cups. Altogether a very impressive collection. – MONUMENTS. Sepulchral slab with foliated cross outside the S wall of the church; inscription in French (cf. St Breock, Little Petherick, St Merryn, St Buryan). – Between chancel and N aisle free-standing monument to Thomas Vivian, the last Prior of Bodmin but two, 1533 (cf. Rialton). The monument comes from the priory church. It is of black Catacleuse stone and grey marble. Recumbent effigy on a chest decorated with figures of the Evangelists. Cherubs with shields, and coarse Italianizing balusters (the earliest example of the effect on Cornwall of such metropolitan work as the tomb of Henry VII, completed fourteen years earlier). – Richard Durant † 1632 and his wives and twenty children, slate slab. – Peter Bolt, 1633, one of the finest incised slabs in the county. – Michael Bennet, 1821 by *William Behnes*. – Capt. Oakley, 1835, also by *Behnes*, very restrained, with Greek helmet and shield. – Displayed in the s aisle, the BODMIN CASKET, ivory, of Spanish Mudéjar style,* C12. It may be the casket in which relics of St Petroc were handed back to the Prior of Bodmin in 1177, after having been stolen.

CHAPEL OF ST THOMAS BECKET, in the churchyard, E of the parish church. Of the building, which was licensed for worship in 1377, the crypt survives, and large fragments of the upper walls, with a fine Dec E window of three lights.

CHURCH OF THE HOLY ROOD. Only the mid C15 Berry Tower survives.

Of the once great FRANCISCAN FRIARY founded *c.*1240 or later the only fragments which survive are part of a gateway incorporated into a shop in Fore Street and two pillars, one in the churchyard, the other in the Public Rooms near the Assize Courts, which are on ground once occupied by the great hall of the friary.‡

(ABBEY OF ST MARY AND ST PETROC (R.C.). By *Vyvyan Salisbury*, 1965. It is at the w end of Bodmin; the adjoining seminary was opened in 1907.)

THE TOWN

The secular centre of Bodmin is MOUNT FOLLY, with the neo-classical granite building of the ASSIZE COURT erected in 1837–8 (by *Burt* of Launceston) and other neo-classical buildings. FORE STREET has some pleasant stucco fronts and shop-windows, and the granite MARKET with Doric piers, three openings, and bulls' and rams' heads in the frieze: 1839. It is now a laundry. – ST LAWRENCE'S HOSPITAL, at the w end of the town, contains a part built in 1818 by *Foulston*. – The former PRISON, 1855, with imposing gateway and massive walls, is now a road transport centre.

The approach to Bodmin is dominated by an OBELISK, 144 ft high, erected to commemorate Lt-Gen. Sir W. R. Gilbert, 1856–7.

* Sicily has also been suggested as the country of origin.
‡ This paragraph contributed by Mr H. J. Willmott.

On CASTLE HILL, Tower Hill Farmhouse, long and low, early
C18 (MHLG).
INSCRIBED STONE, built into a farm building at Lancarffe,
1½ m. NNE. DUNOCATI HIC JACIT FILI MERCAGNI; C5–7 ?
CAMP, at Tregear. A rectangular earthwork, 320 by 260 ft, with
Roman remains. The camp was occupied from the C1 to the
early C2; it was possibly a fort to protect trading and mining.
GLYNN HOUSE. *See* Cardinham.

BODRIFTY *see* GULVAL *and* MADRON

0070
BOKELLY
Near St Kew

Tudor BARN, strongly buttressed, and HOUSE, re-fronted
apparently late in the C17.

0090
BOSCASTLE

A minute harbour, ideally protected by nature, and with two
stone jetties, of which one was destroyed by a mine during the
Second World War. A few cottages and groups of houses close
by of local stone or painted the usual biscuit colour – for the
harbour master and probably sailors. Their low, square forms
contrast strangely with the wild hills on both sides. The village
climbs up the valley of the river Valency.

Boscastle has no church; its mother church is Minster (*q.v.*),
but Forrabury church on the hills to the s is nearer (*q.v.*). Of
the Botreaux castle from which Boscastle derives its name
nothing survives.

3030
BOTALLACK
Near St Just-in-Penwith

Since the C18 one of the most famous of the Cornish TIN MINES
(now abandoned). The engine house stands 30 ft above the
Atlantic, under which the galleries extended.
MANOR HOUSE. 1665, L-shaped (MHLG).

4060
BOTUS FLEMING

ST MARY. Nothing special about the w tower with its diagonal
buttresses (roughcast, alas) nor about the exterior of the rest
of the church. But inside it has a handsome arcade between N
aisle and nave, on octagonal piers whose capitals are studded

with stylized fleurons, an unusual and very successful treatment. Moreover, the second pier has on its w side, carved out of the granite of the pier, a projecting base and canopy for a figure, and the two adjoining piers also have brackets for statues. The same motif occurs in Devon. – FONT. Of Purbeck table-top type, with seven flat little blank niches with pointed heads on each side. – MONUMENT. In a recess a cross-legged Knight, badly preserved, probably one of the Moditons, whose seat was close to Botus Fleming.

In a field to the NE of the church an OBELISK 12 ft tall to the memory of William Martyn, 1762, who, being 'a Catholic Christian, in the true, not depraved Popish sense of the word', knew 'no superstitious veneration for church or churchyard' and therefore preferred to be buried in unconsecrated ground.

MODITONHAM. *See* p. 121.

BOYTON 3090

HOLY NAME(?). Unbuttressed C14 tower, partly rebuilt in 1692–4 (cf. the round-headed top windows). Nave and s aisle only. Arcade of Cornish C15 standard. Wagon roofs, good in the aisle. Windows straight-headed. – FONT. Plain Early Norman, of the same irregular oval shape as Morwenstow and Washaway. – ROOD SCREEN. Base only, with tracery of *c.*1500, similar to that on so many Cornish bench ends. – PLATE. Embossed and repoussé Sweetmeat Dish by *SB*, 1663–4; other pieces of 1699, 1721, etc.

(BOYTON MILL. In the mill itself the machinery is still in working order. The miller's house is stone-built and colour-washed. *The Times*, 8 August 1966)

BRADFORD *see* BLISLAND

BRADOC 1060

ST MARY. Small, standing on its own, close to Boconnoc Woods. Two-storeyed W tower without buttresses. The N side still has the early transept and no aisle, the s side an aisle of five bays; standard Cornish piers and arches. The odd arches between nave and N transept are C19. Original wagon roofs in nave and aisle. – FONT. Norman, with four corner faces and large trees of life in between. – PULPIT. Elizabethan. – ROOD SCREEN. The base of two sections, each of six narrow panels, remains. The carved motifs have enough allusions to the coming of the

Renaissance to make a date before 1530 unlikely. – A curious set of PANELS s of the rood screen. What can they be ? They look like *Volkskunst* of the C18, little carved groups in relief of two figures opposite each other, very stiff and quaint, one panel with three faces, one *en face*, two in profile, one panel with a woman holding a snake's tail, and the whole surrounded by panels with Celtic-looking animals. – BENCH ENDS. Very cut about, but obviously originally an interesting set, with a figure of Father Time, two figures of saints, and other saints small on shields with their emblem on a neighbouring shield. – PLATE. An unusually interesting Chalice and Paten, possibly of Marian date, but entirely pre-Reformation in design.

BARROW CEMETERY, $\frac{1}{2}$ m. W of Taphouse and N of the A390. A linear cemetery of eight bowl barrows, none of which appear to have been excavated.

BRANE *see* SANCREED

6020

BREAGE

ST BREACA. The church is entirely of the C15,[*] and entirely of granite. The W tower has buttresses of three stages and set-back grotesque heads and gargoyles sticking out from its top cornice below the battlements. The pinnacles are corbelled out. The interior is entered through a s porch with panelled jambs, battlements, and buttresses. It has a nave and two identical aisles of seven bays with standard Cornish granite piers, plain capitals, and decorated abaci. The arches into the two transepts are of the same type. Both transepts are battlemented too. There is some old timber in the s aisle and the N transept. – ROMAN MILESTONE with inscription referring to Marcus Cassianus Posthumus (258–68). – WALL PAINTINGS against the N wall, uncommonly interesting: St Christopher, the Warning to the Sabbath-Breakers, St Hilary, St Corentine, and St Ambrose. In the splays of windows in the s aisle, St Thomas of Canterbury and St Giles, and other fragments, all late C15. – STAINED GLASS. A few fragments in the N aisle. – CROSS HEAD in the churchyard. Four-holed wheel-cross with Hiberno-Saxon decoration, the only sandstone cross of this kind in Cornwall. Much worn.

[*] Though restored in the C19 (MHLG).

BROADOAK *see* BRADOC

BRYHER *see* SCILLY ISLES

BUDE

2000

Not an attractive harbour-town compared with others in Cornwall and Devon. The church of ST MICHAEL AND ALL ANGELS is of 1835 (by *Wightwick*; enlarged 1876) and unimportant. The old parish church of Bude is Stratton. The VICARAGE is said to have been a manor house of Sir John Arundel of Trerice, and to be of the C15, with later additions. Hall with fine oak beams.* Between river and canal THE CASTLE, a low, castellated stone mansion of c.1850, now the Urban District Council Offices.

(EBBINGFORD MANOR. A stone tablet on the front reads 'R.W, 1758', presumably the date of a restoration or rebuilding in which much of the former material was re-used. C14 doorways and mullioned windows.‡)

BUDOCK

7030

ST BUDOCK. The mother-church of Falmouth. The W tower has diagonal buttresses, a motif not usual in Cornwall. It is of three stages. The S transept is C13, with one lancet window at the E. Its arch towards the nave inside is double-chamfered and rests on shafts with moulded capitals. The N aisle is C15, Cornish granite standard, of seven bays. The S porch has the panelled jambs familiar in this part of Cornwall. The church has BOX PEWS, in the Georgian tradition, now all too rare. – ROOD SCREEN. The base remains across N aisle and chancel, with charming carving and painted saints (cf. Gunwalloe, St Winnow, and Devon). – MONUMENTS. Brass to John Killigrew, 1567, and wife. – Fragment of a monument to Sir John Killigrew, erected in 1617. Limestone and alabaster, with kneeling figures and finely carved ornament.

(ROSEMERRYN. A house of c.1730, two-storeyed, seven bays, with a rather heavy pedimented doorway. Partly slate-hung. GMT)

(THE CRAG, Maenporth. 1865 by *Alfred Waterhouse*, who attempted to incorporate Cornish traditional idioms, e.g. circular granite pillars. Now a hotel. In a fine position on the cliff edge. GMT)

* Information from G. W. Copeland.
‡ Information from B. Stamp.

BURRELL HOUSE
Near Saltash

1621, with a wing dated 1636. Lattice windows towards the garden and a four-centred door arch. The entrance side was altered in the C18 – slate-hung with Georgian windows.

BURYAS BRIDGE *see* TREREIFE

BUSSOW *see* ST IVES

CAERHAYS *see* ST MICHAEL CAERHAYS

CAERWYNNEN *see* CAMBORNE

CALENICK *see* KEA

CALLINGTON

The little town, not specially attractive, is dominated by the great chimney of a disused mine on Kit Hill to the NE, looking from the distance like one more Wellington Testimonial.

ST MARY. The mother-church of Callington is South Hill, 3 m. N – just as St Stephen is the mother-church of Launceston, St Martin of Looe, etc. St Mary was consecrated in 1438, an ambitious building with a three-staged W tower whose buttresses are set back and end at the top of the second stage. They are there replaced by three-eighths projections on demifigures of angels, and on these projections rise the pinnacles. The nave is flanked by N and S aisles of four tall, wide bays, and an outer N aisle added in 1882 by *J. D. Sedding*. The rest is early C15 and seems earlier, for it still has the simple square piers with four attached shafts that characterize C14 work in Cornwall. The capitals are simply moulded, the arches have two concave chamfers. There is a clerestory, a feature most unusual in Cornwall. Its windows are ranged with the spandrels of the arcade, not with the apexes of the arches (cf. St Germans, Fowey, Lostwithiel). The wagon roofs are old. Outside, the church is battlemented, so that the clerestory can hardly be seen. – FONT. A coarse example of the type of Altarnun, St Thomas Launceston, etc., with faces at the corners and rosettes in circles. – DOOR of the C15, with simple hinges and closing-ring. – PLATE. Chalice and Paten by *Jons* of Exeter, 1570–2; Chalice and Paten by *IH*, 1678–9. – MONUMENTS. Brass to Sir Nicholas Assheton and wife, 1466. –

Alabaster monument to Sir Robert Willoughby de Broke, Steward of the Duchy of Cornwall and Lord of the Manor of Callington, 1502. Effigy in armour with Garter robes and folded hands, feet against a lion; two tiny figures of friars appear beneath it. Evidently imported. – Large slate ledger stone with a relief of a kneeling woman to Ann Holiday, 1753, signed by *John Burt* of Callington. – CROSS in the churchyard. Lantern type, late medieval, on a plain octagonal shaft; very worn.

(RECTORY. Good stone house of the early C18 (*c.*1719). G. W. Copeland)

NEW BRIDGE (river Lynher), 1¼ m. SW. Late C15; round arches of granite. Widened in 1874, partly rebuilt in 1898.

DUPATH. *See* p. 64.

CASTLEWICH HENGE, 1 m. SE. A circular ditch with outer bank encloses an area some 300 ft in diameter. A single entrance occurs on the S.

CALSTOCK

4060

ST ANDREW. Not very promising externally, with the usual late three-storeyed W tower of regular granite blocks and with lancet windows of typical early C19 appearance. The E end, however, has for its N as well as its S side two very domestic-looking windows of three lights with straight tops and a transom across. Behind the N one is the Edgcumbe Chapel with two MONUMENTS: to Pears Edgcumbe, 1666, good white and grey work without figures, and to Jemima, Countess of Sandwich, 1674, with two mourning figures and a rather large coronet. – The arcades of the two aisles are different in a historically significant way: early and late C15 – the N arch square piers with attached demi-shafts, the S arch the Cornish standard design; the N arch plain double-chamfered, the S with a much more complex moulding.

(RECTORY. By *Decimus Burton*, 1853–4. Howard Colvin)

(HAREWOOD HOUSE. Late C18 or early C19. Square granite house of two storeys, in a fine position overlooking the river Tamar. GMT)

(RAILWAY VIADUCT. Across the Tamar. Twelve arches.)

CAMBORNE

6040

ST MARTIN AND ST MERIADOCUS. The church stands at the end of the town. It is of granite throughout, C15, with a W

tower with double set-back buttresses, and inside standard
Cornish piers (with large horizontal leaves to the capitals;
cf. Gwinear) and four-centred arches. There are two identical
aisles, each of five bays, with two lower bays for the chancel
(cf. Bodmin). The four- and five-light windows have four-
centred heads to each light and no tracery, not an unusual
feature in this part of Cornwall. An outer s aisle was added in
1878. – ALTAR SLAB in the present altar, almost certainly
C10. It comes from Chapel Ia, Troon, and has a key border,
Anglo-Saxon lettering referring to the donor Leuiut, and five
crosses* on the (present) under-surface. – REREDOS with
Commandment Tables and three cherubs' heads in the pediment; 1761. – PULPIT. The coat of arms would date it c.1480,
though there has been some restoration (A. J. Vincent). –
MONUMENTS. Sir William Pendarves, 1726, with a medallion
bust, by *James Paty the Elder* of Bristol. – Anne Acton, 1780,
with gracefully carved urn, by *F. Robins* of Bath. – Edward
William Wynne Pendarves, 1853, with a large bust at the top,
by *E. H. Baily*.

The town is not specially attractive. The nicest building is the
LITERARY INSTITUTE, 1829, with a Tuscan centre *in antis*
and lower wings, all severe granite.‡

(ROSEWARNE HOUSE, Tehidy Road. Granite, c.1810(?).
Italianate and gloomy. Central block with gabled projecting
wings joined by a colonnade to first-floor height (GMT).
LOWER ROSEWARNE. A complete C15 hall and cross-
passage house, with another hall added longitudinally c.1500.
Now largely enclosed in C18 additions (Professor Charles
Thomas).)

(CAERWYNNEN QUOIT, 2 m. s of Camborne. A good specimen;
three legs and a large capstone. Dr Athelstane Hill)

HUT CIRCLES, on the sw slope of Caerwynnen hill. Both huts
lie just above the 600 ft contour and are marked by low banks
overgrown by bracken and gorse. They are approximately
50 ft in diameter. The huts have produced sherds of Iron Age
B pottery.

GWITHIAN TOWANS. *See* Gwithian.

ROMAN VILLA, discovered in 1931, at Magor, near Camborne.
Of winged corridor type; probably late C2. No Roman villa
has yet been excavated further w than this.

* They refer to the C12(?) change from frontal to mensa. Not now visible
(Professor Charles Thomas).

‡ A BEAM ENGINE for pumping water from a mine is well preserved
alongside the main road through the town.

CAMELFORD

Not a specially attractive town: grey houses, chiefly along one long descending street. Towards the bottom, the TOWN HALL, 1806. Until recently Camelford had no parish church – the same typically Cornish state of affairs as at Launceston. Wadebridge. etc. The parish church of Camelford was Lanteglos. The new church of ST THOMAS, consecrated in 1938, is by *Sir Charles Nicholson*.
(SIR JAMES SMITH'S COMPREHENSIVE SCHOOL. 1962 by the County Architect, *F. K. Hicklin*.)

CAPE CORNWALL

Near St Just-in-Penwith

ST HELEN'S CHAPEL. Remains of a small medieval chapel, used as a farm building.

CARCLEW *see* MYLOR

CARDINHAM

ST MEUBRED. Granite W tower of three stages with thin setback buttresses. The nave has two wide, light aisles on tallish piers of Cornish standard granite design. The s aisle is of six bays, that on the N of five. The E end of the chancel was damaged in the Second World War. In its N wall a low E.E. sepulchral niche. – WAGON ROOFS in aisles and porch. – Good set of typically Cornish C15–C16 BENCH ENDS. – ROYAL ARMS with strapwork decoration; 1661. – MONUMENTS. Brass to Thomas Awmarle, Rector, *c*.1400 – whole figure in gown and hood.* – Glynn Family, 1699. Epitaph with little angel figures on top; very conservative. – CROSS in the churchyard: one of the best in the county. $8\frac{1}{2}$ ft high; four-holed head, with knotwork on the front face. Shaft in three panels, top with inscription, below plaitwork. Back face with beautiful interlace, back shaft with coarse scrolls. C9 or C10. – Several INSCRIBED STONES: in the churchyard (RANOCORI FILI MESGI); s of the churchyard, in the wall of a wagon shed; at the crossroads $\frac{1}{4}$ m. NW of Welltown (VAILATHI FILI UROCHANI; c6 or c7), and beside it another (OR P EP TITUS; c6 or c7).

* An exceedingly rare example of a cleric in civil dress (cf. High Halstow, Kent). (Information from F. A. Greenhill)

(GLYNN, near Bodmin Road station, in Fowey Valley. Fine, large stone house, rebuilt in 1805. W front of nine bays, engaged pillared portico. In the grounds, the remains of two CROSSES. G. M. Trinick and G. W. Copeland)

CARGOLL *see* ST NEWLYN EAST

CARLYON BAY *see* CHARLESTOWN

CARNANTON *see* MAWGAN-IN-PYDAR

6040
CARN BREA

CARN BREA HILLFORT, 2½ m. WSW of Redruth and ¼ m. S of Carnbrea village. Roughly oval, of bivallate construction, enclosing some 36 acres, with entrances on the N and S. A number of hut circles are visible in the interior. Traces of Neolithic occupation have also been found on the hill.
The MONUMENT to Lord de Dunstanville is of 1836.

CARN EUNY *see* SANCREED

6030
CARNMENELLIS

HOLY TRINITY. By *J. Hayward*, *c.*1849. – FONT from Sithney, Late Norman, circular and small; not of special merit.

CASTILLY *see* LUXULYAN

6060
CASTLE-AN-DINAS
2 m. ESE of St Columb Major

An approximately circular fort defined by four concentric lines of ramparts cut by a broad entrance on the SW. Excavations have revealed two structural phases: the first consisted of a univallate structure (second rampart from the exterior) provided with at least six entrances, to which were added in the second phase the three remaining lines of fortifications. Sherds of Iron Age B pottery were found in association with the structure.

4030
CASTLE-AN-DINAS WEST
2 m. N of Gulval

TOWER, erected by a local landowner *c.*1800. It is a sham castle with towers, built for the magnificent prospect of St Michael's

Bay, Mount's Bay, and Penzance. One finds it sometimes mentioned as Rogers's Tower. ½ m. away is the Iron Age village of Chysauster, for which *see* Gulval.

CASTLE DORE
2½ m. N of Fowey

1050

A roughly circular bivallate earthwork, the inner rampart enclosing an area 320 ft in diameter. An entrance on the E is defended by a secondary enclosure. The site is well preserved and the ramparts still survive to a height of 7 ft. Excavation revealed two main structural phases: in Phase I both ramparts were of dump construction, but in Phase II the inner fortifications were provided with a vertical outer stone face. A series of circular huts are located in the interior.

CASTLE HORNECK *see* PENZANCE

CASTLEWICH HENGE *see* CALLINGTON

CHACEWATER
5 m. W of Truro

7040

(ST PAUL. A church was built in 1828, repaired in 1886, greatly damaged by lightning in that same year, and entirely rebuilt (except the tower) by *Edmund Sedding* in 1892. The church is a few yards s of the road on a steep knoll. The tower, a gaunt shaft, bare of windows except in the uppermost of four lightly indicated stages, is impressive. The lofty interior is remarkable for the colour of the unplastered walls of local stone, buff, grey, yellow, and brown setting off effectively the shallow-sea-water green of the octagonal shafts of polyphant stone and granite arches. The nave has a wagon roof 43 ft high, the aisles lean-to roofs. An arched recess in the E wall provides a bent eyebrow to the five-light E window whose bright STAINED GLASS comes from St Mary, Truro. There are lancets in the clerestory and square-headed windows in the aisle walls which have shallow recesses inside and corresponding projections without. A satisfying sense that Sedding here knew what effect he wanted to get; and got it.)*

CHAPEL POINT *see* MEVAGISSEY

CHARLESTOWN

0050

Nine inhabitants in 1790, 281 by 1801 – thanks to the establishment of a tiny port by the 'spirited and meritorious exertions of

* From *Collins Guide to English Parish Churches*, ed. John Betjeman, 1958.

Charles Rashleigh'. A few nice terraces of cottages by the harbour, and one substantial house, no doubt the harbour master's.

ST PAUL. 1849, by *Eales*.

At CARLYON BAY, W of Charlestown, a number of modern flat-roofed houses by *Marshall Sisson*.

CHUN CASTLE *see* MORVAH

CHYSAUSTER *see* GULVAL

CHYVERTON *see* PERRANUTHNOE

6030   CLOWANCE

Plain house of seven bays and two storeys, granite, with a one-storey Tuscan porch of four columns. Mr Colvin tells me that there was work here by *R. Mylne*, 1776. The house was partly rebuilt *c*.1838 and completed after a fire in 1845.

8060   COLAN

ST COLANUS. A small church in a lonely, sheltered spot between trees. The building is essentially C13 and can perhaps be connected with the date 1276, when a Cardinham gave it (through the Bishop) to Glasney College, near Penryn. Of the C13 are in fact S wall, S chancel wall, and S transept (cf. its single-chamfered arch into the nave). On the N side a standard C15 arcade of three bays plus two for the chancel. The chancel part of the aisle is separated from the nave part by an arch just like those of the nave arcade; that is, Cornish standard. The W tower was rebuilt in 1879. – ROOD SCREEN. The base only survives. – STAINED GLASS of 1887, 1884, etc., by *Gibbs & Howard*. – BRASSES. John Cosowarth and family, 1575, the same composition of inscription, figures, and shields as, for example, on the Arundell brasses at Mawgan-in-Pydar and St Columb Major. – The Bluett family, with twenty-two children, *c*.1580.

2060   COLDRENNICK
                      Near Menheniot

Half-timbered black and white Herefordshire- or Cheshire-looking Victorian mansion by *C. F. Hayward*, 1870.

COLQUITE   0070
Near St Mabyn

Below the house, the ruin of a manor house, possibly of the late
C15, with two doorways and a window opening remaining on
the ground floor, and five window openings on the upper floor.
It might have been a first-floor hall-house. A detailed study has
been made by F. Chesher, *Cornish Archaeology*, VI, 1967.

COME-TO-GOOD   8030
Near Feock

FRIENDS' MEETING HOUSE. 1709, a whitewashed, thatched 16a
cottage from outside, with stables for the churchgoers' horses
on one side under one roof with the house. Inside the familiar
arrangement of the meeting house with its plain benches and
raised gallery.

CONSTANTINE   7020

ST CONSTANTINE. An impressive church in a commanding
position on the hills N of one of the N creeks of the Helford
river – large, and all of regular granite blocks.* The W tower
is tall, of three stages, with buttresses set back from the
corners, panelled pinnacles, a lozenge decoration of the top
cornice, and heads carved at the tops of the buttresses. The
W door has leaf-scroll decoration exactly as at Mawgan near
by, and a hoodmould with heads as label stops. The aisles are
also buttressed; so is the S porch, which possesses the panelled
jambs usual in the district, and a niche above the entrance
arch. Apart from the N and S aisles of seven and six bays
respectively, there is an outer N aisle of three bays. The tower
arch is provided with shafts to the responds as at Mawgan.
All piers are square with four attached shafts. – PLATE.
Chalice and Paten of 1575–7; other plate of the C18. –
BRASSES. To Richard Gerveys, 1574, and family, a palimpsest
with, on the reverse, the upper part of a large Flemish C14
brass.
N of the church the old SCHOOLHOUSE, dated 1733.
CROSS. Trevease Farm, 1¾ m. NNW. With a circular head and a
very primitive Crucifixus with horizontally stretched-out arms.
The feet are standing on a cross with two top bars.

* It is C15, restored in 1859–1901 (MHLG).

(MERTHEN. Fine two-storey porch with a Tudor arch. Granite, with mullioned windows. Three three-storey C18 windows on the S front. GMT)

TREWARDREVA. Originally an E-shaped manor house of *c.*1600, remodelled in 1719–49, that is, re-faced with ashlar, and the mullioned windows replaced by sash windows. Stables added in granite. The W wing was pulled down in 1860. Some additions of 1936. The interior contains a fine staircase and some C18 panelled rooms with moulded plaster ceilings, the best of these on the first floor.

TREWARDREVA FOGOU, just opposite the entrance to Trewardreva. The structure consists of a slightly curved passage, 66 ft long and between 5 ft 6 in. and 6 ft 6 in. in height, roofed by lintels and revetted by dry stone walling. Access to the fogou is from the SW, although the original entrance has been destroyed. The fogou originally stood within a fortified enclosure, and traces of the rampart are visible to the E of the structure.

CONSTANTINE BAY
W of St Merryn towards Trevose

8070

Ruins of a chapel with nave and chancel, one aisle, and tower, dated by Henderson *c.*1390.

COPPERHOUSE *see* HAYLE COPPERHOUSE

CORNELLY

9040

ST CORNELIUS. Standing all on its own, with a wide view. A slim little W tower, as Mylor would be if it did not have its heavy buttresses l. and r. The ground floor slate, with a tiny lancet window in the W, no doubt C13; the second stage granite. The N side of the little church also is C13, with one lancet window. On the S side the windows were replaced by Perp windows, and a S porch (wagon roof preserved) was added, but on the whole the church can still give an impression of the scale of a Cornish parish church of the C13. – FONT. Granite, octagonal, as primitively carved as if it were Norman, yet no doubt post-Reformation, and hardly intended to be revivalism – just a rustic carver's handiwork. – PULPIT with crudely painted panels with coats of arms; C17. – MONUMENT to Jane Reeves, 1783, with excellent portrait bust of the young woman in an oval medallion.

COTEHELE

The most extensive and important Tudor house of Cornwall, picturesquely placed in woods above the river Tamar, and picturesque also in its architecture, the product of growth more than plan. Cotehele was the chief seat of the Edgcumbe family before Mount Edgcumbe opposite Plymouth replaced it in the favour of Sir Richard Edgcumbe. Cotehele, as we see it today, is essentially the work of his father, Sir Piers Edgcumbe, † 1539, and his grandfather, Sir Richard, † 1489. Of an earlier date (the house came into the family by marriage in 1353) much of walls survives, sandstone rubble as against the later granite ashlar, and a few details such as small round-headed windows in the S and W ranges and a door in the courtyard to the l. of the chapel window. The courtyard is reached through the main GATEWAY, with a granite tunnel-vault divided by transverse ribs, as if it were a timber wagon roof. The chapel window is on the l., the GREAT HALL right 48 opposite. Its door, curiously enough, does not lead into the screens passage. The hall has an early C16 roof with arched 49 principals steadied by purlins and kept taut by braces – a rather conservative technique at a time when hammerbeam roofs were already popular. It is the same technique as appears at Penshurst, Ockwells, Cothay, etc., and also at Trecarrel. Beyond the hall is another smaller courtyard and a further range of rooms with the NW tower, dated 1627, projecting beyond the front. Out of the hall lead three doors into the offices, and on the other side was the solar. Beyond this follows the CHAPEL. It dates from the late C15 with much C19 restoration. The E window is new, but the S windows are original, with early C16 GLASS. Original also the SCREEN, the simple ceiled wagon roof, and the white and green floor tiles. The PEW ENDS are old too, but were brought in from elsewhere, as were also the two German PAINTINGS of c.1500 l. and r. of the reredos. Behind the altar a Flemish triptych of the Adoration of the Magi; early C16. The ALTAR FRONTAL is a beautiful piece of appliqué work, silver on purple, with the twelve Apostles and the arms of Sir Piers Edgcumbe. In the chapel a copy of the MONUMENT to Sir Richard † 1489, at Morlaix in France. On the outside the chapel has a little bellcote of granite with pinnacles, looking like a holy well building.

CHAPEL ON THE CLIFF, 70 ft above the Tamar, marking the spot where Richard Edgcumbe jumped into the river to escape from Sir Henry Trenowth (1483). Restored in 1620 and 1729. Still intact, but rather neglected. Original three-light E window and two-light N and S windows and W door. Ceiled roof, probably C15, with linenfold panelling and four BENCH ENDS. (A. S. B. New and G. W. Copeland)

CRANE GODREVY see GWITHIAN

CRANKAN see GULVAL

7060

CRANTOCK

ST CARANTOC. A curious building with an interesting history. Of the Norman church the plan of the nave and the two transepts, and some masonry, remains. The central tower of this building collapsed in 1412. A college was instituted at Crantock church by Bishop Brewer of Exeter c.1236. This required an enlargement of the chancel. What the C13 chancel looked like we do not know, but it is worth mentioning that the Norman arches of the transepts open into the chancel aisles. In its present form, however, the chancel is C14, higher than the nave, with lean-to roofs for the two aisles (the nave has no aisles) and arcades on octagonal piers and two-centred, single-chamfered arches. The C13 chancel was larger than the present chancel. The W tower is roughcast, with battlements, but no pinnacles. It has buttresses on the lower stage which meet at r. angles at the corners, and not, as was usual later in the south-west of England, leaving the corners free. The lower stage is therefore probably C13. – FONT. Norman, of the type of Mawgan-in-Pydar, St Columb Minor, St Wenn, re-tooled in 1474(?), and with that date inscribed in large script. – ROOD SCREEN. Mostly modern (by E. H. Sedding, who restored the church c.1893), but it is recognizable that the old screen had no tracery at all between the uprights. A specially airy and graceful type; cf. Mawgan-in-Pydar. – SCULPTURE. Fragments of a Virgin and two saints of the C15 inside the S wall of the tower. – PLATE. Chalice and Paten probably by Avery of Exeter, c.1576.

KELSEY HEAD PROMONTORY FORT. The headland is defended by a single bank and ditch which encloses an area of 2½ acres. A single entrance occurs in the middle of the fortifications.

CREED

ST ANDREW. W tower of three stages with buttresses set back
from the corners; rebuilt in 1734. The church has a N transept, and in the N walls traces of Norman masonry. The S
side has a C15 aisle with very lavish windows, especially the
E window, and a S porch with fluted jambs, decorated capitals,
and a pointed barrel-vault with transverse arches inside.
Badly carved heads as the boss of the central arch. The W
window of the S aisle is Dec. The arcade of the aisle is of five
bays, quite tall and spacious, with standard Cornish piers.
The aisle still preserves some parts of its old wagon roof. –
PISCINA (N transept). For the antiquarian the most interesting
object in the church – a Norman pillar piscina with chevron
decoration of the pillar, placed under a C13 trefoil arch. –
The chancel PISCINA looks early C14. – FONT. C13, of
Catacleuse (?) stone, octagonal, with two shallow blank niches
with pointed heads to each side. – ROOD SCREEN. Only a
little preserved, but of interesting design, with flamboyant
blank tracery of the panels. – STAINED GLASS. Minor
fragments in the S windows. – PLATE. Chalice and Paten by
P. Symonds of Plymouth, 1720–1; Flagon by *Étienne Rongent*,
1732–3. – MONUMENT to T. Ducys † 1559, wife, and son
† 1602. Slate, with inscriptions and coat of arms; well
engraved, not rustic.

(PENNANS. A charming house of *c.*1720. Granite, five-bay
centre with projecting wings. Pedimented doorway. GMT)

(GARLENICK. Stone house of two storeys and five bays, with
embattled parapet; *c.*1810. GMT)

CREEKVEAN see FEOCK

CROAN

Near Washaway

Manor house of two storeys and seven bays with a hipped roof,
built *c.*1696 for a prosperous attorney.

CROWAN

ST CREWENNA. All granite, severely restored in 1872, with a W
tower of three stages, unbuttressed. The inside has a remarkable N arcade (similar to St Ives) with standard Cornish
granite piers, but capitals of sufficient height to house shield-
holding angels on all four sides. Their escutcheons allude to a

St Aubyn marriage of 1398. The arches are two-centred.
There are three of these bays; the three following are Elizabethan. The s arcade was added late in the C17, but swept
away in 1870 and replaced by one of Cornish standard. –
FONT. Granite; plain, square bowl, quatrefoil section of shaft,
base with extremely primitively carved lions *passant*; probably
late medieval, not Norman (cf. St Ives). – MONUMENTS.
Brasses to Geoffrey St Aubyn and wife, *c.* 1420, Geoffrey
St Aubyn and wife, *c.*1490, Thomas St Aubyn and wife,
*c.*1550. – Damaged monument to Col. Thomas St Aubyn
with a small standing figure, *c.*1650. – Sir John St Aubyn
† 1714. Tomb-chest with black marble inscription plate on
top. – Sir John St Aubyn † 1772, by *Joseph Wilton*, with two
life-size putti and an urn. – Sir John St Aubyn † 1839, with a
life-size mourning woman by an urn; dull. By *Behnes*.
(CHURCH HOUSE. An interesting example of a C19 medium-
sized house built in the Scottish Baronial style – unusual for
Cornwall. Mullioned windows, steep-pitched roof, gable
parapets, massive chimneystacks. MHLG)

7050   CUBERT

ST CUBERT. W tower with bold buttresses on the lower stage,
only just set back from the angles. A broached spire finishes
the relatively low tower, an unusual feature in Cornwall. The
tower was rebuilt in 1852.* The arch from the tower into the
nave is narrow, pointed, with a moulding of the arch which
confirms that the whole tower was built originally *c.*1300. Of
the same date and moulding the arch into the N transept and
the plain N door into the nave. Then, in the C15, a s aisle was
added, of six bays, with a s transept to its s, the detail standard
Cornish granite design. The s side of the s transept has a niche
for a tomb. Chancel and aisle have their original wagon roofs.
Most of the windows were inserted by *Street*. Sedding noted
that 'the only old windows left are the two-light C14 window
in the N wall of the chancel, and one of three lights in the s
wall of the aisle'. – FONT. C13, circular, on the usual five
supports (the outer with shaft-rings), the sides of the bowl
with chip-carving of rosettes, stars, etc. – PULPIT. Made up
of bench ends of standard design. – MONUMENTS. Extremely
pretty slate plate for the 'exuviae Arthuri Lawrence plebei'
and his sons. They died in 1669 and 1699. The inscription is

* Mr Nairn tells me of a restoration by *G. E. Street*, 1846–9.

flanked by boldly incised columns, with a rich scrolly pediment with plenty of floral decoration above. – Fine, sharp inscription plate with urn above to John Hoskin † 1810, by *Isbell* of Truro. – INSCRIBED STONE in the w wall of the tower: CONETOCI FILI TEGERNOMALI. Date c7 at the earliest: cf. the Hiberno-Saxon letters.

CUBY

9040

ST CUBY. 1828, with the C14 W tower of slate, in two stages, with diagonal buttresses and a two-centred arch to the w door. The N side with the N transept still exhibits some of the medieval masonry. The s porch has a pointed tunnel-vault with transverse arches, and in the apex of the middle one two heads of kings as a boss. The hoodmould of the porch doorway also has two kings as label-stops, and two more kings are walled into the porch. The tracery of the windows is typical of the pre-antiquarian early C19. – FONT. Late Norman, Bodmin type, with the same heads at the corners, and motifs of animals, knots, and trees of life between. – INSCRIBED STONE. At the s end of the w side of the s aisle: NONNITA ERCILINI RIGATI . . . TRIS FILI ERCILINI; C6 or C7.

CURY

6020

ST GUNWALLOE. The main point of interest is the Norman s doorway of one order of columns, with a key band on one side and zigzag on the other side of the columns; tympanum with a series of interlaced rings surrounded by zigzag and beads. The s wall altogether has the earliest features of the church, Norman and C14 probably. A squint connects s transept and chancel. It consists of an octagonal pier taking the place of the corner of the two parts (cf. Landewednack, Mawgan-in-Meneage). The N arcade of six bays and the N aisle are later, yet, as the N window of the same design as at Sithney, Mullion, and Gunwalloe shows (also with the same charming panelling of the inner arch), not later than the early C15. The piers of the arcade are Cornish granite standard, with the familiar horizontal leaves along the abaci. The w tower is of two stages only and unbuttressed. A stair-turret rises in the NW corner to above the pinnacles. Simple w door and window above, both with heads as label-stops (cf., for example, Manaccan). – FONT with crude corner shafts and shallowly carved star or rosette medallions between. A variety of the Bodmin type.

(BONYTHON. Late c18. A delightful granite house of basement and two storeys. Five bays. Eight wide steps with curving handrails rise to the doorway (cf. Pengreep), with fanlight above and wide rusticated surround. The central bay is brought slightly forward. Venetian window above, and a slight pediment with small fan-shaped window. Four stone balls on hexagonal pillars cap the parapet (as at Clowance). Exceptionally elegant. GMT)

BOCHYM. *See* Helston.

₁₀₈₀

DAVIDSTOW

ST DAVID. The church was so much restored in 1875 (by *Hine* of Plymouth) that little original work remains inside. It is a large building with an unusually wide nave and wide aisles. The three E windows are of five lights each, wider also than the standard. The W tower is tall, of three stages, and with buttresses which leave the corners free. The parapet is unembattled. – A few BENCH ENDS remain in the E part of the S aisle; one shows a man with bagpipes, another a saint, a lion, and the kneeling donor (?).

₀₀₈₀

DELABOLE

A long straggling village, with the slate quarries noticeable everywhere.

ST JOHN. By *Hine & Odgers* of Plymouth, c.1880. – PLATE. Chalice and Paten by *A. Chetier* of Paris, rather a fine piece; c18.

METHODIST CHAPEL. 1863, with a broad, crazy Italianate porch.

₇₀₃₀

DEVORAN

ST JOHN. 1855–6 by *J. L. Pearson*, unaisled and unattractive, with a polygonal chancel and E.E. detail, all rather cheap-looking inside. – PLATE. Chalice, foreign, c16, and Paten, foreign, c.1700.

DOBWALLS *see* LISKEARD

DONIERT STONE *see* ST CLEER

DULOE

St Cuby and St Leonard. A plan not unique in Cornwall, but rare enough, and only surviving where it had been adopted in the earlier Middle Ages. The tower is not at the w but attached to the s transept. It dates from the C13 and is exceptionally well preserved, although its Perp top stage was taken down in 1861. The pyramidal roof is C19, but no doubt an approximately correct imitation of the original top. The strong two-staged buttresses at the foot are also indicative of a date at any rate earlier than the Perp style. A STOUP of the same date is in the Colshull Chapel. The s door into the tower has a C13 surround, with colonnettes and simply moulded capitals. The arch between transept and tower was blocked up at an early date. That from the nave into the s transept however is Perp, of the same design as the N arcade of four bays, a design not quite Cornish standard: instead of the simple shaft–hollow–shaft profile of the piers there are two fillets l. and r. of the hollow, as at St Martin-by-Looe, St Cleer, Lewannick. The two bays of the N aisle adjoining the chancel are a little lower, but very much more sumptuous, owing to the fact that the chancel aisle was built as the Colshull family chapel at the end of the C15. Sir John Colshull † 1483 was buried in it, and his MONUMENT still survives, a tomb-chest with shields in quatrefoils in circles in squares as its chief decorative motif (exactly the same as in the octagonal FONT). On the w side this is replaced by a Crucifixion. On the chest lies a plate of dark elvan stone, and on this lies Sir John in armour. The carving of the figure is disappointing, especially when compared with the exquisite detail of flowers, leaves, and grapes in the arcades of the chapel. The E arch rests on a demi-figure of an angel. The chapel is enclosed by a PARCLOSE SCREEN, evidently not entirely in its original state. It is quite conceivable that it is made up from pieces of a rood screen. But the armorial devices prove its connexion with the Colshull family. In the exterior view also the chapel is singled out from the rest of the building by buttresses, battlements, and pinnacles. – PLATE. Chalice and Paten by *Jons* of Exeter, 1575; Paten on foot, by *J. Rand*, 1717–18. – OTHER MONUMENTS. Slates in the Colshull Chapel to Anna Coffyn, 1592, in Elizabethan dress; to two unknown wives and their children, also Elizabethan, and especially pretty in the way the figures kneel on cushions floating nowhere, with foliage trails as a surround; to John Killiow † 1601 and wife, tomb-chest with coat of arms against the brick wall; and to Mary Arundell, who died young in 1629 (Maria Arundell | Man a dry laurel | Man to a Marigold compar'd may bee | Man may be likened to the laurel tree | Both feede the eye, both please the optick sense | Both soone decay, both suddenly fleet hence | What then inferre you from here name but this | Man fades away, man a dry laurel is). – Henry Bewes, 1793 by *William Adron*. His best work: relief of a woman with portrait medallion of the dead man.

(HOLY WELL, ½ m. down the hill towards Looe. The exterior is modern.)

STONE CIRCLE, near the church. A small circle of eight stones with a diameter of 38 ft. The present setting represents the work of restoration in the C19. The circle may originally have enclosed a cairn, all traces of which have disappeared. One or more cremations in urns were found at the bases of the stones.

DUPATH
3060
Near Callington

HOLY WELL. In a square little granite building, probably of the C15, with a sunk basin at the far end, and the water coming in from the front side, running in a conduit into the basin, and out into the open at the back. Steeply pointed tunnel-vault with one transverse arch, forming the gabled roof as well, and crowned with a bellcote-like turret over the entrance.

EBBINGFORD MANOR *see* BUDE

EGLOSHAYLE
0070

ST CONAN (?). Wholly Perp, with the exception of some earlier masonry in the N wall and a N doorway and two windows of *c*.1300. The W tower is over 80 ft high and impressive, specially from the other side of the river Camel. It has buttresses set back from the corners, and a door commemorating the gift of the tower by John Loveybond (*see* Wadebridge). The door has roll-mouldings in the jambs in the form of snakes (a curious Celtic survival), and on the N side cognizance of 'Loveybound'. Nave of six bays, S aisle, fragmentary (never completed) N aisle, N transept, S porch. Nave piers of granite with the usual Cornish profile; capitals moulded. In the S aisle good Perp windows, especially the E window of five lights, exceptionally grand for Cornwall. GLASS in the E window, 1930 by *G. Cruttwell* and *T. Hamilton*. The s aisle roof of the usual wagon type, ceiled. The purlins and ribs are finely carved, and some of the supporting angels survive. – FONT. Norman, Purbeck table-top type, with plain blank arcading on the sides. – PUPLIT. Octagonal, Caen stone, C15, with carved emblems of the Passion and some more emblems referring to John Loveybond. – MONUMENTS. Dame Barbara Molesworth † 1735. Large, of white and grey marble, with bust, and obelisk in relief behind; evidently of metropolitan workmanship, although the inscription says, not very complimentarily: 'To deliver to Posterity a Description of the Beautys of her Mind would be as equally Vain as the Sculptor's Attempt in the above resemblance of her Face. The one was superior to Art, the other to Imagination.' – Sir A. D. Molesworth † 1824, by *Richard Westmacott, R.A.* – Also neo-classical minor wall-monuments, for example by *Shepherd* of Plymouth.

EGLOSKERRY

2080

ST KERIA. Standing in the middle of the village. Of the Norman church the N wall and N transept (with jambs of the arch towards the nave) survive, and also the N and s doorways. The N one is blocked and has a tympanum with a dragon snapping at its own tail. The s tympanum is now walled-in inside: a lamb *passant* and a cross standing in front of it. The s aisle is separated from the nave by a standard Cornish arcade of five bays. The W tower is C15, of three stages and unbuttressed. s porch of granite with a wagon roof. – FONT. Plain Norman, with cable-moulding at the top. – PISCINA, s of the altar. Norman (a rarity). It is a block capital on a short shaft, with a little palm-leaf decoration in the corners between the characteristic lunettes of the block capital. – PLATE. Chalice and Paten by *Coton* of Barnstaple, Elizabethan; Italian Cup and Cover, c.1700. – MONUMENT to a layman, in a niche at the E end of the aisle. Alabaster effigy, in a bad state of preservation.

PENHEALE. *See* p. 135.

ERTH BARTON *see* SALTASH

1050

ETHY
Near Lerryn

Georgian house of seven bays and two storeys, the centre flanked by giant pilasters.

8030

FALMOUTH

Modern Falmouth covers quite a large area, and the beach with the largest hotels faces Falmouth Bay to the S, whereas the old harbour faced N. It is an excellent wide harbour for smaller ships, protected by Henry VIII's two castles: Pendennis and St Mawes. But the real development of Falmouth begins only with Sir John Killigrew (died 1584), whose family mansion, Arwenack, still partly remains, and who saw the possibilities for a prosperous town in the then fishing village. The visible history starts with the C17 and C18 cottages off the main streets, behind Market Street and down Fish Strand Hill and Quay Hill. The conversion into a town came chiefly in the thirty years after the incorporation (1661) with the building of the church and Church Street.

CHURCH OF KING CHARLES THE MARTYR. 1662–4. Partly paid for by Sir Peter Killigrew. The W tower, oddly narrower in its E–W than its N–S dimension, was built about 1684 (top stage and pinnacles, 1800). The nave was originally 66 by 66 ft in size and separated into nave and aisles by the tall granite
19b columns with Ionic capitals in plaster which still exist. In the strangest contrast to this classical splendour are the windows, in two tiers of typically Cornish Perp design, and the three separate, long, panelled roofs, equally typical of the Cornish late Middle Ages. A chancel was added in 1684, but this came down in 1813. Galleries were put in in 1686, 1695, and 1702, somewhat spoiling the grand simplicity of the former interior design. The new E end of 1813 was much longer than the previous one and had a Venetian window at the E. Finally in 1896 *E. H. Sedding* made several further alterations. The result is the present church, without N and S galleries and with an entablature above the columns. – PULPIT. Made up of C16 and C17 carvings; origin unknown. – SCREEN. Granite, from St Paul, Penzance, where it served as a communion rail. – CREDENCE TABLE with the Killigrew arms; 1759. – STAINED GLASS. Some old glass above the Lady Altar, bought in Italy in the C19. – E window by *Taylor* and *Clifden*, 1913. –

ALABASTER relief of the Flagellation in the vestry. – MONU-
MENTS. Thomas Corker † 1700. Prettily written inscription
on a convex oval shield. – Richard Lockyer † 1789. Standing
mourning woman by an urn against a dark obelisk; by *Paty*
of Bristol. – Capt. James Bull † 1821, exactly the same composition in reverse, by *Isbell* of Truro. – (The Rev. Lewis
Mathias, 1837 by *Jacob* and *Thomas Olvers* of Falmouth.)

ALL SAINTS, Killigrew Street. 1887–90 by *J. D. Sedding*.* Not
an appealing exterior, though the w end with five lancets and
two bold buttresses is impressive and very much in Sedding's
style. Inside a large and wide arch, very tall piers connected
by round arches, and narrow aisles in which the pointed
Gothic windows look odd enough, framed by the semicircles
of the arcade.

ST MARY IMMACULATE (R.C.), Killigrew Road. 1869 by
J. A. Hansom; tower and spire 1881 by *J. S. Hansom*.)

ST MICHAEL, Penwerris. 1827 by *R. Crout*, with a curious
castellated façade towards the water, and a little turret on the
w gable: a plain rectangle inside.

CHURCH STREET dates from the late C17, but of that the
exteriors of the houses betray little. Of C18 development also
little of interest survives, chiefly a few good brick houses at
the far end of ARWENACK STREET and the beginning of
GROVE PLACE: chequerboard patterns of brick and vitrified
headers. Other C18 terraces deserve no special mention.‡ The
main growth came apparently with the early C19. To this
phase belong the most noteworthy public buildings: the
CUSTOM HOUSE, the ROYAL CORNWALL POLYTECHNIC 63a
(1833, in Church Street),§ and the former FALMOUTH
CLASSICAL AND MATHEMATICAL SCHOOL (1824, in
Killigrew Road), all Greek Doric. Of the same time some of
the places of worship other than of the Established Church,
for example the SYNAGOGUE in Vernon Place, 1816. A little
earlier the ROYAL HOTEL in Market Street and the best
private houses: for example GROVE HILL HOUSE, *c.*1790,
the older parts of the GREENBANK HOTEL by the water, and
MARLBOROUGH HOUSE in Marlborough Avenue, built in 59b
1805–15 by Captain Bull, with a pretty pavilion with lantern.
The front has an Ionic colonnade, the interior a handsome

---

* Sedding thought this his best work, according to Mr P. Anson.

‡ Except perhaps Nos. 1–3 BANK PLACE (MHLG).

§ Gunnis records there a bust of the Prince of Wales by *Nevil Northey
Burnard*, 1848.

curved staircase. Of terraces of this time it is sufficient to mention STRATTON TERRACE, Penwerris.

(In addition ALBERT TERRACE: colour-washed brick with doors and windows with pointed arches; FLORENCE PLACE and FLORENCE TERRACE: complete groups of thirteen and fifteen houses; STRATTON PLACE, TEHIDY TERRACE. MHLG)

ARWENACK HOUSE. The manor of the Killigrews is at the far end of Grove Place, opposite the severely plain OBELISK to the Killigrew family erected in 1737. Of the large Elizabethan house only a shadow remains. Chapel and Hall were destroyed in the Civil War. Additions to the ruined building were made after 1786.

(TRESCOBEAS SECONDARY MODERN SCHOOL, on the Trescobeas Estate. 1957 by *Lyons, Israel & Ellis*.)

PENDENNIS CASTLE. *See* p. 134.

8030   FEOCK

An unusually pretty village, of Devon rather than Cornish character, overlooking Carrick Roads.

ST FEOCA. The w tower alone remains of the old church, C13, one-storeyed, with a pyramidal roof. The opening towards the nave was low and pointed. It stands detached from the present church, which is all C19, except the standard Cornish arcade with plain capitals and four-centred arches. The furnishing of the chancel must have cost a great deal of money – STAINED GLASS. E window by *Beer* of Exeter (TK). – FONT Late Norman, of Catacleuse stone, crisply carved, circular with a frieze of two tiers of diagonal crosses above and circles with trees of life below (cf. Ladock, Fowey, etc.). – PULPIT With four late C16 Flemish panels with religious scenes. – The LYCH GATE with a slate-hung upper storey, presumably a vestry room or schoolroom, is early C19. – CROSS, in the churchyard. Still the old Celtic type with the circular head Crucifixus not yet with crossed feet. Yet the foliated cross at the back seems to prove C13 workmanship.

(CREEKVEAN, E of Feock on Pill Creek. A holiday house by *Richard Rogers* and *N. & W. Foster*, 1967.)

COME-TO-GOOD. *See* p. 55.

FERNACRE *see* ST BREWARD

FLUSHING

The village was founded in 1661, and one terrace of houses (CLONMORE, with triangular pediment and plastered front, and CLINTON HOUSE, similar, but with a straight canopy over the door) seems indeed to belong to the C17.* It might stand in any town. Around it there are a few pretty cottages and one more fine Georgian house, ROCKSIDE, slate-hung, in fact a warehouse, converted in the C18. The church of ST PETER is of 1842. ORGAN formerly in Exeter Hall, London (information from P. Laws).

FORRABURY

CHURCH. Exposed on a bare hill S of Boscastle. A short, plain W tower of 1750, still completely in the medieval tradition, even with battlements and very plain pinnacles. The little church has a Norman S wall and S transept with the Norman imposts at the opening towards the nave. The nave is short and has a N aisle with depressed two-centred arches on odd, thick, vaguely classical columns. The S porch is covered by two big slabs of granite. – FONT. Norman, cup-shaped, with diagonal criss-cross on the cup (cf. Tintagel, Minster). – S of the churchyard a CROSS of a usual elementary type.

WELLTOWN. The manor house of c.1640 has its porch, some very heavy-looking mullioned windows, the staircase, and a few rooms still intact.

FOWEY‡

This small town rising on the hillside by an excellent natural harbour close to the mouth of the river Fowey was once one of England's busiest ports. Its ships during medieval times carried away tin, were employed in the King's service, and indulged in piracy. In 1457 the French burnt the town, after which disaster two blockhouses were built on either side of the harbour: between these stretched a chain. Henry VIII in connexion with his systematic fortification of the S coast (cf. Pendennis and

* Or early C18, according to Lady Redwood, who also draws attention to No. 22 TREYEW ROAD, large, with bow windows on two floors at each end of the front, and to NEW QUAY HOUSE, slate-hung upper storeys, side elevation semicircular, the entrance doors altered.

‡ Information on Fowey has been checked and considerably amplified – partly from unpublished sources – by Mr John Keast. I am most grateful to him.

St Mawes) added a stronger fort: ST CATHERINE'S CASTLE (restored 1855).

18 ST NICHOLAS. The arrangement of nave of five bays, N and S aisles (of unusual width), two-storeyed S porch, and W tower is Cornish standard, but the execution differs from the usual pattern in many ways, owing to its date. While the vast majority of interiors one sees in Cornwall are C15, St Nicholas was re-dedicated in 1336. The plain octagonal piers running without any capitals into the plain double-chamfered pointed arches indeed fit the early C14 and are probably inspired by friars' architecture. The contemporary clerestory has windows ranging with the spandrels, not the apexes of the arches (cf. St Germans, Lostwithiel, Callington), and starting below these. The aisles with their windows may be contemporary with the clerestory of the late C15, the exceptionally fine carved wagon roof, and the S porch, which has (as against the usual arrangement) open archways to W and E, and an eight-ribbed vault. The tower has four stages and buttresses leaving the corners free. It is richly decorated (cf. Launceston): plinth with two bands of ornament, first stringcourse with two bands of ornament, second and third stringcourses also two bands, pinnacles in relief against the top parts of the buttresses, pannelled top pinnacles, ornamented battlements. The four-light S windows and the five-light chancel window are C15 or early C16. They have colonnettes in their inner jambs. –

26a FONT. Norman, of Catacleuse stone, with rosettes in circles and an upper border of crossed zigzag lines. Good workmanship. The same workshop supplied very similar fonts to Ladock, Feock, and St Mewan. – PULPIT. Hexagonal; 1601. – MONUMENTS. Brasses to a civilian and wife, and another to a civilian, c.1450. – John Rashleigh, 1582. – Alice Rashleigh, 1602. – Incised stone plate, late C16, the figure consciously archaic. – More interesting the monument to John Rashleigh of about 1610, lying on a chest with ruff and berret. The back plate with strapwork in a separate place. – Another Rashleigh monument is of 1683 and has an architectural background with columns, garlands, and a broken segmental pediment.

50 PLACE. The seat of the Treffry family, immediately NW of the church, and with its high walls, battlements, and Cornish vegetation forming a delightful ensemble with it. The house is an overwhelming display of early C19 to Early Victorian Gothic, the work of *J. T. (Austin) Treffry* of between 1813 and 1845. Of the old house not much was left untouched. The best

piece is the early c16 bay window in the courtyard, two-storeyed, with transoms and all the lights arched. The ornate canted bay of the E front is re-erected with old materials. It is reminiscent of Launceston church and was originally on the S side, where it was replaced and a yet bigger and showier bay window added. The towers also are c19. It is of an ambitious, somewhat elephantine Walter Scottian romanticism. Inside, the showpiece is the Porphyry Hall of 1841–3 above the library, with its polished porphyry walls. The staircase must be late too, for here Georgian details get mixed up with Gothic ones.

ALMSHOUSES, W of the church. c17.

At the lower end of Lostwithiel Street, facing into Trafalgar Square, is the SHIP HOTEL, a c15 house renovated in 1570 (carved oak fireplace and panelling, vaulted plaster ceiling), being then the town house of the Rashleigh family. Front rebuilt in the late c19. An existing doorway in the upper storey formerly communicated with a room in the arch or 'bow' which used to span Lostwithiel Street until 1876. This was the toll gate or south gate of the town. The house opposite is probably c14, with c16 and c18 alterations – stone windows subsequently filled in and plastered over.

E of Trafalgar Square the TOWN HALL, erected in 1792. This embodies part of an older building with c14 windows – which Henderson suggested may have been a guild chapel: later used as the town 'clink' (iron grille still in place). Opposite in DOLPHIN TERRACE are remains of the lower course (Pentewan stone) of the Broadgate, one of the defence gateways of the town in medieval times. The c18 houses adjoining probably occupy the site of a large castellated building which Leland mentions in the middle of the c15 as 'facing quadrately onto the harbour', possibly the Haveners Hall mentioned in earlier documents.

There is a c14 window and door in a house in WEBB STREET adjoining the King of Prussia inn: below the latter is the old market space, fronted by granite columns.

In FORE STREET the LUGGER of 1633 with modern frontage; then NOAH'S ARK, probably a merchant's house of the c16, with remains of a carved plaster ceiling; and at the bottom of CUSTOM HOUSE HILL a large early c18 house, modernized. The original porch still exists, with a carved shell hood.

Other c16 and c17 houses which have recently been restored may be seen in NORTH STREET, UNION PLACE, and LOSTWITHIEL STREET.

Menabilly. *See* p. 116.
Penquite. *See* p. 135.

5020

GERMOE

St Germoe. The usual three-stage w tower of regular granite
blocks. The pinnacles are corbelled out, as at St Ives. The s
wall is the earliest part of the building. A Norman w window
in the s transept. The exterior of the chancel also seems to a
large extent Norman. Other s windows of the c14. The n aisle
also belongs to the c14, low, with Cornish standard piers.
The arch to the n transept is of the same kind, whereas the s
transept is divided from the nave by a pier of the same section,
but placed diagonally. In the c15 a s porch was built, its gable
resting on two animals and crowned by a Crucifixus. – font.
Very primitive Norman, with three faces, one hardly recognizable. – stoup. Fragment in the n transept, Norman,
scalloped.

St Germoe's Chair (or King Germoe's Throne). An interesting little building in the churchyard wall, like an c18 covered
seat but probably medieval;* it is entered by a twin arch with
a circular pier and has three seats at its back, with blank
pointed arches separated by shafts with moulded capitals. The
central arch has a crowned head, badly carved, at its top.

Tregoning Hill. China clay was discovered first here in
1768.

Pengersick Castle. *See* p. 134.

8030

GERRANS

St Gerent. From the sea the e side with its two roofs and the
spire appear behind fine old pine-trees; for St Gerent
possesses one of the rare Cornish spires, octagonal, with one
ring of quatrefoil decoration mid-way up. The lower part has
diagonal buttresses and is of slate (except for the w front on
the ground floor), probably c14. In the n wall are two small
lancets (restoration ?).‡ The s aisle is an addition, the arcade
on square piers with four attached shafts, and depressed
pointed arches. – font. Norman, square, with four shallow

* c15, according to the mhlg.

‡ With the exception of the tower, the church was entirely rebuilt in 1849
by *William White* of Truro. As far as possible the original stones and windows
were re-used in an exact replica of the old church. Only the sacristy was
added. (*Ecclesiologist*, October 1849, p. 246.)

blank niches on each side (a simplified version of the Egloshayle type). – BENCH ENDS. Only a few. – PLATE. Chalice
and Paten by the same maker as St Anthony-in-Roseland,
dated 1595; also a pretty Falmouth-made Porringer of c.1700,
signed *IP*. – MONUMENT to Edward Hobbs, 1718 by *Weston*
of Exeter, with two allegorical figures in garments as chastely
undetailed as if they were of 1820.

GIANT'S HOUSE *see* ZENNOR

GIANT'S QUOIT *see* TRESLOTHAN

GLYNN *see* CARDINHAM

GODOLPHIN   6030

ST JOHN THE BAPTIST. 1849–50 by *J. P. St Aubyn*.)
GODOLPHIN HALL. The home of the Godolphins, who rose 56b
into prominence under Henry VIII and were knighted about
the middle of the C16. The present building is approached
from the N and consists of three wings around a square courtyard and the front wall of a further building on the S side of
this. Originally the main buildings extended S of this wall,
with two projecting wings to the S. Of the early C16 a room
remains in the E range with some linenfold panelling and
prettily patterned ceiling beams. Opposite the hall range is a
Jacobean range with a fireplace (*ex situ*) inside. The most
rewarding part is the castellated N side, with a loggia of seven
bays on the ground floor. It has fat, heavy Tuscan columns.
The windows above are mullioned and transomed and have
the same hoodmoulds drawn on as a continuous stringcourse
as at Lanhydrock. This looks mid C17, and makes the accepted
date of after 1712 for Godolphin seem highly unlikely, even
for Cornwall. Farm buildings and remains of quite an ambitious garden can still be seen in the solitude which surrounds
present-day Godolphin.

GOLANT   1050
Parish of St Samson

ST SAMSON. The E side faces the Fowey river down the hill.
The church is small but full of interest. It seems to have been
built all at one go and was consecrated in 1509. Low W tower
of rough granite blocks, in two stages, battlemented but not

pinnacled. HOLY WELL in the corner between tower and porch, with straight-headed windows on the S and N. Inside the church a fine wagon roof in the nave and an equally fine ceiled cradle roof in the aisle. The arcade between the two is of seven bays with low standard piers. – BENCH ENDS, made up into a pulpit and stalls. They are uncommonly varied, especially noteworthy is a series with little figures of apostles on one shield and their emblems on the other; also one large figure of St Samson. Of other motifs there are for example two crowned heads on little castles, a fool's head, a coat of arms of the Colquite family. – MONUMENT. Slate plate to Edmund Constable † 1716 ('Short blaze of life, meteor of human pride | Essay'd to live but liked it not and died'). – SCULPTURE. Head of Christ, looking up; marble; Italian Baroque? – STAINED GLASS. C15 figures of St Anthony and St Samson, fairly well preserved.

GOLDEN

9040

The farm contains the traces of a hall-house of the late 1530s refronted and probably much reconstructed a century later and again added to in the C18. A stone overmantel remains from the C16 house, with carved tritons.

There is also a splendid BARN with its original roof timbers (upper cruck trusses – cf. Tintagel Old Post Office) and one original round-headed window in the S wall at first-floor level. A stone newel stair to the upper storey raises the question of whether this might once have been a dwelling house with a first-floor hall; but if there ever were any other features to corroborate this, they disappeared when the barn was partly rebuilt in the C19 (V. M. and F. J. Chesher).

GONVENA see WADEBRIDGE

GORAN HAVEN

0040

ST GORANUS. The village, at the time of writing a still completely unspoilt Cornish fishing village, was called Porthjust in the past. The church, largely rebuilt in 1885, consists of a slim W tower without buttresses or pinnacles, and a nave with Perp windows. The nice S door arch with a niche above should be noted.

GORRAN

T GORAN. A surprisingly big and important church, with a W tower 90 ft high and a S aisle eight bays long. The tower is of regular granite blocks, in three stages, with buttresses set back from the corners; wholly late C15 or early C16. The S aisle has three-light windows and a four-light E window. The arcade inside is of white Pentewan stone, the piers with the same variation of the standard section as St Ives, namely a concave–convex–concave curve instead of the normal simple hollow.* The moulded capitals and two-centred arches also point to the early C15. The S porch is battlemented with two pinnacles and has panelled jambs. The wagon roof in the porch is original. Of the other timbers bits of wall plates have been made up into a lectern. The N side of the church is older; the (blocked) N door is especially clearly of the C13 (with a head at the apex and two heads as label-stops), and the arch from the nave to the transept probably is too. – FONT. Norman, on five supports, with corner faces and, as chief ornamental motifs between, the unusual motif of streaky flowing hair and rosette, tree of life, etc.‡ – STAINED GLASS. Tiny fragments in the E window of the S aisle. – BENCH ENDS. Fifty-three altogether, more than in most other churches, but not specially interesting in the motifs. Some have two, some one motif to an end. There are many initials, many of the familiar Instruments of the Passion, and also some ornamental motifs clearly belonging to the Renaissance. – PLATE. Chalice and Paten, probably Elizabethan; also a Flagon by *Freeman*, 1705–6. – MONUMENTS. Head of a coffin-shaped slab with foliated cross. – Brass to an unknown kneeling woman, *c.*1510. – Richard Edgcumbe of Bodrugan † 1604. A purely Italian frame with scrolly pediment, impossible in England at that date; either foreign or later, say *c.* 1670.

GRADE

HOLY CROSS or ST GRADA. It is a pity no better church was designed in 1862 to replace a small building with an old

* The Rev. J. H. Adams points out that the arcade was built in three stages. The last three piers and capitals are of granite, and therefore more rudely carved, and there are three slightly different forms of base.

‡ Two points suggest that the font may not be Norman: the Bodrugan arms on the E face (which could possibly have been added later, of course) and a curious, un-Norman round-faced monster right at the base (Rev. J. H. Adams).

tradition, in a position so bare and prominent as to be visible for miles around. The roof pitches especially are quite out of keeping with Cornish traditions. Of the old church only the w tower remains: regular serpentine blocks, two stages, no buttresses (just like the neighbouring churches of Ruan Major, Landewednack, and Mullion). Inside is a FONT of the C13, a variation on the Bodmin type, similar to Cury: thick short corner shafts and four shallowly carved stars, rosettes etc., in circles. – BRASS to James Erisey † 1522 and family, an early example of a type often found in Cornwall (see Mawgan-in-Pydar, etc.).

9040

GRAMPOUND

CROSS in the market place, late medieval, 12 ft high, on step and pedestal; unornamented. (CHAPEL OF ST NUNN. Rebuilt in 1869 on its C15 site. A. S. B. New)
TRENOWTH. See p. 227.

GREYSTONE BRIDGE see LAWHITTON

GUGH see SCILLY ISLES

4030

GULVAL

ST GULVAL. At first sight it appears a new church;* only the w tower is obviously old: of regular granite blocks, in three stages, with no buttresses. We are here in the rare position of knowing its date. It had just been completed in 1440. The N parts of the church are new, the s parts only heavily restored: s aisle with octagonal piers, their capitals decorated with shield-holding angels, as at St Ives. The date there would correspond to that of the tower of Gulval. – The FONT also is of St Ives type, but with only one severely stylized angel holding a shield. – PLATE. Paten, 1685–6 by *TC*, prettily inscribed; Paten, 1809 by *J. Edward*. – MONUMENTS. Fragmentary monument with two kneeling figures: John Davill † 1627 and Arthur Harris † 1628. – William Harris † 1766, prettily Rococo. – William Arundel Harris † 1826, by *Scott of Penzance*; rather reactionary for its date.

INSCRIBED STONES. One s of the churchyard with cable, key, and interlace decoration, another at Barlowena Bottom, to

---

* It was restored in 1892 by *J. P. St Aubyn* (G. Spain).

wards Madron (QUENATAUCI IC DINUI FILIUS), *c.*C6 or C7. The lettering transitional between Roman and Hiberno-Saxon.

BODRIFTY IRON AGE SETTLEMENT, at the foot of Mulfra Hill. The settlement consists of a series of hut circles surrounded by the remains of a stone enclosure wall now much overgrown by bracken and gorse. The whole complex occupies an area of approximately 4 acres. A number of the huts have been excavated and produced Iron Age A pottery. To the E are further huts and a CELTIC FIELD SYSTEM.

CHYSAUSTER. This, the best preserved group of courtyard houses in the county, consists of eight houses arranged in pairs on either side of a 'street'. Each consists of an oval court enclosed within a massive stone wall in which are a series of rooms and cells opening on to the court. Finds from the houses indicate that occupation continued into the Roman period. (There is a ruined fogou below the village.)

CRANKAN COURTYARD HOUSES, ⅔ m. SW of Chysauster. Two ruined houses are still visible in this settlement, the larger having a maximum diameter of 91 ft with walls still over 6 ft high. To the E is a terraced FIELD SYSTEM.

COURTYARD HOUSE, ¾ m. W, on the hillside above Try Farm. A single, well preserved house, 66 ft in maximum diameter, having a courtyard and round and long rooms. It is entered by a doorway on the SW. There are traces of a possible second house to the SW.

STANDING STONE, S of Try Farm. The stone projects 8 ft above the ground. On the E side was a cist containing a handled Beaker.

GUNNISLAKE

4070

NEW BRIDGE. Built *c.*1520, the best of all the Cornish granite bridges. Large, regular blocks. 182 ft long, of seven arches.

GUNWALLOE

6020

ST GUNWALLOE. Close to the sea, but sheltered from it by a bluff. The tower of an older church, built into the rock, stands on its own, two-storeyed, with a pyramidal roof and no buttresses; of slate, not of granite. The church was rebuilt in the C14–C15. The S porch has panelled jambs, the N aisle an E window of the same design as at Sithney, Mullion, and Cury. There are two aisles of five bays and identical design, with standard Cornish piers, plain capitals, and thinly decorated abaci. Old wagon roofs in the s aisle and s porch. – FONT. Fragments of the type of Buryan and Wendron. – ROOD SCREEN. The most important feature of the church is two panels of the old rood screen, C15, with painted figures of apostles below (cf. Budock, St Winnow, and many Devon examples) and beautiful flamboyant tracery above. They are used inside the N and s doors.

GURNARDS HEAD *see* MORVAH

7040

GWENNAP

ST WENNAPA. The odd feature of this church is its isolated tower with a pyramidal roof (of what date?). The church itself was rebuilt in 1862.* – Some nice MONUMENTS of the 1840s inside, for example by *Pearce* of Truro.

GWENNAP PIT. Stepped amphitheatre, perhaps originally caused by mining subsidence, in which Wesley preached several times – first in 1762. The present form of the amphitheatre is early C19.)

PENGREEP. *See* p. 135.

5030

GWINEAR

ST GWINEAR. A rather neglected church with a w tower of granite, in three stages, with buttresses set back from the angles and a NE stair-turret rising above the battlements and pinnacles. It was in course of erection in 1441. The windows at the bell stage are straight-headed. The chancel has a typical window of *c*.1300, five lancet lights, and tracery of the intersecting type. The interior effect is confused by the existence of the Arundell Aisle, an outer N aisle of three E bays. The inner N aisle follows the nave all the way; the s aisle starts two bays from the w. The latter has piers of four major and four minor shafts and unusual capitals, plain mostly, but in two piers decorated. The arches are nearly semicircular. The N arcade is Cornish standard, with large horizontal leaves on the capitals for the first bays, for the further bays with capitals showing four angels holding shields (cf. Crowan).

* The Rev. Frank Hastings tells me that the sw corner is C13 and that the s aisle, chancel, and nave are C14 and C15. He notes also a C14 trefoil PISCINA.

This motif is repeated in the arcade of the Arundell Aisle, which is otherwise (at the time of writing) in a sadly squalid state. The windows are Perp, those of the s aisle of four lights each with a four-centred head and no tracery at all. – FONT. Granite, 1727, an early case of antiquarian imitation of the Norman style. – PULPIT. Made up of bench ends, with one motif for each end. – LECTERN and KNEELING DESK also made up from bench ends. – ROOD SCREEN.* The base is left, with well-carved ornament, chiefly in each panel a vertical foliage serpentine.

(LANYON FARM, ½ m. SW of Gwinear Road Station. 1668, with later additions. MHLG)

P OLKINGHORNE FARM, ¼ m. W of Lanyon Farm. C17, with C18 and C19 additions. MHLG)

GWITHIAN   5040

St GOCIANUS. As at Perranzabuloe, or rather St Piran's church, there was at first an oratory in the sands. It still exists, but after excavation in the C19 has again been left to itself. It was rectangular, and may date back to Celtic Christianity. Its existence at Gwithian is not surprising: Hayle, near by, was the chief port of disembarkation of Irish saints. The present church was built in 1866 by *E. Sedding Sen.* A few fragments of the C15 are incorporated into the lychgate. It has its old W tower of regular granite blocks with panelled pinnacles. The C13 chancel arch is said to be preserved or copied in the present double-chamfered arch. – FONT. If it is medieval at all, it must be so much tampered with as to be wholly unrecognizable. It is square, with neat motifs of snake, rosette, cross, in medallions (cf. Phillack).

GWITHIAN TOWANS, ½ m. N of Gwithian village. An extensive Bronze Age farm with huts and fields was recovered by excavation. Nothing is now visible on the ground.

CRANE GODREVY, I m. N of Gwithian village. The ruins of a small manor of the C11–17 are built into the corner of a small fortified enclosure of the Late Iron Age.

HAREWOOD HOUSE *see* CALSTOCK

HARLYN *see* ST MERRYN

* Early C15 (MHLG).

4060
HATT
Near Saltash

Square red brick house of two and a half storeys, built about
1720.

HAWKSTOR DOWN *see* BLISLAND

5030
HAYLE

For the parish church, *see* Phillack.

St Elwyn. 1886–8 by *J. D. Sedding*, not up to the standard of
the architect of Holy Trinity, Sloane Street. Rather loud
outside, with the apse of the aisle coming forward like a
bastion, and dull inside. The buttress on the w side dividing
the w window in two is characteristically Late Victorian.

(Trevassack Manor, ¼ m. NE of Hayle Station. Mostly
C17–18; date-stone, 1700. Two-storeyed, three bays, low
and wide. MHLG)

(Bodriggy House. Long and low, granite; *c.* 1710.)

5030
HAYLE COPPERHOUSE

(In a field a few yards from the road at the top of Steamer Hill is
the Engine House of the first steam-using railway in Cornwall, built in 1834 to carry ore from the mines near Hayle to
smelting works at Redruth. It was horse-drawn from Hayle
to the foot of the hill, then hauled up by a stationary engine.
Dr Athelstane Hill)

9040
HELIGAN
Near St Ewe

Of 1603 originally, mostly rebuilt in 1727,* and with additions
of 1810. A plain three-storeyed front of six bays, with the two
central ones slightly projecting. No special decoration.
Attractive mid C18 Stable Block with bell tower.

0070
HELLAND

Church. Largely rebuilt. The s arcade is old, four bays, plain,
of Cornish granite standard. – Font. Plain, cup-shaped; is it

---

* Also rebuilt in 1692–3, Mr Colvin tells me.

c13? – MONUMENT. Very worn-off incised slab to H. Calwodley, early c16.

BRIDGE. One of the best medieval bridges in the county. c15, with four pointed arches springing from water level; double rings of thin slate voussoirs (cf. Lostwithiel).

HELLIGAN
Near St Mabyn

0070

Old farm buildings and part of the doorway and staircase of a house dated 1679.

HELSTON

6020

ST MICHAEL. Built at the expense of the Earl of Godolphin in 1751–61. The designer was *Thomas Edwards* of Greenwich. The interior is disappointing, with a gallery round three sides on short iron columns, a flat ceiling, and a lower chancel with a curved ceiling.* The outside has a w tower of granite blocks, Cornish in feeling, but with pilasters instead of buttresses, round-headed windows, and obelisks instead of pinnacles. The nave has five round-headed windows. A granite porch with pilasters was added in 1830 on the s side, with a pretty staircase inside up to the gallery (and a BRASS to T. Bougins † 1602 and family). – CHANDELIER. Of brass, dated 1762. – PLATE. Chalice and Paten by *WB*, 1630; other pieces of 1694, 1712, 1717. – MONUMENTS. John Trevener, 1825, and Peter Hill, 1837, by *Thomas Denman*.

MARKET HOUSE in the centre of the town, 1837–8 by *W. Harris* of Bristol, severely classical, of granite, with Doric columns on the upper floor, in shape not dissimilar to the Market House at Penzance. Two main streets run down from it and carry water down in open conduits: the main street, called COINAGEHALL STREET (from the special stannary coinage), in a slight curve with houses l. and r. on a pleasant scale, three old-fashioned hotels, and only one eyesore, the METHODIST CHURCH of 1888. (Emphasized by the MHLG, apart from the hotels, Nos. 15, 29, 43, and the house on the N side of the Bowling Green.) At the bottom end of the street the MONUMENT to H. M. Grylls, 1834, a Gothic entrance lodge to a public park, which is the site of the CASTLE. CHURCH STREET runs down and

* Mr H. Dalton Clifford has pointed out to me its resemblance, internally, to St Alfege, Greenwich.

up again, ending by the church. (Note No. 20, of the C17–18. MHLG)

(The ANGEL HOTEL, formerly the Godolphins' town house. Part of it is C16, including the Assembly Room, with a minstrels' gallery. Dr Athelstane Hill)

(Also stressed by the MHLG: in CROSS STREET, Nos. 1, 10, and the Vicarage; in GODOLPHIN ROAD, Nos. 28–34; No. 9 LADY STREET; Nos. 1–3, 4–6, 13, 30, 51–53 MENEAGE STREET; Nos. 19–23 and 61–65 MONUMENT STREET; and a cinema in WENDRON STREET, a former Nonconformist chapel in the Norman style of c.1840.)

(BOCHYM MANOR, Cury Cross. Large and irregular; C16–17. Two storeys. The entrance side has three gabled bay windows. The occurrence of the motif of vertically set, keyed-in ovals suggests the later C17. Among the outbuildings is an embattled clock tower. What is its date?)

(JUNIOR AND INFANTS' SCHOOL, Parc Eglos. 1965 by the County Architect, *A. J. Groves*.)

(TRENETHICK BARTON, 1 m. NE. Elizabethan farmhouse of granite with mullioned, hoodmoulded windows, a two-storeyed porch, and a separate granite gatehouse. Supposed Norman masonry at the back. Dr Athelstane Hill)

PENROSE. *See* p. 136.

HERODSFOOT
2060

ALL SAINTS. 1850. Contains a C14 font, not of specially good workmanship, but of interesting design, with a circular bowl and a frieze of foliage scrolls along the upper rim. It is from the ruined chapel of St Martin at Respryn, St Winnow.

HESSENFORD
3050

(ST ANNE. 1832, rebuilt in 1871 to designs by *J. P. St Aubyn*.)

HORSE BRIDGE *see* STOKE CLIMSLAND

HUGH TOWN *see* SCILLY ISLES

THE HURLERS *see* ST CLEER

ILLOGAN
6040

ST ILLOGAN. The parish was the centre of C18 mining, but the church is in entirely rural surroundings. A C14 granite tower of two stages with diagonal buttresses is all that survives of the old church; the new was built away from it in 1846, with octagonal piers, by *St Aubyn*. – FONT. Granite, with the old Cornish motif of faces at the corners, completely re-tooled. – ROYAL ARMS. Richly carved; late C17. – MONUMENTS.* Stone relief with four excellent kneeling figures and a shield above, from a monument to the Rev. John Collins, Rector of Illogan, 1632–84. – Mary Collins † 1743. Pretty tablet with two putti on top. – Francis Basset † 1769. Good, with medallion portrait above a sarcophagus in relief. – Lord de Dunstanville † 1835, with frontal bust in medallion by *Westmacott*. – John Basset † 1843, his disconsolate children standing by a locked door. – Frances Baroness Basset † 1855; young woman feeding the poor. – John Francis Basset † 1869. Standing angel in a plain, rather dull Gothic frame, by *J. S. Westmacott*.

INCE CASTLE 4050

The present building is a perfect square of two main storeys, with four square corner towers, built of brick with granite dressings, overlooking the Lynher estuary opposite Antony. The towers are now slate-hung (covering original chequer-patterned brickwork), and with pyramid roofs, but originally battlemented. It has a wide granite external stair to the main entrance at the first floor. It was probably built in the early C17 (in spite of the supposed date 1540 alleged from a Courtenay cartouche over the entrance). Even at this later date its layout is of some interest, with its illusion of a gatehouse (it never was one), with no main hall, no main staircase (the towers have narrow spirals to their upper floors), perhaps instigated by the plans (but certainly not the elevations) of some French early C16 châteaux.

The wing between the towers at the back was added when the house was refurbished in the 1920s. The whole, in spite of its symmetry, is eminently picturesque, thanks to its variety of materials and colours, and its setting.‡

JACOBSTOW 1090

ST JAMES. Pleasantly situated in a hollow. W tower of granite, unbuttressed, with carvings on the plinth as at North Tamerton

* Mr F. A. Greenhill has drawn my attention to a brass to James Basset and wife, 1603, very good for its period.
‡ I owe this entry to Professor Martyn Jope.

and Week St Mary. Granite porch, castellated, with tunnel-vault. The nave and aisles a little earlier: C15. Arcades of four bays, Cornish standard shafts, rather low, and four-centred arches. The aisle windows are original, the Cornish three-light standard. – FONT. Norman, the type of Altarnun and St Thomas, Launceston, with faces at the four corners and stylized six-petalled flowers in niches on the four sides. – PULPIT. Made up of old bench ends. – ALTAR. An Elizabethan communion table with bulbous legs. – The NORTH DOOR is original. – PLATE. Chalice and Paten by *Jons* of Exeter, 1577; Paten by *H. Bateman*, 1788.

8040   KEA

OLD CHURCH. Only the tower survives: three-storeyed, with thin diagonal buttresses and battlements. A small mission church was added to the tower in 1863.

ALL HALLOWS. Built in 1802 by *James Wyatt* and pulled down in 1895. The church replacing it is by *Fellowes Prynne*, very un-Cornish, but attractive, with a lead spire and a steep tiled roof, starting low down. Inside, the main object of interest is the FONT. This is Norman, of Bodmin type, with five supports, heads at the four corners, and on the sides the tree of life twice, and once a cross and a lion *passant*. – PLATE. Chalice and Paten with the arms of René d'Amboise, datable either 1514–15 or 1537–8. A very similar piece was given by Henri III to Chartres Cathedral.

(CALENICK HOUSE. C18, with traces of a much older building inside. Very similar to Trereife, but smaller. Two storeys, seven bays. Simple door with pediment. Slate-hung upper storey. Separate clock tower with cupola, dated 1752. Information from Major H. Carey Morgan and GMT.)

KILLIOW. *See* p. 85.

KELSEY HEAD *see* CRANTOCK

8040   KENWYN

ST CUBY. Over the lychgate an upper storey, slate-hung; probably a schoolroom. From the churchyard a fine view of Truro with the viaduct in the front and the cathedral in the centre. The W tower of three stages has buttresses set back from the angles. The N side with N transept belongs to the C14 or an earlier date. The S side is C15, aisle and chapel

separated from the nave and chancel by an arcade of seven
bays with slim standard Cornish piers and four-centred arches.
The arcade to the N transept is later still. Figures of a bishop
and an angel attached to the capitals.

BISHOP'S PALACE (formerly Vicarage). 1780.

KERRIS FARM see PAUL

KILKHAMPTON   2010

ST JAMES. A stately church, on the whole Cornish standard: 19a
W tower with buttresses set back from the angles, aisled
interior of seven bays with standard shafts and four-centred
arches, wagon roofs, and S porch, built probably under John
Grenville, who was rector from 1524 to 1580. It was certainly
he who dated the S porch 'Porta Celi 1567'. The most important feature of the church is its Norman S doorway, four
arches with colonnettes in three, zigzag, beak-head, and
interesting capitals, two with fir cones (cf. Morwenstow). –
BENCH ENDS. Of c.1500–60, with abbreviated representations
of the Instruments of Christ's Passion, typical of the county:
Flagon and Chalice; thirty pieces of silver; pillar, cords, and
scourges; lantern, lance, and halberd; cock on pillar, etc.
(cf. Poughill, Launcells). – ORGAN. Some parts by *Father
Smith*, recased. – ROYAL ARMS. By *Michael Chuke* (1679–1742)
(cf. Stratton and Launcells). With strapwork decoration: an
early case of Jacobean Revival, or an imitation of the Royal Arms
at Poughill church? – PLATE. Chalice and Paten, 1637–8. –
MONUMENTS. John Warminster, 1700, Richard Westlake,
1704, John Courtis, 1705, all by *Michael Chuke* of Kilkhampton, who is said to be a pupil of Grinling Gibbons. They are
of indifferent quality. – Sir Bevill Grenville † 1643, erected in
1714 ('Thus slain thy valiant ancestor did ly | When his
one Bark a Navy did defy', etc.).

(ALDERCOMBE. C17 and earlier. The two-storeyed house with
its two wings forming a courtyard has mullioned windows of
three to five lights. Fine Tudor-arched gateway to the courtyard, surmounted by three stone pyramids. GMT)

STOWE. *See* p. 216.

KILLIOW   8040
Near Kea

Square granite house with a shallow bay in the middle of the two-storeyed front and tripartite windows l. and r. Late C18 and c.1850. COACH HOUSE of seven bays with cupola.

KING ARTHUR'S HALL *see* ST BREWARD

LADOCK

ST LADOCA. A specially well proportioned W tower of regular granite blocks, in three stages, with buttresses leaving the corners free. On the N side much remains of the C13 church, of which it is said that it was consecrated in 1268. The S aisle is C15 with a S porch with heavy decoration and a curious, very primitive face boxed in a narrow frame over the S door. Is it Norman? And what did it belong to? The S arcade of six bays has slim piers of standard design and unusually elaborate arch mouldings. The N chancel aisle is of the same date and design. The S porch has its old wagon roof. The chancel was severely restored and embellished by *Street*, 1862–4: E window with French Gothic detail, elaborate roof, rich marble and tile polychromy. – FONT. Exactly as at Feock, Catacleuse stone, sharply carved, Late Norman, circular, with an upper border of two tiers of crosses and trees of life in circles below. – ROOD SCREEN. The massively carved base survives, across nave and aisle, with two entrances, and altogether sixteen panels, rather broad and with large, heavy leaves. – BENCH ENDS. A few made up into a lectern. – STAINEDGLASS. Except for St Germans this is the only *Morris* glass in the county: the chancel E window of 1862[*] characteristically different from the later, richer S aisle E window (1869–70) and the W windows (1896, 1897).

LAMORRAN

ST MOREN. The most southerly church in the British Isles, it is small, cruciform, C13, but virtually rebuilt by *White* in 1845. The one-storey building in the SW corner of the churchyard may be part of an isolated tower. – FONT. Circular, Norman, on five supports, with four corner faces and no other ornament. – PLATE. Cover Paten of 1576 by the same master as at Perranarworthal, St Blazey, Stithians. – MONUMENT to John Verman † 1658 and wife, uncommonly large, with four

[*] The earliest known instance of Street collaborating with Morris, his former pupil (Dr Royston Lambert).

arches, two for the figures and two for the inscriptions. –
CROSS, in the churchyard. Gothic, specially fine, with foliated
head broken.

MANOR HOUSE. A farmhouse below the church by the water
has one C16 doorway and very little else preserved.

LANCARFFE see BODMIN

LANDEWEDNACK

ST WINWALLO. In a pretty village close to the Lizard. Low
w tower of the local serpentine, 'blue, glossy green and velvet
black', two stages without buttresses, like all the surrounding
churches. The s porch is battlemented and has a rib-vault
inside, resting on angel corbels and with a larger angel as a
boss. Can it really be late C13 (Sedding) or C14 (Henderson)?
The s door sheltered by this porch is Norman, with serpentine
columns and zigzag and circles to decorate the voussoirs. s
transept and chancel have C14 windows, the N aisle of five
bays and plain Cornish standard arcades. Perp windows without tracery. From the s transept a squint is open into the
chancel in the way typical of this part of Cornwall: the corner
is simply cut off and replaced by a squat pier of standard
Cornish design. – FONT. With an inscription recording the
name of a rector, no doubt the donor of the font. His dates at
Landewednack are 1404–15; the type with the short corner
columns is a simplified version of Bodmin. – PLATE. Chalice
and Paten, 1576–7, nice, of the usual beaker type.

LANDRAKE

ST MICHAEL. In the village, on a hill, with a tower 100 ft high
which can be seen from far away. It is of the usual three
stages with buttresses set back from the angles. In the NE is a
stair-turret of three-eighths plan rising above the pinnacles.
The s side of the church must still contain Norman masonry;
at any rate it contains a s doorway with Norman colonnettes.
The chancel almost touches the village street (an arrangement
very unusual in Cornish villages). The N has a C15 aisle
buttressed outside, with a pinnacled, shallow N porch. The
interior is tall and spacious, rather short, with good original
ceiled wagon roofs and an arcade of four wide bays, the piers
of an unusual variety of the standard Cornish profile, with

three-quarter instead of demi-shafts. The s transept arch belongs to the same date; the chancel arch is C19. From the transept to the chancel and the rood-loft stairs runs a squint-like cut. – FONT. Norman, of Altarnun type, with corner faces and large rosettes in circles. – MONUMENTS. Brass to Edward Cowtney, Lord of Wotton in Landrake, † 1509; small and unimportant. – Two slate plates of 1607 in the N wall of the chancel.

4060

LANDULPH

ST LEONARD. As a record of the connexion of the church with the Lower family of Clifton it contains a MONUMENT to Sir Nicholas Lower † 1655, a beautiful large black marble plate with inscription and coat of arms on a tomb-chest, and (more valuable still) the panelling of the FAMILY PEW, c.1600, now displayed against the W walls of N and s aisles, with linenfold ornamental carving and many coats of arms. The pew was at the E end of the s aisle, beyond the ROOD SCREEN, of which the base is original, with comparatively simple carving of the panels: quatrefoils and the blank tracery with mouchettes which is so characteristic of C15 Cornish bench ends. Landulph church has a number of such BENCH ENDS also, with the usual motifs – and a few unusual ones: a boar's head, a fox, a goose, a rabbit, a bird of prey.

Architecturally the church needs little attention. W tower of three stages with buttresses only just leaving the angles free. They are replaced by thin diagonal buttresses at the top stage. A three-eighths stair-turret rises above the pinnacles. The exterior of the church is roughcast, not a very pleasing treatment. The arcades of five bays have octagonal piers and a fairly simple profile of the arches (two concave chamfers). Good wagon roof in the N aisle. – FONT. Plain, octagonal, on five supports. – In the s aisle an INSCRIPTION records the death and burial of Theodore Palaeologus, a descendant of the medieval Christian Emperors of Byzantium, who died at Clifton in 1636.

2080

LANEAST

ST SATIVOLA VIRGIN or ST MICHAEL. Of the cruciform Norman church the masonry of chancel, N wall, and N transept remains. In the N transept is an E window with the original jambs. The N window in the same transept is a small E.E. triplet. The C14 W tower has diagonal buttresses; its third stage is C15, as is the S aisle, completely of granite. The S porch also is of granite. Both S porch and S aisle have fine wagon roofs. The arcade is simple Cornish standard, low, with four-centred arches. The aisle windows are of three lights, with Cornish standard tracery. – FONT. Norman, of Altarnun–St-Thomas-Launceston type, that is with faces at the corners and stylized six-petalled flowers in circles on the four sides (cf. also Jacobstow, Warbstow, Landrake). – BENCHES nearly complete, though restored; a remarkable sight. The bench ends are carved in the usual Cornish way, but with not much of the symbols of the Passion; mostly just interlaced knots, stars, coats of arms. – ROOD SCREEN across nave and aisle. About 9 ft high, with unusually wide bays, each of four lights. – Some C15 GLASS in the chancel: fragments of Christ crucified, St Christopher, St Catherine.

HOLY WELL in a little C16 building, S of the church.

BRIDGE, by Gimblett's Mill. 1847, odd, with six square openings.

LANHERNE see MAWGAN-IN-PYDAR

LANHYDROCK   0060

The house of the Robartes family is one of the grandest in Corn- 54
wall and certainly the grandest of its century. Sir Richard Robartes, a Truro tin and wool merchant, bought the estate in 1620 and probably began building at once. He was a prosperous and proud enough man. In 1625 Buckingham, having received £10,000 in return, had him created a peer. The dates 1636 and 1642 appear in two places on the fronts of the house, but the gatehouse was completed only in 1658. Originally there were four wings with a central courtyard; the E wing, however, was removed later. In 1881 a large part of the house was burnt. It was re-erected on the old lines after the fire with the addition of new parts at the back (architect, R. Coad). The composition is completely symmetrical, with a central entrance into the W wing. In the N wing a gallery 116 ft long with a 55
shallow tunnel-vault, a plaster ceiling with pendants, flying ribs, and manifold panels surrounded by broad bands and filled with scenes of the Creation and other Old Testament subjects. There is a scene with figures in deep relief over each

fireplace. The work was no doubt done by the plasterers who
worked at Barnstaple and Rashleigh Barton (North Devon).
In axis with the porch is the gatehouse, and towards the gatehouse leads a splendid avenue of beeches and sycamores,
planted in 1648. The windows are mullioned, on the main,
that is upper, floor all of six lights, but all without transoms.
The roof disappears partly behind battlements. All this is still
entirely pre-classical. Only in the gatehouse appear a few
allusions to columns and Renaissance niches. The outer
doorway into the gatehouse is semicircular; the detail of the
inner might come straight from a Perp Cornish church. The
gatehouse is crowned by a profusion of stumpy obelisks, and
such obelisks also articulate the walls of the beautifully kept
inner gardens.

The church of ST HYDEROC stands immediately behind the
manor house, as close to it as is, for example, Mawgan-in-
Pydar church to Lanherne. It is small and not specially
interesting, and its main charm is its position in the shadow of
the house. W tower unbuttressed, of three stages, of regular
granite blocks, as is the rest of the church. N and S aisles of
four bays with Cornish standard piers. The tracery of the
windows looks a C17 interpretation of Perp. – ROYAL ARMS.
Plaster; 1621. – MONUMENT to Lady Essex Speccott † 1689,
not of specially remarkable design but of fine, certainly not
local, workmanship. – CROSS in the churchyard. About 8 ft
high. Wheel broken off the head. Decoration of the Hiberno-
Saxon type, with interlacings and a very crude foliage scroll.

RESPRYN BRIDGE (river Fowey). Partly medieval; the smallest
arch is C15, the two to the W are modern.

(TREBYAN QUOIT, 1¼ m. SW. A large capstone leaning against
an upright, and another large upright. In the same field, a
stone-lined PIT. Dr Athelstane Hill)

LANIVET

ST NEVET. A surprisingly ambitious church with a tall stone W
tower, very sheer, without angle buttresses (the buttresses
leave the angles free) or pinnacles, and with N as well as S
aisles of six bays. The piers of the arcades are circular with
four attached shafts, the S arches simply double-chamfered,
the N arches with concave instead of straight chamfers. Large
Perp windows of varying design. – FONT. Octagonal, with
elaborate C14 tracery panels. – WALL PAINTINGS. Destroyed

during the C19; one of them was the familiar Warning to Sabbath-Breakers (cf. Introduction). – MONUMENT. Slate plate to John and Richard Courtenay, with life-size bearded figure; 1632. – CAPITAL. Late C12, large (about 31 by 29 in.), perhaps from Bodmin Priory.

Lanivet is one of the most rewarding places in Cornwall for information, or at least impressions, of the Dark Age from the C6 to the C10:

PILLAR STONE, by the S porch of the church. Inscribed in Roman capitals: ANNICU. C6 if not C5.

CROSS SLAB, in the churchyard. A cross partly in relief, partly incised. A rare type; cf. Temple, Towednack, Wendron.

COPED STONE, in the churchyard; that is, a hogback-shaped tombstone. Top and sides with key patterns; at head and foot of the top, four dog-like or bear-like beasts; knots at the ends. C10? (Cf. St Tudy, Phillack, St Buryan.)

CROSS in the churchyard. 10 ft high, with very primitive incised decoration including a man with a tail (cf. Penzance). The iconography is not sufficiently explained, and a connexion with pagan fertility rites is likely. The style also deserves a closer analysis than Hencken's 'curiously childish'.

CROSS, in the churchyard. A wheel-cross, 10½ ft high, with interlacings and a crude foliage scroll (cf. Lanhydrock).

ST BENET'S. See p. 158.

LANIVET QUOIT. A much damaged chamber now represented by three upright stones, the largest 15 ft long and 9 ft wide. The latter may be the displaced capstone.

LANLIVERY

ST BRYVYTH (BREVITA). An exceptionally proud church, overlooking the far-stretching Fowey Valley. Its W tower is 97 ft tall and can be seen for miles around. It is of regular granite blocks, in three stages, with Perp windows and buttresses set back from the angles. These buttresses cease at the top of the second stage, and the polygonal pinnacles on angels, beasts, etc., as corbels start as low down as that, accompanying the whole third stage – an original and successful idea. The body of the church has two Dec windows, that on the N side of the N transept, and the W window of the S aisle (new, or reused?). The other windows are Perp, large, and not of the most usual design (E window, 1520). The S aisle is of six bays with wide arches on slim, tall Cornish standard granite piers and a little stylized decoration on the abaci. The arch from nave to transept appears earlier than any of the others. The s aisle and s porch have their old wagon roofs. – FONTS. Fragments of a Norman font in the vestry, Catacleuse stone, of Fowey type. – In the church an uncommonly large, octagonal font, with shields in quatrefoils; C 15.–MONUMENTS. Mary Cotes, 1758, not specially interesting in design, but of good, probably not local, workmanship. – Anne Wynter, 1839 by *J. Theakston*.

PELYN. See p. 132.

See p. 132.

1050

LANREATH

ST MANARCK (MARNACH) AND ST DUNSTAN. The nave N wall and the transept walls are probably Norman. Of the time of the re-dedication (1321) nothing survives. The present appearance is wholly Perp, and specially complete and satisfying. *Bodley*'s restoration in 1887 is tactful and sound. Nave of five bays, s aisle, s porch, N transept at the fourth bay, chancel, W tower with thin buttresses, set back from the angles. Piers of standard Cornish section. Capitals with elementary ornamental carving, arches low and four-centred. On the N side traces of Norman masonry, but later windows. Good wagon roofs in nave and aisle, in the nave with large simple bosses. – FONT. Norman, of Catacleuse stone, Fowey type, that is, cup-shaped. Uncommonly rich, with zigzag, plait, palmettes, etc. – COVER. Handsome shape and decoration; Jacobean. – ALTAR STONE. Norman. – ROOD SCREEN. Right across nave and aisle. Ten traceried bays. Restored in 1905, but much of the old work survives. Painted saints on the bottom panels, *c.*1520 (cf. St Winnow). Cornice of three carved strips. Coving new. The type is more Devonian than Cornish (cf. in Cornwall St Ewe, Budock, St Winnow). – CHANCEL STALLS. With excellent crowning figure sculpture, much of it Jacobean, the rest *c.*1500. – PULPIT and ALTAR TABLE in the transept; Elizabethan. – BENCH ENDS in the transept; Jacobean. – Elaborate MONUMENT to Charles Grylls and wife, 1623. Husband and wife kneel frontally on a tall chest with a relief of eight children. Four Corinthian columns support a canopy with arms, cherubs, and cartouches. All carved in wood (a great rarity), though entirely in imitation of current stonework. Very rustic workmanship.

COURT, s of the church. Of *c.*1610, much restored in 1899. This is an exceptionally good manor house with a projecting gabled entrance bay asymmetrically placed. Low, six-light windows l. and r., and four-light windows above them. In the carving of one room inside appear the arms of the Grylls family.

The terraces of COTTAGES and the INN opposite the church make a specially pretty group.

LANSALLOS

ST ILDIERNA. C15 church, with nave of six bays, S aisle, incomplete N aisle (taking in at its W end an older transept wall), S porch, W tower of three stages with tracery decoration at the foot of the buttresses. Piers of Cornish standard section, coarsely carved capitals, low four-centred arches. Good carved wagon roofs. Windows mostly renewed in the C19. – FONT. Norman, square, with 'Tree of Life' and odd fleur-de-lis ornament. – BENCHES and BENCH ENDS. Thirty-four of the early C16, with carved arms, heads, a 'triciput', etc. – VESTMENT CUPBOARDS. Jacobean. – PLATE. Chalice and Paten, 1606. – MONUMENTS. Fragment of a C14 knight and lady; stone. – Margaret Smith † 1579, slate slab by *Peter Crocker*.

LANTEGLOS-BY-CAMELFORD

ST JULITTA, 1½ m. from Camelford (to the SW), but until recently its only parish church. Large, with nave and S aisle of six bays. Slim piers of Cornish granite standard, with depressed four-centred arches. The aisle is all granite, with three-light windows of a tracery pattern different from the usual. The E window is of five lights, as is that of the chancel, the latter with an unusual flamboyant motif in a circle as the centre of the tracery. This window and the whole granite facing of the E wall of the chancel belong to the time of the aisle, as also does the granite S porch. But the masonry of the chancel and the N transept are Norman (cf. the original imposts of the transept arch). The W tower is unbuttressed, with a NE stair-turret and a nice C14 W doorway with heads as label-stops of the hoodmould. – Elizabethan (i.e. very early) COMMANDMENT BOARDS. – STAINED GLASS. Small C15 fragments in the tracery of the S aisle windows, for example Christ, St Andrew, St James. – PLATE. Chalice and Paten, 1576. – Pretty MONUMENT to W. Inch † 1815, by *R. Isbell*, with a relief of a woman standing by an urn under a weeping willow.

PILLAR STONE in the churchyard, with a Saxon inscription: AELSELÐ 7 GENEREÐ WOHTE ÐYSNE SIBSTEL FOR AELWINES SOUL 7 FOR HEYSEL. Probably C10.

₁₀₅₀   LANTEGLOS-BY-FOWEY

ST WILLOW. An interesting church which in some ways departs from the universal Cornish village convention. Its nave of five bays has octagonal piers of Pentewan stone (cf. Fowey), with very simple capitals and bases and plain round arches. These piers are certainly C14, and to the same date belongs most of the unbuttressed four-storeyed tower, opening in tall arches of simple double-chamfered section into nave as well as aisles (cf. St Keverne). The four-light aisle windows were compared by *E. H. Sedding* (who restored the church in 1904) with Somerset. He points to the fact that the church was appropriated in 1284 to the Hospital of St John at Bridgwater The W and E windows are modern. What the church looked like before the C14, we cannot say. Sedding when restoring thought he could discover traces of Norman work in the corners of the tower piers. The jambs of the S doorway are Norman anyway. The S porch, Sedding suggested, may have been rebuilt in the C17. The roofs are of special importance: that of the N aisle with only chamfered, not moulded, timbers, and probably C14; the nave roof moulded; the S aisle roof more elaborately moulded. – FONT. Early C13, on a Purbeck base with moulded capitals and bases. The bowl of Pentewan stone has stiff-leaf foliage. – STAINED GLASS. A little of Late Perp date in the E window of the S aisle. – E window, with the Adoration of the Shepherds and saints, N and S chancel windows by *Kempe*. – W window and S aisle W window by *Kempe & Tower*. – ALTAR TABLE. A Mohun gift, of 1634. – BENCH ENDS. A considerable number of *c*.1500. – Also fragments of Jacobean PEWS with coats of arms. – MONUMENTS. Tomb-chest in a canopied recess in the S chancel aisle. On the chest a small brass to Thomas de Mohun, laid down *c*.1440. – Close by a brass of *c*.1525 to John Mohun and wife, who died 'ex infirmitate vocata Sudye' (that is, the sweating sickness) in 1508. The chancel aisle was probably a Mohun chapel. Bodinnick and Boconnoc were both seats of the Mohuns. – XP STONE. Built into the Norman doorway; C8 at the latest. – CROSS in the churchyard. Gothic, of lantern type, on octagonal shaft, the faces with tracery.

LANYON FARM see GWINEAR

LANYON QUOIT see MORVAH

LAUNCELLS

2000

ST SWITHIN. Delightfully placed in a wooded valley away from all traffic, with ST SWITHIN'S HOLY WELL opposite the S entrance across a little bridge. Exterior with an unbuttressed W tower and four very tall corner pinnacles. Interior very light, too light perhaps, with white walls and a white plastered wagon roof to the nave (something of an early C19 character). Nave of five bays with tall slim shafts of standard Cornish section, with standard capitals (pretty fleur-de-lis crenellation) and four-centred arches. The N arcade is of granite, the S of polyphant, and their sections differ (the N arcade is a little later than the S). The windows have Perp tracery. – The pride of Launcells is the carved BENCH ENDS, over sixty of them, with abbreviated representations of Christ's Passion, for example table with flagon and loaves for the Lord's Supper; flagon, dish, and towel for the Washing of the Feet; open coffin and spice boxes for the Resurrection; footprints and, higher up, cloud with two feet and the end of a robe for the Ascension, etc. The same workshop supplied bench ends to Kilkhampton and Poughill. – Specially interesting are the ENCAUSTIC TILES in the chancel, C15 Barnstaple ware, with fleur-de-lis, Tudor roses, lions *passant* and *rampant*, pelican, etc. – ALTAR. First half of the C17. – COMMUNION TABLE. From the Dockyard Church, Devonport. – FONT. Very plain Early Norman with cable-mouldings. – ROYAL ARMS with strapwork decoration, by *Michael Chuke* (cf. Kilkhampton and Stratton). – WALL PAINTING of the Sacrifice of Isaac, large, on the W wall of the S aisle, very dim; Tudor. – MONUMENT to Sir John Chamond of 1624; standing wall-tomb with semi-reclining stiff effigy in armour, and two small kneelers at the head and feet.

TAMARSTONE BRIDGE, 2¼ m. E. Brick, 'Gothic', 1809.

LAUNCESTON

3080

Launceston in the Middle Ages was the main town of Cornwall, with one of the most important castles, and one of the most important monastic houses. It was the county town until 1835 and in the early C16 was enriched by the most spectacular church W of Exeter. The town lies on a steep hill, with the market place between church and castle. To the N is the Kensey, hardly more than a brook. It is crossed by a medieval BRIDGE of five little arches (originally higher, because of the accumulated mud) with a roadway only 4 ft wide. The bridge owes its preservation to the building of an C18 bridge lower down stream. Further N the road climbs up to St Stephen, the mother-church of Launceston (*see* p. 200). The name Launceston was originally confined to St Stephen. The present town was called Dunheved. It outgrew the old Launceston in importance during the C13 and C14. Of the town walls a part is preserved on the S side, with the SOUTH GATE (two entrances, one for carriages, one for pedestrians).

ST MARY MAGDALENE. The tower on the SW with a higher SE stair-turret is the only survival of the chapel which is all that Launceston was allowed before the present church was built. It dates from the late C14, is not of spectacular height, and stood separate from the body of the church until quite recently, connected to it only by a shop. It has the standard Cornish buttresses set back from the angles. The chapel attached to it had a steeper roof-pitch than the church of today, as can be seen on the E. The chapel was obviously not a mean building. The church as we see it now is entirely the work of Sir Henry Trecarrel (cf. Trecarrel). It was built in 1511–24, wholly of granite, 103 ft long, and externally decorated with barbarous profuseness. The main motifs are fully described by Cox: on the plinths quatrefoils, with coats of arms and fleur-de-lis alternately, then above these tracery, with coats of arms and letters. The letters, from the chancel door eastwards, read: AVE MARIA GRACIA PLENA DOMINUS TECUM. SPONSUS AMAT SPONSAM. MARIA OPTIMAM PARTEM ELIGIT. O QUAM TERRIBILIS ET METUENDUS EST LOCUS ISTE. VERE ALIUD NON EST HIC NISI DOMUS DEI ET PORTA CELI. Above the legends a course of rose and thistle ornament. Then come the large three- and four-light windows, flanked by ornamented buttresses. By the sides of the windows are palm leaves, in the spandrels roses. Above the windows is some scroll ornament. The battlemented parapet has rose, thistle, and pomegranate. At the E end is a recumbent figure of the Magdalen in a niche below the central window, with four kneeling figures on the l. and four on the r., chiefly angels playing musical instruments. At the top of the E gable are the royal arms. The S porch with an upper

24

storey has in front the date 1511 and the arms of Trecarrel and Kelway; also reliefs of St George and St Martin to the l. and r. of the central niche. The porch is particularly thorough in its ornamentation. The outer side walls are panelled all the way through without any caesura. Most of the panels are repetition work, impressive more by their numbers than their quality. The motifs are partly familiar from contemporary bench ends of the special Cornish type. The style and the extreme lavishness are not wholly original either. Trecarrel evidently went to masons busy on such elaborately decorated exteriors as those of the w tower and Place, Fowey, or (even more likely) St Mary Truro (begun in 1504), and told them that he wanted his decoration still bigger and better. Inside, nave and chancel of eight bays (an exceptional length) and N and S aisles. A w tower in the normal position was planned but not executed. Slender circular piers with four groups of three attached shafts (a unique pattern in Cornwall). Capitals of the usual Cornish Perp type. The arches are pointed, with the exception of the fifth bay, which is wider than the others and has a depressed four-centred arch (a hint at a transeptal centre). The wagon roofs are new. As the piers are slim and the windows large, the room has an even light and a feeling of comfortable width, but it is not in its proportions specially moving – a little disappointing in fact, after the all-out display of the exterior. – FONT. Of c.1525. – PULPIT. Wood, splendidly carved, easily the best in the county.* – BENCH ENDS. 1893–4 and exceptionally good (Arnold Fellows). – ORGAN FRONT. C18. – PLATE. Cover Paten by *Jons* of Exeter, 1580; other pieces of 1637, 1726, 1745, 1770. – CHURCHYARD CROSS with carved head (cf. Lostwithiel). – MONUMENTS. Fragments of a monument of c.1650, with two kneeling figures facing each other with praying-desk between. – Captain Philip Piper † 1677. Not up to much; the same pattern, with columns, swags, and a broken curved pediment. – Granville Piper and Richard Wise (cenotaph; they are buried at Bath), 1731. Sumptuous, uncommonly classical, and uncommonly good. It should be possible to recognize its master. Tall plinth and two storeys, white and a little dark marble. Busts of the deceased, and standing allegorical figures (Charity, Faith, Justice, etc.) in two tiers. – Carved ROYAL ARMS. 41

* It is thought to be pre-Reformation. At the time of writing (1968) it is being restored: the existing black paint is to be removed and the original colour underneath left untouched (Canon W. G. Steer).

AUGUSTINIAN PRIORY. Founded in 1136. Scanty remains
exist behind St Thomas's church: a fragment of the plan and
some small architectural fragments, the most conspicuous of
which is a doorway transferred to the WHITE HART HOTEL
in the Market Place, simple, of one order with colonnettes.*

ST THOMAS. Originally a chapel of ease to St Stephen. Norman
25b   tympanum built into the s porch. Good Norman FONT (the
largest in Cornwall) of the type with corner faces and rosettes in
circles (cf. Altarnun, Callington, etc.). Unbuttressed w tower,
C14 in its lower stages. The rest is Perp (of Cornish standard):
five bays, s aisle, s porch; piers of the usual profile; roofs new.
Altogether much restored (1874). – TOWER SCREEN with
some old linenfold panels. – WALL PAINTINGS. Two at the
E end of the s aisle. – SOUTH DOOR with C13 (or early C14)
ironwork. – PLATE. Cup and cover by *EM*, Elizabethan, of
beautiful shape and much decorated.

ST STEPHEN-BY-LAUNCESTON. *See* p. 200.

CASTLE. Mentioned in Domesday Book; in the C13 the chief
castle of Henry III's brother Richard, Earl of Cornwall.
Repaired by the Black Prince and then neglected. It is recorded
in 1650 that hall and chapel were 'quite level with the ground'.
Only the chief tower and one gatehouse were then still in a
reasonable state. The castle consists of a bailey, since 1840 a
public garden, whose wall adjoined the town wall on the NW
and SE. There are two gates, the (C12?) SOUTH GATE, of
which only the s portion with part of the gateway and two
flanking towers remains, while the outer barbican and an
inner projection into the bailey have gone,‡ and the NORTH
GATE (C13), with a pointed tunnel-vault divided by two
transverse arches (the position of the two portcullises can still
be seen) and an additional C14 building, used later as a prison.
When Howard visited it in 1779 it had no chimney, no water,
no sewers, and damp floors. The prisoners were chained
together. The CHAPEL was in the middle of the bailey. The
KEEP lies on a high mount, reached up a flight of steps with a
round tower at the foot to defend them. It was originally a
shell tower, 50 by 59 ft, with walls 12 ft thick at the foot and
rising to 29 ft in height. In the C13, probably by Richard, a
round tower was built within the shell and the ring between
it and the shell roofed over. The round tower rises one storey

* According to Henderson, the doorway may have come from the castle
chapel.
‡ The side walls of the barbican of the s gatehouse still remain.

above this ring and contained a lower and an upper chamber (with a fireplace).

HOUSES. Some good Georgian brick houses in CASTLE STREET (CASTLE HILL HOUSE and Nos. 3–13). Also one just SE of 58 the church. – PANIER MARKET, Market Street. 1840. (In addition the MHLG stresses Nos. 1–11 Angel Hill; ORANGE CAFÉ and Nos. 26 and 28 in CHURCH STREET; Nos. 4, 6, 11, 13 HIGH STREET; DOCKACRE HOUSE in HORSE LANE, which is long, low, and gabled, C16–17; and Nos. 1–14 NORTHGATE STREET, 2–6 and 5 SOUTHGATE STREET, 22–26 WESTGATE, and the late C18 BAPTIST CHAPEL in Madford Lane.)

NEW BRIDGE (river Tamar), 1¾ m. NE. Early C16, granite ashlar, of four arches, the three large ones of 25 ft span.

ST LEONARD'S BRIDGE (river Kensey), 1 m. E. Footbridge, built by Launceston town in 1580.

LAVETHAN
Near Blisland

0070

House of 1653 incorporating C15 parts. The archway was brought over from another site.

LAWHITTON

3080

ST MICHAEL. A small church with an unusual plan. The tower stands in the place of a S transept. It is of the C13, in three stages, without buttresses, but lessening in dimensions from stage to stage. The C15 S porch (with an old wagon roof) comes close to the tower. There is a N aisle with straight-headed windows; the S windows are Perp, of three lights. Inside, the N arcade of five bays is relatively tall, with piers of standard section and multiple moulded capitals. – FONT. Norman, of Altarnun type, but with unbearded corner faces. – BENCH ENDS. Just a few, not specially interesting. – PULPIT. Dated 1665, yet still entirely in the Jacobean style. – PLATE. Chalice by *Mathew* of Barnstaple, Elizabethan. – MONUMENT. R. Bennet † 1683. Slate, with ornamental writing and a handsome coat of arms. – Richard Coffin † 1796, of Coade stone, that is the patent terracotta ware made by *Coade & Sealy*, whose signature is on the monument. Figures such as the mourning woman on the sarcophagus and the two somewhat oversized putti to the l. and r. could be ordered from the catalogue (cf. the putti at St Michael Caerhays).

GREYSTONE BRIDGE, $1\frac{1}{2}$ m. SE, on the Launceston–Tavistock road. Built in 1439 and still in good condition. 225 ft long, of five arches. The roadway, 10 ft wide, was paved.

LELANT

5030

A seaport in the Middle Ages, until outdone by St Ives.

ST UNY, the church, is in a prominent position, with its s side broadly facing the sea. The building is wholly of rough granite, the w tower of three stages with diagonal buttresses, growing very thin higher up. The interior has remains of a Norman N arcade, one round arch on two short circular piers with scalloped capitals of an unusual variety, with the scallops tied together by bands above and below. The bay to the w of the Norman one has a plain two-centred arch, just to connect the Norman part with the tower, the three bays to the E and the whole s arcade square piers with four attached demi-shafts and two-centred arches. A few capitals are decorated with large horizontal leaves in the Devonshire fashion. All windows are Perp, on the N quite plain three-light openings without tracery. The s door has nice fleurons in jambs and voussoirs and tracery decoration in the spandrels. – FONT. Octagonal, on nine supports; the simplest of ornament, almost undatable. – MONUMENTS. William Praed † 1620 and his family, slate with kneeling figures and flowers, sand-glass, skull; strapwork as decoration. The Praed family came from here (Trevethow) and by the s porch is a large, severely plain sarcophagus to William Praed † 1833.

(THE ABBEY, Lower Lelant. Long and low C16 building with C18 renovations; L-shaped. MHLG)

LERRYN

1050

BRIDGES. Two, both C16, both of two arches, the one at the head of the creek rebuilt in 1575.

ETHY. *See* p. 66.

LESNEWTH

1090

ST MICHAEL. In a very pretty position, on so steep a hillside that the road close by runs at roof level of the church and only the tall unbuttressed w tower is seen, with its stair-turret (with tiny quatrefoil openings) on the N side. The churchyard slopes down to the little stream below. *St Aubyn* in 1865 built a new nave with the vestry treated as a double transept with two gables. The church replaced by St Aubyn had both its Norman transepts (a rarity in Cornwall). – PLATE. Chalice and Paten by *NH*, 1638, the chalice of unusual shape, with snakes at the top of the stem; Maidenhead Spoon of *c.*1560.

LEWANNICK

ST MARTIN. The oddest thing architecturally about this church is the tracery of the windows: two mullions and one transom high up in the arch. It has been thought to belong to the reconstruction after a fire in 1890, but can be proved to have existed before. It probably belongs to the C18. The W tower is of regular granite blocks in three stages with buttresses set back from the angles, and ending on the second stage. On the third the three-eighths plan of the pinnacles starts. The W side is one of the most charming in Cornwall: a W door with fleurons in jambs and voussoirs and flowers and scrolls in the spandrels, and above it a W window with a crocketed ogee canopy and finials on the sides. The E windows have their four-light Perp tracery of the design which unites two lights under one main arch and is especially popular in this district. The church has N and S porches. Inside, the N aisle is of five bays and one small and narrow one for the chancel. The piers are standard. The S side has five bays and the piers show an unusual section, the same as found at St Cleer. – FONT. Large, octagonal, Norman, with some unusual ornamental motifs, for example a coil (labyrinth?), and twice a pentagram. – INSCRIBED STONES. Two with inscriptions partly in Roman capitals, partly in Ogham lettering, that curious script used mainly in south Ireland and occasionally taken over in England in the C5 to C7. It consists entirely of unconnected vertical strokes (cf. St Clement, St Kew). One stone is in the church (inscription: . . . IACIT VIIAGNI . . .), the other S of the churchyard (. . . INGENAUI MEMORIA . . .). – CRESSET STONE with seven cups for tallow, with wicks to give light (cf. Marhamchurch).

LEWARNE
Near St Neot

A rich Victorian seat of the Grylls family, built in 1869 in a neo-Tudor style.

3070

LEZANT

St Michael. w tower of regular granite blocks in three stages. Of the same date the s aisle with its Perp windows. The N aisle in its masonry must be considerably earlier – cf. the N door with its plain chamfered arch and the cusped little lancet window in the w wall (Sedding regarded the window opening itself as Norman). The N and s arcades, however, are identical, with standard piers. Original wagon roofs (ceiled) in both aisles and nave. Another survival of the earlier period, C13 or even C12, is the chancel walls, with the E buttresses and the s window (two lancets in a deeply splayed opening). – FONT. Norman, of Altarnun type, but with the corner faces carved off so that the shape is now octagonal. – MONUMENTS. Trefusis family. An altar tomb at the E end of the s aisle, with slate front and top, a slate back, and also an upright back plate against the s wall of the s aisle. The kneeling figures appear there; otherwise there are inscriptions, coats of arms, and ornament. – Monument to a Lady stiffly reclining, in an aedicule, with two small allegorical figures on the top cornice.

3070

LINKINHORNE

St Melor. An all-granite church, entirely of the large regular ashlar blocks characteristic of the last fifty years of the Perp style.* It has the second highest tower in Cornwall (120 ft high), but its four storeys are not conspicuous, owing to the position of the village. The design is of the usual pattern, with buttresses set back from the angles. The fairly sumptuous re-building of the tower is said to be due to the generosity of Sir Henry Trecarrel (see Trecarrel and Launceston). Nave of five bays, N and s aisles, s porch. The nave has a wagon roof with the E bay slightly lower, that is a kind of separation of the presbytery from the rest. Granite piers of standard section. Capitals carved with foliage. Arches four-centred. The windows Perp. The entrance to the s porch has curious figure-of-eight ornament in jambs and voussoirs (a Celtic survival, one is inclined to say). Little of interest amongst the furnishings, etc. – FONT of polyphant stone. C13, cf. Egloshayle, that is, a square top with narrow pointed blank arcades. – ALTAR SLAB with five crosses, now in the s aisle. – A few BENCH ENDS. – Some STAINED GLASS (in the tops of the aisle windows). –

* At the restoration in 1891 part of a Norman capital was discovered.

WALL PAINTINGS. In the s aisle, the Seven Corporeal Works of Mercy, with Christ presiding in the centre under a canopy; w of this, fragments, probably part of the Seven Deadly Sins.* C15, discovered in 1891. – PLATE. Chalice and Paten by *Jons* of Exeter, 1570–2, especially handsome; Dutch Paten on shell feet by *Regnier Brandt* of Amsterdam, 1755 or 1780. – In the churchyard are several GRAVESTONES by *Daniel Gumb*, who lived with his wife and children in a lonely cottage near the Cheesewring rock and died in 1776.

Near the village the HOLY WELL OF ST MELOR, exceptionally well preserved, in a little C15 building.

PLUSHA BRIDGE, 1½ m. SW. Late C15, granite, of three round-headed arches.

RILLATON ROUND BARROW, ½ m. N of Minions. A bowl barrow, 120 ft in diameter and 8 ft high. It covered a cist (still visible) which contained an inhumation burial accompanied by a bronze dagger and a handled Beaker of gold which is stylistically similar to vessels of gold and silver from Mycenaean Greece.

LISKEARD   2060

The town lies in a picturesque hilly position, with the church on one hill, separated by a valley from another, on which the Regency period built The Parade.

ST MARTIN. The second largest church in Cornwall (the largest is Bodmin), but not happy now with its new tower‡ of neo-Cornish design (1903, by a local architect, *Sanson*) and its neat Victorian-looking interior (new roof 1878, restoration of chancel 1890, etc.). What is visible now is, under its Victorian trim, mainly Perp. Of the Norman church there are only fragments built into the tower to make up a w doorway (treble zigzag) and upper windows. The supports of the tower parapet are also Norman. A deeply splayed Norman opening in the w wall of the present N aisle, its apex only about 7½ ft from the ground. The present church has an overall length of 140 ft. Nave of five bays, chancel of two bays, lower than the nave and separated from it by a chancel arch (an arrangement very unusual in Cornwall; cf. Bodmin, Crantock), N and s aisles, N and s porches, and an extra outer s aisle (Lady Chapel). The date

* For this information, and much more, also relating to wall paintings, I am indebted to Mr E. C. Rouse.
‡ Originally there were two w towers.

of the Lady Chapel is 1428–30, that of the N aisle 1477. There are records of agreements between the Prior of St Stephen, Launceston, and the Mayor of Liskeard about these. The nave arcade is tall, with side openings and slim piers of Cornish standard moulding and two-centred arches. The impression, though airy, is not lofty, for the height up to the springing of the (new) wagon roof is less than the width of the nave. All windows are Perp, of four and five lights (the E window of the chancel new). The S porch has an upper floor with a small window and niches, similar to Bodmin. The N porch is the first of three curious bay-window-like projections which accompany the outer wall of the aisle from W to E. Inside they do not tally with the nave arcades. They are as high as the aisle, and each is covered with a depressed tunnel-vault, with three transverse stone arches across. Outside, the aisles and these projecting bays are battlemented. – FONT. Plain, probably C14. – PULPIT. 1636. – Thirteen CONSECRATION CROSSES on the outer walls of the S and N aisles, unique in Cornwall. – Largely early C19 COMMANDMENT BOARDS with ornamental script; relegated to the N exterior walls. – No MONUMENTS of importance, though many minor neo-classical works by the usual regional purveyors: *Isbell* of Stonehouse (Lieut. Hawkey † 1809, quite elaborate and rather tasteless), *Shepherd* of Plymouth, *Crocker* of Plymouth.

(OUR LADY AND ST NEOT (R.C.), West Street. 1862–3 by *J. A. Hansom.*)

The domestic architecture is pleasant, without highlights. The one ambitious building is WEBB'S HOTEL, 1833 by *Foulston* of Plymouth, with a Tuscan porch and a symmetrical plan with low central hall, pleasant white staircase, and dining room at the back right across. It is the best of several Late Georgian and Early Victorian houses around THE PARADE. Some are stuccoed, some stone-fronted, some slate-hung. In the steep street down from The Parade towards the church the MARKET HALL of 1821 with a convex front and the TOWN HALL of 1859 (by *Henry Rice*), Italianate with a clock tower, rather jarring.

The WORKHOUSE (now Lamellion Hospital), outside the town on the way to the station, is by *Foulston* of Plymouth, 1839.

STUART HOUSE is said to have been built by Trecarrel (to whom Launceston church is due). Some granite windows and a granite fireplace survive.

(In Well Lane, PIPE WELL, originally late C16, now mostly

early C19. – In Barn Street, UPTON COTTAGES, slate-hung, but originally C17. MHLG)

DOUBLEBOIS HOUSE, Dobwalls, 3½ m. W of Liskeard. Of c.1885, by *Christopher White*.)

TREWORGEY. *See* p. 231.

LITTLE PETHERICK

9070

ST PETROCK. The main interest of this tiny church is Anglo-Catholic of the last fifty years. Of the insignificant C14 church the only reminders are two BELLS, some BENCH ENDS, a C15 FONT, and the C13 Purbeck marble SEPULCHRAL SLAB to Sir Roger Lemporu ('gist ici'), with a foliated cross and a human head above it. In 1858 the church was rebuilt by *William White* for Sir Hugh Molesworth, the then rector, and a Tractarian. The Molesworths were also the patrons of the church, and from 1876 to 1898 another Molesworth was rector. In 1898 Athelstan Riley (later Seigneur de la Trinité, Jersey) became patron. To him we owe the introduction of *J. N. Comper* to the church. Comper re-restored it in 1908, and added the HIGH ALTAR with REREDOS and the ROOD SCREEN and loft. Then, c.1916, a chapel was added on the N to commemorate the Hon. Mrs Riley, née Molesworth, with a rich bronze MONUMENT and a Flemish C17 relief behind it. Mr Riley also collected a considerable number of vestments, altar furniture, etc., for example a chasuble with Spanish C15 embroidery, a chasuble with Spanish late C16 embroidery, two late C16 Italian copes, an Italian silver cross perhaps of the C13, two C16 chalices and patens, one Elizabethan the other foreign, a C16 Venetian processional cross, a Spanish C17 painting of the Magdalen, and a chalice and paten by *S. Hennell* (1812–13).

LIZARD LIGHTHOUSE

7010

1000 yds E of Lizard Point

The lighthouse was built in 1751, but altered in 1903, when the balance of the two hexagonal towers, placed at either end of a symmetrical block, was slightly upset by the dismantling of the W light. White walls, tall black chimneystacks, cowls and foghorns (K. Woodbridge).

LOOE

ST NICHOLAS, West Looe. Very small. Mainly 1852 and 1862. Before then used as a school, and after the Reformation as a guildhall. Endowed before 1330. PISCINA of the C14, the windows and wall on the S partly C15. The arcade is of timber from a wrecked ship; C19.

(ST MARY, Church End, East Looe. Rebuilt by *Street* (begun 1851 and later). The exterior is dull. Inside, nave, N aisle, and apsidal chancel. Four large, impressive bays to the nave arcade. The interior is spacious, tall, and well detailed. Marble and polychrome decoration in the sanctuary, and a good PULPIT (all this must be very late 1850s). Dr R. Lambert)

(CHAPEL, East Looe. The lower parts of the tower are probably medieval, the upper C19. Victorian the body of the church with polygonal apse and late C13 to early C14 window details. G. W. Copeland)

BENEDICTINE PRIORY. Remains partly excavated opposite Looe Island, including a chapel in its core Celtic, but enlarged c.1200 and again in the C14. Other foundations were found recently.

The old town of East Looe still has a fairly picturesque HIGH STREET with some side lanes. Several old houses survive, for example one dated 1632, with two six-light oriel windows on the first floor. Old GUILDHALL with gabled porch and outer stair. East and West Looe were connected prior to 1853 by a magnificent BRIDGE* of thirteen arches, built in 1411–18. In West Looe, the JOLLY SAILOR INN (oldest parts C15) and the MARKET HOUSE (now a shop), six-sided, with a bell turret.

LOSTWITHIEL

12a ST BARTHOLOMEW. A sizable town church, the outstanding feature of which is the spire. The tower with its lancet windows is clearly of the C13. On the ground floor until 1878 a public way passed through from N to S. The spire was added in the early C14 with the interposition of a bold, ruthless transition from square to octagon. It is broached and has dormer windows on four of its eight sides. Round its foot is an octagonal screen with on each side double lights, quatrefoil tracery, and a gable.

---

* The present bridge was built in 1853 with seven arches. It was widened in 1960.

The double lights are divided horizontally (transom fashion) by a panel of four diapers. The NE side has a wheel (St Catherine) motif instead. The body of the church, with nave of four bays, N and S aisle, chancel with narrower and lower arcades, and S porch, is C14 too, though later than the spire; in the same unusual style as Fowey lower down the river. The piers are octagonal and have no capitals, the arches are double-chamfered, the clerestory has groups of three lancet windows (perhaps renewed in the C17) placed in line with the spandrels, not with the apexes of the arches (cf. also St Germans, Callington). The E window of five lights is one of the most sumptuous in Cornwall, evidently of the same date as the spire, with trefoils and quatrefoils, mostly round but also pointed. The roofs are all new. In the aisles they are of the lean-to type. The S doorway with colonnettes with shaft-rings and hoodmould on two head corbels also looks early C14. To the same period belongs the FONT. Octagonal, of outstanding quality. On the bowl, panels with carved figures: huntsman and hawk, a head with leaves sprouting from the mouth, a grimacing head of distinctly evil features, wolf and hound, and lions. The style of the carving is so 'metropolitan' that one may have to remember that in the C13 Lostwithiel was the capital of Cornwall and belonged with Restormel to Richard of Cornwall (a candidate for the Imperial throne) and his son Edmund (†1300). The Crucifixion is of a distinctly inferior quality, perhaps re-carved later on. For the dating of the font the tracery panels are instructive: their use of ogees makes a pre-C14 date impossible. – ALMS BOX. Oak, 1645, in the shape of a standing figure with a shield, folk art, inscribed W. T. Maier. – ALABASTER PANEL. Flaying of St Bartholomew. – STAINED GLASS. Faith, Hope, Charity, by *Willement* (TK). – PLATE. Good and typical set of mid-Georgian pieces (two Chalices, Patens, Flagons, and Almsdishes) by *W. Grundy*, 1775–6. – In the churchyard the head of a CROSS with figures; late medieval (cf. Launceston). – MONUMENTS. In the outer S wall between porch and tower, two sepulchral recesses. – Brass of Tristram Curteys, 1423. – Inside, on the N wall, esquire in armour. – Also two pretty Elizabethan wall tablets. – Neo-classical monuments, for example by *Bedford* of London, *Isbell* of Stonehouse, *Shepherd* of Plymouth.

The town has not much character. An early C14 bridge of five pointed arches with double rings to their voussoirs (cf. Greystone and Horse Bridges) leads over the river (parapet, 1676).

Close to the river a certain amount remains of the STANNARY COURT, especially the heavily buttressed Coinage Hall, and further N more ancient masonry and a doorway. The fragments have not been sufficiently investigated. The Stannary Court was the centre of the royal authority over tin-mining and 'coinage' meant the knocking off of the corner or quoin of each block for the benefit of the Duchy of Cornwall. The small GUILDHALL is of 1740 and has an arcaded ground floor. Some good four-square Georgian granite houses. One brick and stone house of 1688 (No. 9 FORE STREET). (The MHLG emphasizes the old GRAMMAR SCHOOL* of 1781 in Queen Street; the MUNICIPAL OFFICES close to the Guildhall, also late C18; Nos. 21–23 NORTH STREET; a late C18 house in THE PARADE; and No. 3 DUKE STREET.)‡

Outside the town: ST FAITH'S HOUSE OF THE SISTERS OF MERCY (now a Youth Hostel), by G. E. Street, 1864. Grey sandstone and black slate. Severe three-storey centre block with square-headed windows randomly placed, articulated by two large buttresses culminating in a large chimneyshaft (partly demolished), and further along a large projecting bay through which a buttress runs into an ornate overhanging gable. The whole effect is hard, austere, angular, and original, genuine Victorian rather than reinterpreted Gothic. House to the W, simple, non-Gothic windows. Chapel to the E, E.E., undistinguished except for the painted, tiled, and alabaster REREDOS. (This paragraph was contributed by Dr R. Lambert.)

₅₀₃₀   LUDGVAN

ST LUDGVAN AND ST PAUL. A re-dedication took place in 1336. To this period some of the chancel with its N window may belong.§ The rest is C15. W tower of three stages, granite blocks with buttresses set back from the angles, the pinnacles corbelled out as at St Ives. Below the battlements heads like gargoyles (cf. St Erth). The tower arch inside has panelled

* Mr J. T. Smith suggests that the building looks exactly as if it had been designed as a market hall. When and how might it have been used as a school?

‡ At the corner of the former MALT HOUSE is a stone of 1658 recording a three-thousand-year lease dating from 1652.

§ Mr T. W. French asks: Can the one and a half blocked windows in the chancel with splayed jambs and semicircular rere-arches be as late as 1336? The MHLG considers the tower to be C14, and notes that it was over-restored in 1888. The carved granite panel over the porch, said to represent S Ludgvan, is of unknown date.

jambs. The s aisle is of four bays, its piers with four major
and four minor shafts and moulded capitals. The N aisle has
six bays with piers of the same design but C15 capitals. The S
aisle is a little earlier. – FONT. Norman, of an unusual design
with scalloped sides, a chip-carved moulding along the top, a
cable-moulding below. – STAINED GLASS. In the S aisle the
three l. windows by *Lavers, Barraud & Westlake*, 1868–73. –
PLATE. Chalice and Paten, Elizabethan, probably by the same
maker as Stithians; excellent set of Chalice, Patens, and two
Flagons with the Godolphin arms, by *Blackford* of Plymouth,
1727–8 (*see* Perranuthnoe). – MONUMENTS. Slate to John
South † 1636 and family, very appealingly infantile. – Brass
inscription plate to Christopher Borlase, † 1749 ('By the
smallness of this table | judge not, Reader, of that loss which
it deplores', etc.), fine engraved script. – Memorials of William
Borlase, and of Sir Humphrey Davy and his parents.

LUXULYAN *0050*

ST CIRICIUS AND ST JULITTA. A large, all-granite church, and
all of large regular granite ashlar. w tower, without buttresses
or pinnacles, with a very tall NE stair-turret; rather military-
looking. The Perp windows are large and well proportioned.
The S porch is battlemented, with an exceptionally handsome
tracery-panelled pointed tunnel-vault inside. The even granite
surface is particularly impressive on the E side of the church.
The interior has N and S aisles of six bays and very similar
design, both with standard Cornish granite piers, and both
with the same arch mouldings. Only the capitals differ. Some
of the old timbers of the wagon roofs are preserved. – FONT.
St Austell type, almost identical with St Austell. – STAINED
GLASS. Old fragments in the w tower window. – The chancel
window is a memorial to Sylvanus Trevail, the architect,
† 1903. – PLATE. Fine Chalice and Paten by *Jons* of Exeter,
1576; Paten and Flagon by *W. Tuite*, 1771–2.

(HOLY WELL (St Cyr). Small, with a nice little moulded doorway. G. W. Copeland)

(The TREFFRY VIADUCT, crossing the Luxulyan Valley, is of
granite, 700 ft long, nearly 100 ft high, and has ten arches. It
was built by J. T. Treffry *c*.1825–30. It carries a large stream,
white with china clay, a footpath, and the remains of a disused
light railway. Dr Athelstane Hill)

PRIDEAUX. *See* p. 146.
METHROSE. *See* p. 118.

CASTILLY HENGE MONUMENT, 400 yds S of the Bodmin–
Truro road, near Lower Woon Farm. The monument consists
of an oval ditch with external bank having a maximum diameter of 217 ft. The site is well preserved, and the bank still
survives to a height of 6 ft. There is a broad entrance on the
NNW and a smaller gap on the SSE. Excavations have shown
that the present form of the site represents a remodelling of
the original Neolithic henge to form a medieval amphitheatre,
for the presentation of religious plays.

MABE

7030

ST LAUD. The church lies outside the village, entirely on its
own. The usual W tower of regular granite blocks, in three
stages, with no buttresses.* The rest of the church is granite
too, with a specially fine S porch, its outer doorway with
cable decoration outside and a repeated motif of a lily in a
vase inside up the jambs and along the arch. The frame of the
S door itself is of limestone, that is much more finely worked,
with leaf-scrolls along two orders of jambs and voussoirs and
decoration in the spandrels too. The W door to the tower has
similar decoration in granite. N and S aisles separated from the
nave by octagonal piers with capitals evidently made for
Cornish standard piers. The tower arch has responds with
attached shafts and heads instead of capitals. To the l. and r.
of the modern reredos, fragments of an alabaster ALTAR of the
C15 (Annunciation, Nativity, Last Supper). – PLATE. Good
Chalice and Paten of 1576; very handsome Tazza of 1577–8,
one of a pair, the other at St Agnes; plain Tankard of 1750.

MADRON

4030

ST MADERN. The mother-church of Penzance, a sizable building, all granite, with a W tower of only two stages, but the
lower one very tall. At its upper end a corbel table. The tower
is unbuttressed. In the chancel is a one-seat SEDILE with
PISCINA next to it which belongs probably to the early C14
(re-dedication of altar, 1336). The S aisle could also belong to
this period: piers of four major and four minor shafts, and
two-centred arches (of limestone). The N aisle is C15, with
taller piers and carving all round some of the capitals. Both

* Tower and porch C15; otherwise the church was almost entirely rebuilt
in 1866 (MHLG).

aisles are of six bays. Much of the old carving is incorporated into the new wagon roofs. Outside, two of the s aisle windows have very primitive granite carved heads as keystones. The s porch is c19. – ROOD SCREEN. Some panels of the base are original and keep some of the original colours. Each panel is of two lights, with a tall crocketed gable, the design reminiscent of Somerset (Dunster), as Bligh Bond observed. – BENCH ENDS of standard two-shield design, but with beasts resting on the tops. – PULPIT. Plain, good c18 oak. – ALTAR RAILS. Good, solid early c18 work. – TOWER SCREEN. Jacobean, the balustrading characteristically coarser than that of the altar rails. – CARVED PANEL with a group of nine angels, c15, in the s aisle (where from?). – PLATE. Flagon, 1791 by *Edward Fennell*; a finely proportioned ewer. – MONUMENTS. Brass to John Clies, Mayor of Penzance, and his family, 1623 (s aisle, floor). – Slate plate to John Maddern † 1621, very *Volkskunst*, and to Thomas Fleming and his family † 1631, with two couples carved on top of each other and their children kneeling below, just like playing cards. – The Rev. Duke Pearce, 1720. Two kneeling figures facing each other across a prayer desk, a type which had been in fashion in the c16 and must in 1720 have appeared extremely outmoded. – In the churchyard the very heavy, severely Greek Price Mausoleum, *c*.1820.

BAPISTERY of St Madron. c14, a plain rectangle, now in ruins, but with an altar still *in situ*. Near by, ST MADRON'S WELL. Several good houses around the village, but nothing special.

MÊN SCRYFA DOWN, 3 m. NW of Madron, up a side lane on the E side of the Madron–Morvah road. c5 or c6 PILLAR STONE, 8 ft tall, with inscription in Roman capitals: ˏRIALOBRANI CUNOVALI FILI.

BODRIFTY IRON AGE SETTLEMENT, 1½ m. SW of Porthmeor. The principal settlement consists of an irregular enclosure with an entrance on the SW, within which are six or eight hut circles.

MULFRA QUOIT, 3 m. N of Madron. A partially ruined mega-lithic tomb with three of the four original uprights still stand-ing and supporting a partially displaced capstone. There are traces of a circular barrow 40 ft in diameter which originally covered the chamber.

TREWERN STANDING STONE. The surviving member of a pair of standing stones set 10 ft apart. Excavation in the c19 of the area between the two stones revealed a pit possibly con-taining an inhumation burial.

WEST LANYON. This single standing stone, 5 ft high, is all that remains of a rectangular megalithic chamber destroyed in the C18.

MAEN CASTLE *see* SENNEN

MAENPORTH *see* BUDOCK

MAGOR *see* CAMBORNE

4050

MAKER

ST JULIAN. The church stands quite on its own on the high ground adjoining the far end of the Mount Edgcumbe estate. It has a heavy W tower with ornate pinnacles. The buttresses leave the angles free and end half-way up the third stage in little pinnacles in relief. The body of the church has N and S aisles, S porch, and an outer S aisle added as an Edgcumbe family chapel. The piers of the five-bay arcades N and S are Cornish standard of identical design; the Edgcumbe aisle has a slightly different (later) moulding, with more pronounced points between the shafts and the hollows, and more finely moulded capitals and arches. – FONT. From St Merryn. Norman, large, and excellent, of Bodmin type, with five supports, corner busts, and the snake convolutions in between especially wild and disorderly. – MONUMENTS. The only one of the Edgcumbe monuments worth recording is that to Richard Lord Edgcumbe † 1758, a standing wall-monument with a bust above a sarcophagus and against a pyramid. – Sir Richard Hunt † 1787, by *Kendall* of Exeter. Large grey oval plate with white laurel wreath, and inside it a framed inscription plate with urn on top.

(Curious 'embattled' COACH HOUSE near the church. Probably early C19.)

(BLOCKHOUSE, on the edge of Mount Edgcumbe Park. Square; in good order. Probably Civil War rather than C16. G. W. Copeland)

7020

MANACCAN

ST MANACCA. Norman S door, with three little orders of columns and curious fluted voussoirs; obviously not entirely in its original state. At the NW corner of the S transept the top of a Norman shaft has been uncovered. The E window of the

same transept and the s window of the chancel are C13. The
N aisle is C15, standard Cornish granite design, of six bays.
There is a squint between s transept and chancel. The w
tower is of slate, not of granite, two-storeyed, unbuttressed.*
The w door has heads as label-stops (cf. for example, Cury).
– PLATE. Chalice and Paten by *Jons* of Exeter, 1570–3; also
pieces of 1699, 1722, 1732, 1737.

MARAZION

5030

In the first edition of this book Marazion was not mentioned,
because it has no buildings of special interest. But Marazion is
attractive as a whole. John Betjeman in the *Shell Guide* agrees
with me in this.

(The town was a borough until 1883, and a settlement in the
   Middle Ages occupied by Jews who smelted tin. Today it is
   rendered almost uninhabitable by heavy traffic running
   through the long, narrow, and twisty street of which the town
   chiefly consists. Down by where the ferries cross to St
   Michael's are some cobbled pavements and old houses which
   give a look of Lyme Regis to the old centre of the town. There
   is a pretty classical galleried METHODIST CHAPEL of 1862
   and one grand square Georgian house at the w end of the town
   standing back among trees. Much of the little town is tall
   boarding houses with pebbledashed walls, yellow brick dressings, and green-painted gables. The church (ALL SAINTS), a
   hard-looking building of 1861 by *J. P. St Aubyn*, replacing an
   old chapel of ease, has a N aisle altar by *Martin Travers*. From
   the w side of the town there is a splendid view of the outline of
   St Michael's Mount as seen across the flat foreshore.)‡

MARHAMCHURCH

2000

ST MARWENNA. A church of modest size with a tower of
modest height. The tower has diagonal buttresses climbing up
in four stages, and a polygonal NE staircase-turret. Of the
Norman church the masonry of the s transept at least seems
to remain. The N transept was absorbed when a N aisle was
built. The arcade is low, of standard Cornish appearance. Aisle
and nave are of about the same width, both with wagon roofs.
– PULPIT. C17, with tester, in the corner of s transept and

* C14, with C15 parapet and pinnacles (MHLG).
‡ John Betjeman, *Cornwall* Shell Guide, Faber & Faber, 1964.

chancel. – ROYAL ARMS with strapwork decoration, by *Michael Chuke* (cf. Kilkhampton). – CRESSET STONE with four holes on an octagonal pier (cemented into the tower base). – The most remarkable feature of the church is the stonework of a WINDOW in a niche in the W wall. It has a cusped head, a transom, and the lower part divided by a mullion. In all probability it is the opening of an anchorite's cell of whose construction for one Cecilia Moys we hear between 1403 and 1405.

MARHAYS MANOR HOUSE. With two good plaster ceilings. One is similar to the work of *c.* 1680 at Dunsland House in North Devon. The stone mullions of the windows have gone. One C14 doorway is still in use.

MARHAYS *see* MARHAMCHURCH

MAWGAN-IN-MENEAGE

ST MAWGAN. A fine three-storeyed tower of regular granite blocks with ribbed pinnacles on angel corbels (cf., for example, St Anthony-in-Meneage). The W door has a charming leaf-scroll decoration all over one order of jambs and voussoirs. Close to the door the coats of arms of the Carminow, Reskymer, Ferrers, and Vyvyan families. On the S side the porch is attached to the transept (cf. also St Anthony-in-Meneage). The chancel has two E.E. windows, the chancel S and E windows are Dec, the N aisle is clearly Perp, with a fine E window. Inside, the N aisle has an arcade of seven bays of Cornish granite design, with a little decoration of the abaci. The N transept is C19. The S transept is separated from the aisle by two arches on standard piers with moulded capitals. It is connected with the chancel by an elaborate squint similar to those at Landewednack, etc. The cut-off corner is replaced by a three-eighths shaft with a badly carved shield-holding angel. The tower arch has shafts attached to the responds and angels as capitals. The N aisle still possesses much of its original wagon roof. – FONT. Octagonal, with corner shafts coming out in a stove-pipe fashion. – MONUMENTS. In the S transept, a cross-legged knight and a woman wearing a wimple, *c.*1300. – Sir Vyell Vyvyan † 1820. Two children and an urn, a large relief, signed in Greek letters by *Bartolini* (Βαρτολινυς εποιει). – INSCRIBED STONE, known as Mawgan Cross: inscription, CNEGUMI FILI GENAIUS, with Hiberno-Saxon letters, perhaps as late as the C10 and originally with a cross head. The position at the meeting of three roads seems original.

TRELOWARREN. *See* p. 225.

MAWGAN-IN-PYDAR

8060

In a lovely wooded valley, church, house, and village embedded in trees.

ST MAWGAN. A large, low church, with its tower to the S of the S transept. The tower has buttresses set back from the angles and a NE stair-turret rising to above parapet height. Its lower part, the N transept, with its arch into the nave, and the nave are C13. The S aisle was added in the C15, four wide bays and then after some bare wall two more bays for the chancel aisle. The latter are earlier (see their two-centred arches). Yet the piers are already of standard Cornish design. The nave arcades are also standard, with four-centred arches and horizontal leaves carved along the abaci. The nave W window of three lights is *c.*1300; the other windows are good Perp of three, four, and five lights. A squint leads from the N transept into the chancel.* – FONT. On five supports, with circular bowl. The corners with faces, the four sides with a zigzag top border and shields below (cf. St Wenn, Crantock, St Columb Minor). – PULPIT. Of *c.*1530, with panels with large Instruments of the Passion. – ROOD SCREEN. Tall, with loft. The openings have no tracery; their heads are freely cusped. Good cornice with the Arundell arms in the centre. For this specially graceful and airy type of screen cf. Crantock. – BENCH ENDS. Many of the C15, with the usual two shields with monograms, Instruments of the Passion, etc., on the shields. – BRASSES. Very rubbed-off brass of a Vicar, early C15, in the chancel N wall, and fragments of several brasses of the Arundell family. All are incomplete; parts of some are now at Wardour Castle. – The following deserve notice: George A. and wife † 1573, two figures and verses (palimpsest of Flemish early C16 brass); Jane A. † 1577 and Mary A. † 1578, inscriptions and shields only, figures at Wardour (palimpsest of Flemish brass of 1374); Cecily A. † 1578, figure, verses, and shields (palimpsest of 1374, as above); unknown man, late C16. – LANTERN CROSS in the churchyard.

* The church was restored and partly rebuilt in 1860–1 by *Butterfield*. The RECTORY, of about the same date, is also by him, and the present stone SCHOOL by the stream (1863). (Information from the Rev. R. J. Hawkins and Dr Paul Thompson.)

LANHERNE, the house of the Arundell family, and since 1794 a
convent. The front is Elizabethan, the back parts partly late
C17 and partly late C18. In the garden by the main entrance a
CROSS, one of the most elaborate Cornish crosses, with Christ
Crucified and on the r. side an interlaced beast. The inscription
and the beast are very similar to Sancreed. – LANTERN CROSS
35   of soft Pentewan stone. This originally stood near Roseworthy,
Gwinear.

(CARNANTON. Beautifully situated in the Vale of Lanherne.
Late C18, three-storeyed stone house. Severe, unadorned
s front of seven bays. Victorian additions at the back. GMT)

WOODWAN. CROSS HEAD, lantern type, late medieval, with
figure sculpture.

7020   MAWNAN

ST MAUNANUS AND ST STEPHEN.* Far from the village,
amongst trees, with its cemetery overlooking the mouth of the
Helford river. W tower of two stages, unbuttressed, with
window tracery of the Dec style. A narrow lancet window in
the chancel, C14 windows on the N side. Yet the two aisles are
of identical C15 design, with granite piers consisting of four
major and four minor shafts. There is an excellent PISCINA
in the chancel wall, C13, with finely carved heads as label-
stops. The FONT is octagonal, C15. Of the ROOD SCREEN only
four painted panels of saints remain (cf. Budock and Gunwalloe).

1050   MENABILLY
                          Near Fowey

A Rashleigh mansion, built c.1600 and entirely rebuilt c.1710–15,
with a central courtyard. Again much altered c.1821. The
house appears a plain, comfortable specimen of that date. The
staircase and a good plaster ceiling of the 1715 period. Of the
1820s, the splendid landscaping of the grounds, opening up a
vista to the sea. The GARDENS are (or were) famous for their
wealth of sub-tropical plants, unparalleled in Britain. At the
foot of the grounds a GROTTO (1750–60),‡ very neglected. –
INSCRIBED STONE at East Lodge. On the front: CIRUSIUS
HIC IACIT CUNOMORI FILIUS; on the back a T-cross; probably

* Restored by *William White* in 1855 (S. Muthesius).
‡ Or possibly of the 1730s, according to Mr P. Laws; but Barbara Jones
(*Follies*) says c. 1780.

c6. It has been seriously suggested that 'Cirusius' should be read 'Drustaus', i.e. Tristanus ,and that Cunomanus is King Mark.

MENACUDDLE see ST AUSTELL

MENHENIOT

2060

ST LALLUWY. One of the rare Cornish churches with a spire, plain, octagonal, on a two-storeyed tower with battlements and strong three-stepped buttresses set back from the angles. The windows are small, and the battlements project on a corbel table. The whole is probably early c14. Inside there is a difference between the arcades of the N and s aisles, although both are Perp. The s aisle is later (cf. its more elaborately detailed capitals and four-centred elaborately moulded arches). The ceiled wagon roofs are the most enjoyable element of the church, especially the wall plates of the nave. – PULPIT. 1891 by *Hems* of Exeter, who did so many reredoses in Cornish and Devon churches. He is more successful here, where he relates the polar exploits of Vice-Admiral Trelawny-Jago and the *Enterprise*. – PLATE. Flagon, silver-mounted stoneware (tiger-ware) with repoussé decoration, 1578–9; similar stoneware Flagon, similarly decorated, by *Eston* of Exeter, *c.*1576–92; other pieces of 1668, 1695. – Beautifully engraved BRASS INSCRIPTION to Sir Ralph Carmynow † 1386; the earliest brass in Cornwall (F. A. Greenhill). – Other Trelawny MONUMENTS. Semicircular top of a slate tomb to I. T., with good decoration, in particular two oversized, fat putti. – Jonathan Trelawny † 1674, Edward Trelawny, Dean of Exeter, † 1726, with a good bust on the pediment. – Also L. Stephens † 1724, a black marble slab with superb lettering and achievement. – Tablet to Lady Charlotte Carr, by *M. Eames* of Exeter.

COLDRENNICK. *See* p. 54.

MÊN SCRYFA see MADRON

MERIFIELD see ANTONY

MERRY MAIDENS see ST BURYAN

MERTHER

8040

ST COHAN. A small, neglected church,* with a thin w tower

---

* Now disused. The figure of St Anthony and the font and pulpit are now at Tresillian (*see* p. 227).

(cf. Cornelly, Mylor) with heavy diagonal buttresses and two stages; no battlements left. In the N wall two Norman window openings, one with a C14 window put in. Most of the windows are Late Perp, with hoodmoulds. The S arcade is Cornish standard. A little figure of St Anthony in a niche to the N of the altar. – PLATE. Chalice and Paten of 1576, attributed to master *IW* (*see* Bodmin), very nicely decorated; Paten on foot by *E. Jay*, 1788–9.

(The MHLG lists a C16 FARMHOUSE, with C19 and C20 additions. N front with a two-storey projection for the entrance, large, moulded, Tudor-arched doorway, mullioned windows, and one small gable.)

METHROSE
Near Luxulyan

0050

One of the best farmhouses in Cornwall. C16. A four-centred arch in the regular granite wall takes the visitor into a small courtyard with the hall on the r., low-built, with granite walls and dipping slate roof and an oriel window. The date is perhaps late C15 or early C16. In plan it is similar to Tintagel Old Post Office, with an identically placed hall fireplace in the front wall with a window bay beside it (probably rebuilt in the C17), and a two-storey service end (in this case, the upper floor extends over the cross-passage). The chamber beyond the hall has been absorbed into the later 'parlour' wing, which is said by Henderson to have been built by Nicholas Kendall some time between 1622 and 1649. The drip-course instead of hoodmoulds is a feature occasionally used in Cornwall in the middle of the C17.

MEVAGISSEY

0040

Very picturesque and little-spoilt fishing village. Inner harbour (pier, 1770–3) and more recent outer harbour. Houses climbing up on the N. On the W good net-drying and mending houses of characteristic deep plan with central door. On the S (No. 27 Polkirt Hill) a more ambitious five-window pink-granite house of *c.*1730, with central entrance with Tuscan demi-columns and pediment. Modillion frieze at the eaves. (The MHLG also lists another C18 house, Lawn House, in Church Street. Two storeys, three bays, large, low pediment.) The castle of the Bodrugans has disappeared.

ST PETER. The tower has no buttresses. It was restored in a
shortened form and with a saddleback roof after it had
collapsed. The N aisle of four bays is of Pentewan stone. The
piers are of standard section, but the abaci are octagonal and
decorated. Earlier traces are the trefoil PISCINA in the nave,
W of the S transept, and the three-light Dec S window of the
transept. – FONT. Norman, circular, with chip-carved
rosettes, etc., a herringbone moulding above, a zigzag moulding below, and a cable moulding on the base. – MONUMENTS.
Otwell Hill † 1617 and wife ('Stock Lancashier, Birth London,
Cornwall gave | to Otwell Hill Inhabitance and Grave |
Franck, Frugall, Plaisannt, Sober, Stout and Kinde . . .'),
an uncommonly ambitious composition with the two effigies
reclining above and behind each other (cf. Truro Cathedral)
and columns l. and r. with a semicircular top, with inscription
plate and strap and fruit ornament. – Lewis Dart † 1632 and
family, in contrast a humble, local slate with ten kneeling
figures.

CHAPEL POINT. Three houses by *J. A. Campbell*, 1934–9, of
solid local stone (Neo-Rustic).

PENWARNE. *See* p. 137.

MICHAELSTOW

0070

ST MICHAEL. Unbuttressed W tower with NE stair-turret (cf.
Lanteglos-by-Camelford). Nave and aisles, the S aisle of five
bays, the N aisle ending one bay short of chancel and S aisle.
The arcades are standard granite design, except that the four
E piers of the S side have limestone capitals with large horizontal leaf motifs all around. The wagon roofs are original. –
FONT. Plain, octagonal (what date?). – BENCHES. A few
original ones with bench ends with shields. – Several MONU-
MENTS. Slate plates, for example Jane Merifield, 1663, with
nice scrolly lettering and two standing figures in the costume
of the period, incised as primitively as if they were done by a
child. – In the N wall of the chancel is a stone with a quatrefoil
opening, reported to have been the window of an anchorite's
cell, which was attached to the N wall of the chancel.

MILLBROOK

4050

(Ruined CHAPEL of the vanished Inswork Manor House.
DODBROOK MANOR has a two-stage porch, mullioned windows,
etc. G. W. Copeland)

MINSTER

St Merteriana. The mother-church of Boscastle, a mile away across a bleak hill and down into a dip with luxuriant trees. The churchyard is on the steep slope of the dell. Unbuttressed w tower of the usual kind, but unfinished and provided with a saddleback roof instead of the standard battlements and pinnacles.* The church has nave and s aisle of five bays, with Cornish standard piers and four-centred arches. The n windows of the chancel are E.E. – FONT. The bowl with diagonal crisscross lines (cf. Tintagel, Forrabury). – PLATE. A specially rewarding collection. Chalice by *Jons* of Exeter, *c.*1576. – Two Flagons of 1588–9, in their shape interesting stoneware forms. There are no others of the type in the West of England. Maker's mark: *HC* or *HIC*. – Paten by *Bateman*, 1792–3. – MONUMENTS. Several slate plates. – Two little monuments with kneeling figures opposite each other as usual about 1600. The one is 1611, the other (W. Cotton) as late as 1656. – In the chancel: John Cotton † 1703; indifferent.

Priory. No remains.

Redevallen Manor House, 1½ m. ssw of Minster and ¾ m. nw of Waterpit Down crossroads. On an E-plan, with well preserved porch and mullioned windows. Dated 1642. On a hill near by, above the coast road from Tintagel to Boscastle, the medieval farmhouse of Trewhitten, one of the oldest in n Cornwall. It is pre-c14. Small, stone-built. Two storeys each with two rooms. The larger ground-floor room has a stone fireplace and a stone newel stair in a rectangular turret. The smaller ground-floor room was originally a byre. This is a late version of a long house (V. M. and F. J. Chesher).

Worthivale, 3 m. s of Minster and 3 m. se of Tintagel, near Camelford Station. The present house is probably mid c17, despite the date 1703 above the door (V. M. and F. J. Chesher). Among the outbuildings are the remains of a small Tudor house. Near by an INSCRIBED STONE ('King Arthur's Grave'): LATINI IC IACIT FILIUS MAGARI. The lettering is transitional between Roman and Hiberno-Saxon.

Waterpit Down. CROSS SHAFTS (on the r. side of the road from Tintagel to Launceston). Interlaced ornament and defaced inscription. Supposed to be c10.

---

* Presumably dating from 1869–71, when the church was much rebuilt (A. S. B. New).

MITHIAN
7050
6½ m. NW of Truro

(ST PETER. 1861 by *William White*. An impressive, severe
cruciform church with high raftered roofs (Dr Paul Thompson). The tower was rebuilt in 1928.)

MODITONHAM
4060
Near Botus Fleming

Of the castle of the Moditons nothing is preserved. The present
house is Georgian, of seven bays and three storeys, with a
parapet and a Roman Doric porch.

MORVAH
4030

ST BRIDGET or ST MORWETHA. The interest of this church is
less its humble, two-staged, unbuttressed W tower of the
C14 than its nave and chancel of 1828. In spite of their date
these are not in the Commissioners' style (*see* Penzance, St
Day): rough granite, unaisled, and certainly meant to be
Cornish Medieval from outside, though the window tracery
does odd things.

CHUN CASTLE, 1 m. S. This outstanding fortification, the only
true stone-built fort in Cornwall, consists of two concentric
stone ramparts beyond which is a pair of rock-cut ditches.
A single entrance occurs on the SW. The fort is still a most
impressive structure, with ramparts standing to a height of
10 ft. Excavations located a series of stone-built circular and
rectangular houses in the interior of the fort.

CHUN QUOIT, on the same hill as the castle. This is a large
closed megalithic chamber of four uprights supporting a
massive capstone 8 ft square. The chamber lies at the centre
of a round barrow 35 ft in diameter.

GURNARDS HEAD PROMONTORY FORT, 1 m. N of Porthmeor.
The promontory is cut off by two ramparts and three ditches
at its narrowest point. The inner rampart still survives to a
height of 6 ft. Two groups of circular stone huts occur in the
interior on the E side.

LANYON QUOIT, 2 m. SE. The present megalithic chamber of
three uprights and a capstone represents restoration work
carried out in 1824. The chamber lies at the N end of a long
barrow 90 ft long and 40 ft wide. A series of stones projecting
from the S end of the mound may mark the site of a second
chamber.

MORVAL

As at Lanhydrock and Boconnoc, the church and the house lie
close together in the grounds. The HOUSE (of the Glynn and
from the C17 to the C19 the Buller families) is one of the best
in Cornwall, evidently an E-shaped Tudor building originally,
though its central porch has gone, its windows have white C18
glazing-bars, and its hipped roof belongs no doubt to the
same century.

ST WENNA. Small and low behind the rhododendrons, with
an unbuttressed, three-stage W tower of slate. The N side has
an aisle, the S side still the older arrangement without an aisle
but with a transept. One chancel window looks as if it might
have been C13 originally. The N aisle arcade is Cornish granite
standard with large horizontal leaves as decoration of the
capitals. The roof of the aisle is original. – C17 ALMSBOX
with iron hinges and mountings. – PLATE. The only completely preserved Pre-Reformation piece in Cornwall, a Paten
of 1528–9, not particularly noteworthy otherwise; Chalice of
c.1576; some C18 pieces. – MONUMENT to Walter Coode
† 1637, slate, with kneeling parents and children allegorically
expressed by fruits growing out of branches issuing from the
parents. Skulls above the fruits show the death of children
before their parents.

MORWENSTOW

ST JOHN BAPTIST. There are not many Norman parish
churches preserved in Cornwall, and those of which fragments
remain were usually aisleless. At Morwenstow a Norman N
arcade remains on thick circular piers with scalloped and
otherwise ornamented capitals and arches with zigzag and
beak-head decoration. The Norman S door also survives, with
colonnettes and zigzag arches. It was removed from its
original site when a S aisle was added, and the arches were
split up so as to attach one to the outer front of the S porch.
Of the capitals one has two birds, one fir cones (cf. Kilkhampton). The most interesting Norman features are the crude
heads of men and beasts on the porch, and, of very strong
appeal, inside in the spandrels between the arches. The three
Norman N bays are followed by two E.E. bays also with
circular piers. They have double-chamfered pointed arches.
The S arcade and S aisle on the other hand are Cornish late
medieval standard. One bay was re-done in 1564 and bears

that date and intials in capitals and abaci. The wagon roofs of 20 nave and aisles are original. The w tower is unbuttressed, Cornish standard. The way it stands four-square and silent above a combe, facing the sea beyond, is unforgettable. – FONT. Very primitive Norman, egg-shaped, with a simple cable moulding at the foot. – BENCH ENDS with Early Renaissance motifs. – ROOD SCREEN of 1575, reassembled in 1845 by Hawker, with cast-iron tracery and a few original fragments. – Remains of a WALL PAINTING (St Morwenna) on the N wall of the chancel; faint. – PLATE. A good set. Chalice and Paten by *Coton* of Barnstaple, *c.*1572; Paten on foot by *J. Elston Jun.* of Exeter, 1728–9; Flagon by *M. Fox*, 1755–6.

VICARAGE. Built by the eccentric R. S. Hawker, whose poems are so beloved by Cornishmen. The chimneys are in imitation of the towers of the various churches he had been connected with. The kitchen chimney is reminiscent of his mother's tomb.

STANBURY, 1 m. s of the church. L-shaped house of the C16 and earlier. Great hall, etc. Two-storeyed projecting porch; mullioned windows with hoods. Inside, the date 1585 on a stone fireplace. GMT)

MOUNT EDGCUMBE
4050

Burnt out during the Second World War; only the grounds survived intact, and the views towards Plymouth Sound and the Channel remain as splendid as ever. The house is now rebuilt (1960), with octagonal towers at the four corners and a large C18 wing to the w. It was originally built, in a shape of great interest historically, for *Sir Richard Edgcumbe* in 1547–54 from a 'platt' he was to supply, by a Devon contractor, *Roger Palmer* of North Buckland, who had to follow 'alwayes . . . the devyse, advyse and plan' of Sir Richard. It has been much remodelled since, but from the first it had corner towers (then round and slender) and a lofty hall 'rising in the midst above the rest', as Carew tells us (1602), just as at Wollaton in Nottinghamshire thirty years later. So it was a very modern mansion as compared with Edgcumbe's paternal Cotehele, though its hall was the same size and shape in plan, and it had a rather medieval aspect, with no fully symmetrical front. Of the interior nothing, alas, need now be said. The garden has English, Italian, and French parts, a typical early C19

conception, and a pedimented GARDEN HOUSE, with a centre
of before 1735, and late C18 wings. Triangular *Coade* stone
MONUMENT, 14 ft high, to Timothy Brett, 1791. Also a
folly RUIN of c.1750, and THOMSON'S SEAT, with Tuscan
columns and a pediment.*

(HOLY WELL (St Leonard). On the edge of the Park, above the
road, about ¼ m. NW of the church. An attractive little building, well restored. G. W. Copeland)

4020   MOUSEHOLE

Originally called Port Enys; destroyed by the Spanish in 1595,
except for the manor house.

(Nos. 1–2 Keigwin Street form part of the C16 MANOR HOUSE.
Some granite windows remain. Porch on granite columns,
with room over. MHLG)

MULFRA QUOIT *see* MADRON

6010   MULLION

ST MELINA. Mainly important because one of the churches
richest in old BENCH ENDS. They are here to be found with
two motifs and with one motif for each end. Amongst the
representations are, besides the Instruments of the Passion
and initials, also profiles, a jester, a monk, etc. The date must
be as late as 1535 or later, for there are plenty of details indica-
tive of the coming of the Renaissance – cf. for example the
end with the two cherubs with chalice and barrel. Architecturally the church is nothing special. W tower of granite and
the local serpentine; two stages, unbuttressed, similar to Cury,
the same label-stops at the W door. A little relief of the
Crucifixion above the upper window. The S porch has panelled
jambs of the Cury–Gunwalloe type. The S aisle has the same
E window with cusped tracery as at Sithney, Gunwalloe, and
Cury. The N and S arcades are identical, of Cornish standard
design and undecorated capitals. The ceiled wagon roofs
have their original timber. The N and S doors are original too.
– FONT. C13, octagonal, three of the sides with two very
shallow blank trefoiled arcades, the fourth with a serpent
motif. – LECTERN made up of two panels with sibyls of
c.1530–50. – ROOD SCREEN. Very little of the original woodwork left. – ROYAL ARMS of Charles II, well carved.

        * I owe this entry to Professor Martyn Jope.

MYLOR

St Melorus. In an exquisite position, with the churchyard extending N towards the creek. A remarkable church in several ways. It has a turret on its W gable with very thick buttresses l. and r. (the width of the nave behind), and in addition, a little further W, a belfry of *c.*1636 with a weatherboarded upper storey. Moreover, the church possesses two Norman doorways, one on the N in its original position with a Maltese cross in the tympanum and a zigzag moulding up the jambs and along the lintel, and the other transferred to the W, with one order of colonnettes and also a cross in the tympanum. The N walls, including those of the transept, still have some of their Norman masonry. The S side is Perp, with a S aisle divided from the nave by an arcade of six bays on slim piers of standard Cornish design and standard decoration of the abaci; Caen stone. S porch: exceptionally well carved doorway with a pretty openwork tracery head and panelled jambs (cf. St Austell). – FONT. Octagonal, with a plain decoration of crosses. Base and shaft C13; bowl later. – PISCINA. Octagonal pillar with octagonal bowl; the same design as at Bodmin. – PULPIT. Good Elizabethan. – ROOD SCREEN. Well preserved and well and broadly carved. To each section belong four narrow upright panels with undulating foliage; the colours, red and black, are still clearly visible. Above the panels runs an inscription: IARYS IONAI JESW CREST. – The REREDOS has a central panel of glass mosaic by *Salviati* (C. K. Burton). – MONUMENTS. Francis Trefusis, 1680, kneeling in front of an aedicule with a classical segmental pediment, a cartouche with large angels below. – Reginald Cocks, 1805 by *Richard Westmacott*. – Several minor monuments, for example by *Pearce* of Truro and *T. King* of Bath. – In the churchyard the tallest Cornish CROSS, 17 ft 6 in. if part of its shaft were not buried in the ground. Little ornament, chiefly incised circles and concentric circles.

Several nice early C19 houses in the neighbourhood, including ENYS, 1833 by *Henry Harrison*, a plain granite block, two storeys, six bays by three, with a large later wing (GMT).

(CARCLEW. Granite. Gutted by fire in 1934. It was one of the most beautiful houses in Cornwall. Centre of *c.*1740 with portico to full height. The wings with pediments and Venetian windows, joined by colonnades to the main block, were added by *Thomas Edwards* in 1749. GMT)

NANCEALVERNE HOUSE *see* PENZANCE

NANSCOWE FARM *see* ST BREOCK

NEWLYN

The fishing harbour, the quay, and the rising narrow streets not as picturesque as at St Ives or Fowey or Looe.

ST PETER (rebuilt by Mr *Perrow* in 1865 (G. Spain), aisle and transept 1881–6) has good windows with Faith, Hope, Charity, and Dorcas. The E end and font cover are by *Martin Travers* ('Newlyn School'). A good deal of sculpture by the Rev. *Allan Wyon.*

(The OLD MANOR in Trewarveth Street is C17, the MANOR HOUSE in Fore Street C18 granite ashlar of five bays and two storeys. MYRTLE COTTAGE is mid C18 (?). MHLG)

NEWLYN EAST *see* ST NEWLYN EAST

NEWQUAY

Of limited architectural attraction: worth while mostly for those whose interest does not cease when Regency changes into Victorian. The only noteworthy earlier house is the HUER'S HOUSE on the headland, whitewashed, with a little tower and an outer staircase. From it the huer would watch for approaching shoals of pilchards and then cry his 'Heva, heva', and with signals direct the men in the boats.

THE TOWER. The Molesworth family house (now golf club house), built in 1835, with a castellated tower and a private chapel. The Molesworths were one of the leading Roman Catholic families (*see* Little Petherick).

HEADLAND HOTEL. By *Sylvanus Trevail*, but decidedly disappointing, Victorian, yellow and red brick, tall and symmetrical, with pavilion roofs and no redeeming features.

ST MICHAEL. By *Comper*, 1909–11, large, with plenty of window; sober and spacious. The motifs are mostly Cornish. The rood and rood screen very much simpler than at Little Petherick. The exterior well and freely grouped.

WESLEY METHODIST CHURCH. Nice example of the picturesque type of *c.*1900. By *Bell, Withers & Meredith*. The date is 1904.

(BRANCH LIBRARY, just below St Michael's church. 1962 by the County Architect, *F. K. Hicklin*.)

ROUND BARROWS, ¼ m. NW of Trevelgue. These two large
  bowl barrows, excavated in the C19, were found to cover stone
  cists containing inhumation burials, one with a stone battle-
  axe.

NEWTON FERRERS

Plain granite mansion built about 1686–95 (dates on gatepiers)
  for Sir William Coryton. Two-storeyed, with a centre of seven
  bays and two little projecting wings of two bays each. The
  earliest Cornish mansion of classical design, that is without
  any trace of Tudor survivals. Unfortunately two-thirds of the
  house were gutted by fire in 1940. Some of it has been rebuilt;
  the rest stands as a picturesque ruin. – Lead figures and a
  Nymph by one of the *Adam*, French C18, sculptors, on the
  lawn. – Excellent collection of French C18 art brought together
  by Sir Robert Abdy.

NINE MAIDENS see WENDRON and ZENNOR

NORTH HILL

ST TORNEY. A large and specially ambitiously decorated
  church. The w tower and s aisle of regular granite blocks were
  probably done by masons who had come from St Neot. The
  s aisle has the same buttresses, battlements, and pinnacles,
  the same large, wide windows (though of only three lights),
  the same two-storeyed porch, and the same pattern of the
  vaulting ribs inside. The w tower is three-storeyed with
  buttresses set back from the angles, and a very unusual little
  bit of decoration at the sill of the w window. The interior has
  its old ceiled wagon roofs in nave and aisles. They rest on wide
  arches which in their turn rest on slim piers of Cornish
  standard design. The aisles are only four bays long, yet the
  church seems large. All this is of the C15 or early C16. But the
  chancel must be of the C14, that is the Dec style, as is obvious
  from the richly crocketed (very restored) ogee niche in the N
  wall (EASTER SEPULCHRE) and the small ogee statuary
  niches to the l. and r. of the E window and also E of the N and
  s windows. Moreover, the N window has a curious shelf at its
  bottom with little traceried niches against its back. A squint
  connects s aisle and chancel. – FONT. Norman, circular,
  undecorated. – FAMILY PEW. Doors with inlay woodwork,

1724. – MONUMENTS. More, and more interesting, than in
most Cornish village churches. Slate to Henry Spoure † 1603.
Skull (imago mortis) and coat of arms. – Thomas Vincent
† 1606, wife, and fifteen children. Elaborate altar tomb with
slate front and top and a slate back, prettily upcurved, with an
allegorical representation of the Ascension of Christ, and,
below, a figure of death. – Richard Spoure † 1653, also still
slate, with three arches; still wholly of Jacobean proportions.
40   – Henry Spoure † 1688, with sister and parents. One of the
        most endearing monuments in Cornwall: father and mother
39b   kneeling opposite each other, still in the old Elizabethan and
Jacobean tradition, the children standing in niches behind.
The four figures realistically coloured. Standing wall-monument with columns l. and r. and an elaborate entablature and
pediment. – V. Darley and wife † 1791, by *Emes* of Exeter. –
F. Hearle Rodd and wife † 1836 and 1833, identical monuments by *E. Gaffin* of Regent Street.

BRIDGE at Beriow Bridge, $\frac{1}{2}$ m. s, on the road to Liskeard.
Medieval, of three crudely pointed arches. Piers as thick as
the arches are wide. Much widened in 1890.

NINE STONES, on East Moor, $2\frac{1}{2}$ m. NW. A circle of eight small
stones, none more than 4 ft high, surrounding a central stone.

3090
NORTH TAMERTON

Close to a bridge across the Tamar and thus the Devon border.

ST DENIS (?). With an unbuttressed granite W tower with
crude carvings on the plinth: squares with trefoil, quatrefoil,
star, etc., with leaves as infillings (cf. Week St Mary). The
exterior of the S aisle has two granite bands at window-sill and
window-arch-springing level. Interior with nave and S aisle
only, standard Cornish C15 type. A few typical BENCH ENDS.
– PLATE. Chalice and Paten by *Jons* of Exeter, 1576; Set of
1722–3 by *J. White*. – Nice slate SLAB to Walter Robins
† 1706.

OGBEARE HALL. Gabled manor house with mullioned windows.
Partly C15.

OGBEARE HALL *see* NORTH TAMERTON

1090
OTTERHAM

ST DENIS (?). The tower must be Norman in part, for the arch
into the nave rests on Norman imposts. From outside, however, there is nothing in the two stages of the tower which

Prehistory: St Cleer, Trethevy Quoit

(a) *Scenery:* coastline near Lizard Point

(b) *Scenery:* Kynance Cove

(a) *Man-made Scenery:* St Austell, china-clay dumps

(b) *Man-made Scenery:* Roche, rocks and chapel

3

Man-made Scenery: Morvah, engine house of a deserted tin-mine

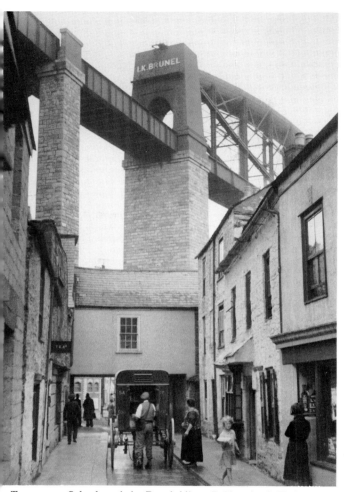

Townscape: Saltash and the Royal Albert Bridge, by I. K. Brunel, 1857–9

(a) *Townscape:* Truro, Lemon Street, begun 1794

(b) *Townscape:* Polperro, the harbour

6

(a) *Cornish Villages:* St Clement

(b) *Cornish Villages:* Lizard Point, cottages

7

Cornish Villages: Veryan, one of the five round cottages

Cornish Villages: Newquay, Huer's House

(a) *Cornish Villages:* Tintagel, Old Post Office

(b) *Church Exteriors:* Tintagel

(a) *Church Exteriors:* St Levan, a church on a hill

(b) *Church Exteriors:* St Just-in-Roseland, a church in a combe

(a) *Church Exteriors:* Lostwithiel, mainly late thirteenth and early fourteenth centuries

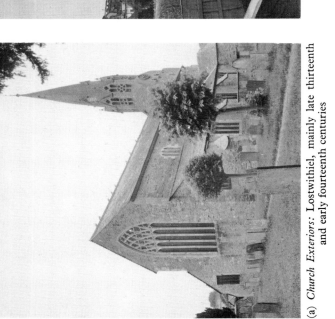

(b) *Church Exteriors:* St Ives, 1410–34

Church Exteriors: St Neot, fifteenth century

(a) *Church Towers:* St Austell, *c.* 1480

(b) *Church Towers:* Probus, *c.* 1520–30

14

Church Exteriors: Truro Cathedral, by J. L. Pearson, 1880–1910

(a) *Nonconformist Chapels:* Come-to-Good, Friends' Meeting House, 1709

(b) *Nonconformist Chapels:* Truro, Methodist Church, 1830

16

(a) *Church Interiors:* Morwenstow, north arcade Norman and Early English, south arcade Perpendicular

(b) *Church Interiors:* Scilly Isles, Tresco Priory, arches, thirteenth century

17

Church Interiors: Fowey, re-dedicated in 1336

(a) *Church Interiors:* Kilkhampton, a typically Cornish late medieval
interior with standard piers and wagon roofs

(b) *Church Interiors:* Falmouth, King Charles the Martyr, 1662–4
(east window 1813)

19

Church Interiors: Morwenstow, a typically Cornish wagon roof

Architectural Decoration in Stone: St Germans, portal, Norman
(Copyright Country Life)

Architectural Decoration in Stone: Morwenstow, detail from the Norman arcade

(a) *Architectural Decoration in Stone*: St Just-in-Penwith, tracery, mid-fourteenth-century Decorated

(b) *Architectural Decoration in Stone*: Mylor, doorway, late medieval

23

Architectural Decoration in Stone: Launceston church, east end, 1511–24

(a) *Architectural Decoration in Stone:* St Ives church, capital, early fifteenth century

(b) *Church Furnishings in Stone: Fonts:* Launceston, St Thomas, Norman

(a) *Church Furnishings in Stone: Fonts: Fowey, Norman*

(b) *Church Furnishings in Stone: Fonts: Roche, Norman*

Church Furnishings in Stone: Fonts: Bodmin, twelfth century

Church Furnishings in Stone: Fonts: Lostwithiel, early
fourteenth century

(a) *Church Furnishings in Stone: Fonts: St Ives,*
probably fifteenth century

(b) *Church Furnishings in Wood: Bench Ends:*
St Winnow, early sixteenth century

29

Church Furnishings in Wood: Stall End: Lanreath, Jacobean

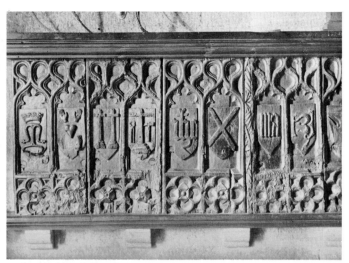

(a) *Church Furnishings in Wood: Bench Ends:* St Austell,
early sixteenth century

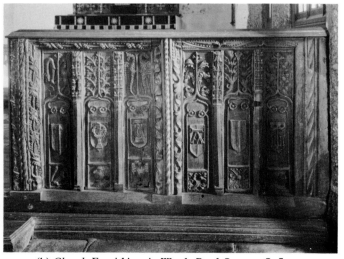

(b) *Church Furnishings in Wood: Rood Screens:* St Levan

31

Church Furnishings in Wood: Rood Screens: St Buryan, early sixteenth century (renewed)

(a) *Stained Glass*: St Neot, Harys window, early sixteenth century

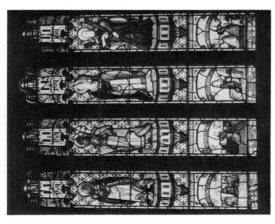

(b) *Stained Glass*: St Neot, detail from the St George window

33

Wall Painting: Breage, St Christopher, fifteenth century

34

Church Sculpture: Mawgan-in-Pydar, Lanherne, Saxon cross

36

(a) *Church Sculpture*: Egloskerry, tympanum, Norman

(b) *Church Sculpture*: St Endellion, tomb-chest,
c. 1400

(b) *Church Sculpture*: St Ive, St Christopher, fourteenth century

(a) *Church Sculpture*: Sennen, Virgin, late thirteenth century

Church Monuments: Bodmin. Prior Vivian 1533

(b) *Church Monuments*: North Hill, Henry Spoure †1688, detail

(a) *Church Monuments*: St Tudy, Anthony Nicholls †1659

Church Monuments: North Hill, Henry Spoure †1688

Church Monuments: Launceston, Granville Piper and Richard Wise, 1731

41

Church Monuments: St Germans, Edward Eliot, by J. M.
Rysbrack, 1722 (*Copyright Country Life*)

42

Church Monuments: Probus, Thomas Hawkins †1766

(a) Michaelstow, slate headstone, 1776

(b) St Cleer, Holy Well, fifteenth century

Castles: Tintagel, twelfth- and thirteenth-century ruins

Castles: Restormel, mainly late thirteenth century

Castles: St Michael's Mount, mainly fifteenth and nineteenth centuries

Manor Houses: Cotehele, courtyard, mainly late fifteenth and early sixteenth centuries

48

Manor Houses: Cotehele, great hall, fifteenth century

Manor Houses: Fowey, Place, early sixteenth century and
between 1813 and 1845

Manor Houses: Rialton, late fifteenth century

Manor Houses: Trerice, *c.* 1572 *(Copyright Country Life)*

(a) Scilly Isles, Tresco, Cromwell's Castle, *c.* 1651

(b) St Germans, Moyle Almshouses, probably seventeenth century

Country Houses: Lanhydrock, c. 1635–50, partly rebuilt after 1881 (*Copyright Country Life*)

Country Houses: Lanhydrock, gallery, *c.* 1640 (*Copyright Country Life*)

(a) *Country Houses:* Trelowarren, fifteenth century, with a bay-window of 1662 and a chapel wing of *c.* 1750 (*Copyright Country Life*)

(b) *Country Houses:* Godolphin Hall, probably mid seventeenth century

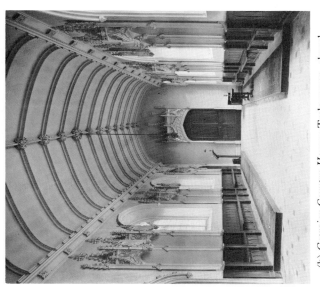

(a) *Georgian Country Houses*: Antony House, 1710–21
(*Copyright Country Life*)

(b) *Georgian Country Houses*: Trelowarren, chapel,
c. 1750 (*Copyright Country Life*)

Georgian Town Houses: Launceston, c. 1740

(a) *Georgian Town Houses*: Truro, Assembly Rooms, 1772

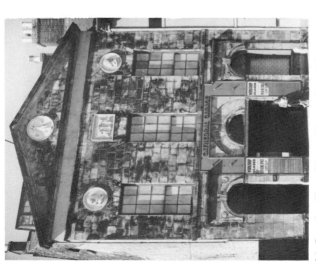

(b) *Georgian Town Houses*: Falmouth, Marlborough House, 1805–15

Georgian Country Houses: Port Eliot, mainly by Sir John Soane, 1802–6 (*Copyright Country Life*)

Georgian Country Houses: Tregothnan, by William Wilkins, 1816–18, and Lewis Vulliamy, 1845–8

(a) *Georgian Country Houses:* St Michael Caerhays, Caerhayes Castle, by John Nash, 1808

(b) *Georgian Country Houses:* Trelissick, by P. F. Robinson, *c.* 1825

(a) *Georgian Town Houses:* Falmouth, Custom House, *c.* 1830

(b) *Georgian Town Houses:* Penzance, Egyptian House, by John Foulston, *c.* 1830

Twentieth Century: Penheale, additions to the seventeenth-century manor house by Sir Edwin Lutyens, 1921 (*Copyright Country Life*)

indicates so early a date. The church was restored severely in 1889; it is of no special interest. The restoration removed the Norman N transept. – FONTS. One plain, octagonal. – Also the remains of a Norman font, the lower part of a tub-bowl ornamented with a simple pattern of large lozenges and a kind of incised roll, not unlike a cable roll, round the base (G. W. Copeland).

PADSTOW

9070

The town embraces the little harbour, a pretty group of houses actually on the quay, of divers materials and colours, from the local stone to whitewash with the quoins and window surrounds picked out, to slate-hanging in grey and biscuit tints, and even to red brick. Several streets stretch up the valley, where at the end of the town are the church and Place, the Prideaux house.

ST PETROC. A sizable church, though not as visibly prosperous as Bodmin or Launceston. The W tower has a heavily buttressed ground floor of the C13 and later upper storeys, three stages in all, with battlements but no pinnacles. There is no W door either. The body of the church is of nave and two aisles. These have five bays plus two lower bays for the chancel chapel (cf. Bodmin). The S chancel chapel is furthermore separated from the aisle by a 'chancel arch'. The piers are all tall of standard Cornish section (limestone and granite). The capitals in the chancel have leaf decoration and stylized flowers on the abacus. In the nave, however, most of the capitals are plain, and there is only a fleur-de-lis crenellation to the abacus. The arches are all two-centred, of C14 design; only the arch from the W tower into the nave belongs to the C13. The E wall of the chancel may be C13 too. The aisles have four-light windows; the main E window is of five lights. The tracery of the S chancel chapel shows it to be of the early or mid C14. It is of the typical leaf pattern. Both aisles have wagon roofs. Outside the S aisle on the buttresses are two animals and one angel with a shield as 'supporters', all damaged. – FONT. Excellent work of the C15, Catacleuse stone, by the Master of St Endellion; octagonal, with demi-figures of angels at the corners and the twelve Apostles in niches in between. It corresponds with the one at St Merryn. – BENCH END of the fox preaching to the geese (cf. St Austell). – PULPIT. Of c.1530, with panels with symbols of the Passion. – IRONWORK. Nice C18 churchyard gates. –

MONUMENTS. Brass to L. Merther, 1421, demi-figure of
priest (chancel floor). – Standing wall-monument to Sir
Nicholas Prideaux, 1627. Base with inscriptions, ornaments
and a chubby child stepping on an old man's shoulder. Above
the four life-sized figures of Sir Nicholas's children, and yet
little higher and further behind, Sir Nicholas and Lady
Prideaux. The parents and the children are facing each other
with prayer desks between. – Dignified simple monument to
Edmund Prideaux † 1693. – CROSS SHAFT, in the churchyard.
Decorated with interlaced plait-work in the Hiberno-Saxon
style; on one side a curious motif similar to a fleur-de-lis.
PRIDEAUX PLACE. The house has been in the Prideaux family
ever since the 1530s. It is in its present form a late C16
building. The E front, of E-shape, survives of that date, though
the gables of the wings were replaced, probably in the C18, by
battlements. Two storeys, plain mullioned windows. The S
front is partly C18, partly of c.1810, when the big bow was
made and the library added at the l. end – both Gothick, in a
very conservative way, rather 1760- than 1810-looking. The
library window is of four lights with intersecting tracery
leaving space for a pointed tracery quatrefoil at the top. Above
this window is a plain quatrefoil window, and the STABLE
also have such windows all along the upper floor. The hall is
now C18, and the screen, which looks c.1600, is imported. It is
suggested to be Spanish in origin. Above the hall is the room
which was the Great Chamber. This has preserved (though
now hidden in the roof) its shallow tunnel-vaults of highly
decorated plaster work. The chief elements of the decoration
are biblical scenes. The whole vault is closely related to that
of the gallery at Lanhydrock and also to Rashleigh Barton in
Devon. The large staircase, the drawing room, and the library
are Gothic of c.1810, but in the reading room late C17 woodwork and a late C17 painting by *Verrio* have been installed.
They are said to come from Stowe. The chimneypiece must be
of c.1740, and hence is too late for Stowe.
    SW of the house is a GARDEN TEMPLE, built in 1738–9. It
has Ionic columns and a pediment.

PANTERSBRIDGE see ST NEOT

PAR

ST MARY. *G. E. Street*'s first church, 1848, and a remarkable
work for a beginner, of a freshness and charm not often

achieved or aimed at by Street.* The steeple on the model of Lostwithiel is low, of comfortable, reassuring proportions. It stands at the W end of the S aisle. The windows of the church are all plain double lancets, and at the SE corner a fine effect is obtained by their three differing lengths. Inside the most curious motif is the little triangular window in one of the SEDILIA niches. Pink stone of a surface which looks mellow and lovable after a hundred years. – STAINED GLASS by *Wailes,* very enjoyable; medallion motifs. – CROSS SHAFT in the churchyard, from a roadside position near Biscovey. Inscriptions, for example, VILLICI FILIUS; lettering and plait-work Hiberno-Saxon, that is, relatively late.

PAUL

4020

T PAULINUS (or St Paul; really St Pol de Leon, the Breton saint). The church was severely damaged by the Spaniards when they landed and burned Penzance in 1595. Traces of restoration in the S and E windows. The W tower is of three stages, with buttresses leaving the corners free, and a stair-turret rising above the pinnacles. The W window has two niches flanking it, and one above it. In the interior there are N and S aisles of seven bays, C15 like the tower, and identical with one exception. The piers are octagonal, the arches double-chamfered. But on the N side, where the rood screen originally went across, the arch is narrower and has two odd shafts of quite a different design, pushed in after the Spanish trouble, it seems, because not really fitting the arches at all. (Where did they come from?) They are of an unusual section with moulded capitals of an unusual design. – STAINED GLASS. E chancel window by *Anning Bell,* 1917. – MONUMENTS. To Capt. Stephen Hutchens † 1709, with two cherubs on the cornice and a cartouche with ships in relief below. – John Badcock † 1784, long inscription and some fine minor decoration, by *Golden* of Holborn. – Grace Marrack, 1810 by *James Isbell* of Truro. – In the churchyard wall, near the SE gate, an obelisk set up by Prince Lucien Bonaparte to commemorate Dolly Pentreath † 1778, who was said to have been the last person to speak Cornish. The Hutchens monument has part of its inscription in Cornish.

---

* The church is local in feeling and achieves much by relying on good proportions, fine materials, and studied simplicity. This is typical of Street's best work in the early 1850s. (Note from Dr Royston Lambert.)

HUTCHENS ALMSHOUSES, by the side of the churchyard. 1709,
two-storeyed, plain, with two doors and six upper windows,
still the early type with two lights and frames of large granite
slabs.

(KERRIS FARM, 1½ m. w of the church. 1721, granite, two-
storeyed. Early C17 parts at the back. MHLG)

PAWTON QUOIT see ST BREOCK

PAYNTERS CROSS see PENTILLIE CASTLE

PELYN
Near Lanlivery

Originally an E-shaped C17 house. Of this one side survives. The
centre was re-done completely in Early Victorian times.

PELYNT

ST NONNA or ST MARY. The chief attraction of this church is
its classical arcade of stately granite columns of the Tuscan
Doric order and depressed segmental arches. They were
erected c.1680 to replace the medieval piers. Otherwise the
church is chiefly Perp, of little architectural interest. The
w tower with corner buttresses and one ogee-headed window
is C14. Nave, s transept, N aisle windows, and all other
windows are Perp. The ceiled wagon roof of the nave has its
old carved bosses. – MONUMENTS. William Achim † 158.
Slate slab with figure in armour; probably by *Crocker*. – John
Buller of Tregarrick † 1615. Tomb-chest with ornamented
top slab and above against the wall another slab, with husband,
wife, and twelve children in flat relief. – Edward Trelawny, by
Robert Wills, 1639; chiefly ornamental. – Elizabeth Vyvyan
† 1640; poor. – Pretty slate plate with inscriptions of home-
spun poetry, 1654 and 1675. – Sir Jonathan Trelawny, the
famous Bishop of Exeter and Winchester († 1721), is buried at
Pelynt. The pastoral staff carried at his funeral is exhibited
the church. – (In the churchyard, Cornish slate HEADSTONE
to William Shuckforth Grigson † 1930, inscribed by *Eric Gill*.
1931.)

ST NONNA'S HOLY WELL, about 1½ m. NE of Pelynt, at Hob
Park.

TRELAWNE. *See* p. 224.

BARROW CEMETERY, ½ m. SW. A nucleated cemetery of both

barrows, ten of which are still visible on the ground; there are further ploughed-out examples detectable only from the air. The excavated sites produced cremation burials in urns, in one case accompanied by a stone battle-axe and in another by a dagger of East Mediterranean manufacture.

PENCALENICK
Near St Clement

8040

The house is by *J. P. St Aubyn*, 1881.

PENCARROW
Near Washaway

0070

Built in 1765–75. Fine Palladian E front of two and a half storeys. Seven bays, with a slightly projecting pedimented three-bay centre. Pediments also to the first-floor windows. The S front is longer and has a different rhythm of windows, but also the window pediments. Rubble, rendered. The staircase has a Venetian window to the N. At the foot of the stairs a cast-iron stove of *c*.1830. Splendid Music Room with Rococo stucco ceiling, but an odd tripartite extension of *c*.1830, making use of a wooden framework which looks a little earlier than the house. The extension was made to house a statue of Venus bought in Rome about 1830. Excellent Molesworth family portraits.

PENDARVES HOUSE *see* TRESLOTHAN

PENDEEN

3030

ST JOHN. Built by the villagers to the design of their parson, 1851.

PENDEEN VAU. C16 farmhouse with an eminently picturesque court at the back and a front of 1670, with nice scrolls to the lower gable-ends. The windows straight, of two lights, with large granite slabs. (Inside, good plasterwork and fireplaces. MHLG)

PENDEEN VAU FOGOU, in the yard of Pendeen Manor Farm. The entrance to the fogou, in the yard, gives access to a sloping passage which runs NE for 23 ft before turning NW for a further 33 ft, terminating in a partially blocked entrance opening on to a field. The main passage is stone-faced and roofed with lintels. At the angle of this passage is a second chamber cut in the clay, 24 ft long.

8030

PENDENNIS CASTLE
Near Falmouth

Pendennis is one of the chain of castles which Henry VIII erected from 1538 onwards under the menace of a French invasion. They extend along the coast from Kent to Cornwall and are designed with a great deal of variety, modifying the theme of the circle and polygon in all-round symmetrical combinations. On their position in the history of architecture and fortification, *see* under St Mawes. Pendennis was begun *c.*1544 and completed in 1546. The circular keep is now the centre of two rings of fortified walls; the outer one with the typical angular bastions of the late C16 (*see* St Mawes) dates from 1583–98 (the very Italian outer gateway is probably as late as 1611), the inner curtain of the time of Henry VIII has sixteen sides. Below on the rocks to the SE was a Tudor 'blockhouse' in addition. This was dismantled in 1654. The keep is approached on first-floor level by a drawbridge with a completely preserved portcullis. The main room on this floor is octagonal, with walls 16 ft thick and ceiling timbers 35 ft long and of a 16 by 16 in. scantling. The gunposts have widely splayed sides and ammunition recesses in them. A spiral staircase in a similar position to that at St Mawes leads to the ground floor, from which the courtyard between keep and curtain wall is reached, and to the basement kitchen. In the courtyard the heavy guns were placed in gunposts with smoke vents; on the curtain walls stood the musketeers firing through the battlements.

PENFOUND MANOR *see* POUNDSTOCK

0070

PENGENNA
Near St Kew

C17 manor house; many mullioned windows with hoodmoulds and a doorway with a four-centred head remain in the old walls.

5020

PENGERSICK CASTLE
Near Germoe

Embattled, late medieval, with two towers. The larger has three storeys, the smaller a newel stair. Loopholes in the walls. Inside some carving and painting (allegories with rhymed inscriptions).

PENGREEP   7030
Near Gwennap

Late Georgian; wing added *c.*1840.

PENHEALE   2080
1 m. NW of Egloskerry

Large manor house of the C17 and C20. Of the medieval house
only one window remains. Gatehouse with loggia on the S
side, the N front of the house, embattled and with rows of
mullioned windows, and the stables all *c.*1620–40. The stables
are dated 1620, the entrance 1636. For the motifs, cf. Lanhydrock and Godolphin. Inside, a sumptuous screen of *c.*1640
in the hall. Behind the hall, parlour, oak-panelled, *c.*1625–30.
The first-floor rooms are made into a gallery. Good plasterwork. One wing of the gatehouse is of the second half of the
C18. No further alterations took place until *Sir Edwin Lutyens*
added the S side beyond the second court. Its main accent is   64
asymmetrical and very bold, a tower-like structure, sheer, and
with two bay-windows, like a London block of flats. Yet it
stands up perfectly to the old work, by virtue of its obstinate
originality.

PENNANCE *see* ZENNOR

PENPONDS   6030

HOLY TRINITY. 1854 by *J. P. St Aubyn.* – PLATE. Almsdish
of brass repoussé, foreign, date 1569.

PENQUITE   1050
Near Fowey

Late Georgian house of two storeys and five bays, with a
pediment over the three central bays. No special decoration.

PENRICE   0040
Near St Austell

Two-storeyed Georgian house with projecting wings of two
windows, the centre with a pediment.

PENROSE
Near Helston

In a splendid position overlooking Loe Pool as if it were an artificial serpentine lake specially made as a vista for the house. This consists of an embattled c17 part with two slightly projecting wings, but c18 windows, and all the rest of *c.*1830 and later.

PENRYN

A town without an old church. St Gluvias to the N is a village on its own, although very near, and of GLASNEY COLLEGE, which lay in the meadows just s of the town, nothing remains. It was founded in 1265 by Bishop Bronescombe of Exeter, who had a manor house at Penryn. With a provost and twelve canons, it was one of the most important religious institutions in Cornwall. Only Tywardreath, Launceston Priory, and Bodmin Priory could vie with it.

The central monument of Penryn today is the tower of its TOWN HALL, dated 1839. Approaching it along the long, friendly main street from the w it looks like a heavy variation on the theme of St Mary-le-Strand in London. The town hall itself, as seen from the other side, is much more modest, 1825, of a country-town appearance. By the side of the town hall the TEETOTAL HALL of 1852, looking exactly like a Nonconformist chapel. BROAD STREET has plenty of nice and no outstanding houses; slate-hung, painted, or of granite, and if they want to appear specially stately, of granite ashlar. Many small Georgian houses adorn ST THOMAS'S STREET to the s. Behind the houses in the backyards are still a few picturesque older bits. (The MHLG draws special attention to the groups 45–55 and 83–101 THE TERRACE; 33–47 ST GLUVIAS STREET; 1–6 THE SQUARE; and several houses in WEST STREET, especially Kernick House.)

(COUNTY SECONDARY SCHOOL. By *F. K. Hicklin*, County Architect, 1961.)

TREMOUGH. *See* p. 226.

PENTEWAN

Known for its building stone, which is much used in Cornwall.

(Terrace above the square, c18 and c19. HILLCROFT is stucco, two storeys, with a wide Venetian window on the ground floor. Nos. 1–4 CHURCH ROW have a slate-roofed veranda along the front, with wooden Doric columns. Then the CHURCH, with a central bowed projection for the doorway. MHLG)

PENTILLIE CASTLE

4060

The castle incorporated a wing of 1698. The C19 building was probably by *William Wilkins Sen.*, completed after 1815 by *Wilkins Jun.* Landscaped by *Repton*. Demolished in 1968, except for the C17 wing. (*Architectural Review*, June 1968.) The building was embattled, with a very tall niche instead of a porch, and was splendidly situated between trees on an eminence above the river Tamar.

A predecessor of Wilkins's client, Sir James Tillie, was buried in a tower which he erected for the purpose on Mount Ararat, N of Pentillie Castle. A memorial is (or was) in the upper room of the tower.

At PAYNTERS CROSS close to one of the gates to the estate is the ESTATE OFFICE, a charming Regency building, only three bays, connected by walls to little wings: Palladio's villa plan *en miniature*. The first-floor veranda is a nice English enrichment of Palladio. Opposite is a group of houses for retainers, stone, in the Tudor style, nicely grouped somewhat like almshouses, but in their detail heavy, if compared to the Regency elegance across the lane.

PENTIRE HEAD

9080

Remains of a cliff castle.)

PENWARNE
Near Mevagissey

0040

Supposed to be a worthwhile farmhouse.)

PENWERRIS *see* FALMOUTH

PENZANCE

4030

Penzance was burned by the Spaniards during their short invasion of 1595. Nothing older survives, and not much either that could belong to the C17.* The chief expansion of the

* Defoe, however, writing in 1724, describes 'A place . . . well built and populous, with good trade and owning many ships. . . . So rich in ore that veins of lead, tin and copper may be seen at low water mark.' Penzance was coinage town from the time of King James.

town is of the early C19. There are some good Georgian and
Regency houses in CHAPEL STREET (interrupted by the
pretentious Italianate WESLYAN CHAPEL with a front of
1864), for example the REGENT HOTEL and the UNION
HOTEL.* On the other side a nice Doric shopfront and then a
63b crazy front in a consistent if not correct Egyptian style, a copy
of Robinson's Egyptian Hall in Piccadilly. The architect was
Foulston of Plymouth, according to Mr P. Laws. (The MHLG
regards as the best houses, apart from those mentioned
Nos. 18, 24, 44, 53, and CHAPEL HOUSE.) The centre of the
town is the MARKET HOUSE, 1837 by *H. J. Whiting*, a digni
fied granite structure on an awkwardly narrow site, with an
Ionic giant portico to the first and second upper storeys. A
dome with Tuscan columns to the drum finishes the com
position, an odd feature of the Penzance skyline. Of the same
period was the MARKET HALL‡ in Princes Street, 1844, and
the two main churches. The main street of Penzance, Market
Jew Street, is rapidly losing its character. There are pretty
terraces a little out W, especially Clarence Terrace, and also
humbler, Clarence Street, Clarence Place, North Parade,
South Parade, and by the sea Regent Terrace. (Regent Square
is a complete little square of twenty-one houses. MHLG) Their
names date them sufficiently. (In addition the MHLG regard
as worth special mention the early C19 Abbey House§ in
Abbey Street; Alverton House and Tredarvah Farm in Alverton
Road, and the Assistance Board offices in Alverton Street
Nos. 7, 8, 10, and Stanley House in Alverton Terrace; Hawke'
Farm in Alverne Hill; Nos. 1–8 in Bullock Market Terrace
Nos. 1–3 and Coombe Cottage in Chyandour; the 'Gothic
eccentricity' of No. 1 Leskinnick Place; Love Lane Farm
house, 1675; and Lower Lariggan House in Lower Lariggan
Crescent, 1810.) (ROSEHILL is of *c.*1810 by *Robert Hitchens*
P. Law)

ST MARY. 1832–5 by *Charles Hutchins*, of regular granite blocks
in a style resembling that of St Luke, Chelsea, in London
that is with a W tower (Cornish in detail) placed tightly be

---

* In the yard of the Union Hotel the remains of a Georgian THEATRE of
*c.*1787 (now a garage). It is identical in size with the theatre at Richmond in
the North Riding of Yorkshire. 'One man must have designed both.'
(D. Sherborn, *Architectural Review*, August 1961.)

‡ Now demolished.

§ Although thoroughly modernized in 1825, it contains a C17 staircase
and panelled room, and parts of the house are certainly older than this
(Information from Mr H. Dalton Clifford.)

tween the two low-pitched gables of the aisles, the aisles as tall as the tall nave, and six long lean windows on the N and S sides and thin pinnacled buttresses between them, not buttressing anything, for inside the tall wooden piers support only the shallow curves of ceilings. A gallery runs round three sides. The fourth has a tall shallow apse. There are plenty of monuments, but none worth mentioning. The ALTAR is a spectacular affair of 1934 by *Ernest Procter*, with a whole prospect including the heavenly host, a corrugated silvery backcloth, jagged rays; all smacking a little of the Wurlitzer.* – MONUMENT to Sarah Bedford, 1832 by *J. Bedford* of London.

ST PAUL, Clarence Street. 1843, enlarged in 1893 by *J. W. Trounson*. – STAINED GLASS by *Willement*, small saints under canopies in large lancet windows, in the style of the early C14.

BAPTIST CHAPEL, Clarence Street. With a horrible but remarkable Norman front: plenty of zigzag, yet as early as 1835–6. By *P. Sambell* of Truro.

CROSS, Morrab Gardens, in front of the library. Very crude circular head with recessed triangle to form a cross. The shaft is chiefly decorated with panels with rows of little holes. The reading of the inscriptions is doubtful.

Outside Penzance. NANCEALVERNE HOUSE, two storeys, five bays, rubble, C18; ROSECADGEHILL HOUSE, C17 (?), granite ashlar, also two storeys, five bays (MHLG). Also CASTLE HORNECK, 1 m. W of the town centre, off the St Just road. A house of *c.*1720 of the Borlase family. Granite, five bays with a pediment. Now a Youth Hostel. Information from Mr H. Dalton Clifford.)

PERRANARWORTHAL 7030

ST PIRAN. Indifferent church of 1884 (by *St Aubyn*). Tower C15, of granite blocks, without buttresses, with its pinnacles on supporting angels (cf. Mawgan-in-Meneage, St Anthony-in-Meneage). Inside the S door a Norman tympanum: lamb and cross with an outer leaf-scroll moulding. – PLATE. Fine Chalice and Paten of *c.*1576–7 by the same unknown master as the Chalice at Stithians.

PERRANPORTH 7050

ST MICHAEL. PLATE. Chalice of Suffolk make, Elizabethan.

* Now greatly toned down, Mr Laws tells me.

(FIRE STATION. 1964 by the County Architect's Department (*A. J. Groves*).)

PERRANUTHNOE

ST PIRAN AND ST NICHOLAS. A small, low church, with the usual W tower* of regular granite blocks, three-staged and with no buttresses. The S side has no aisle, but a transept on plain three-eighths responds with a squint into the chancel. The N arcade is of square piers with demi-shafts. – FONT. C13, granite, with trefoil-headed blank niches.‡ – PLATE. Chalice and Paten of 1576, probably by the master of Stithians and Perranarworthal; Paten by *Blackford* of Plymouth, 1729 (*see* Ludgvan). – MONUMENT to H. Cole † 1775, conventional design of its period, by *Regnart* of Hampstead Road, London, 1800.

(CHYVERTON. Central block *c*.1735, of brick, basement and two storeys, five bays with pediment and small lunette window. The two wings were originally joined by a retaining wall, now by rooms. The W connexion was made *c*.1790, the E *c*.1920. These wing blocks have central stone chimneystacks with granite quoins. The original Delabole scantle slate roof remains. Interior with attractive plaster panelled walls decorated in the early C19. Attractive STABLE BLOCK. GMT)

ACTON CASTLE. *See* p. 35.

PERRAN WHARF

Just S of Perranarworthal. A pretty village of Devon rather than Cornwall type. (The IRON FOUNDRY of the Fox family here was rebuilt *c*.1830 in response to the great demand for steam pumping engines for the Cornish mines: several massive buildings with large windows made up of many small panes. One main door still has a cast-iron arch dated 1791. P. Laws)

PERRANZABULOE

ST PIRAN. Rebuilt in 1804 and made more Cornish Medieval in 1879. The arcade, tower, font, and much else come from the second church of St Piran in the Sands (in Sabulo) (*see* St Piran's). – FONT. A piece of *Volkskunst*, octagonal, with little

---

* C15. The rest of the church practically rebuilt in 1883 (MHLG).
‡ The only granite font in Cornwall (C. K. Burton).

figures of the Virgin and three Apostles in niches; C15
probably. – BENCH ENDS made into a screen at the W end,
early C16, with one motif for each end. – PLATE. Chalice by
Jons of Exeter, 1570–3 (for the Paten belonging to it, cf. St
Agnes); Flagon and Paten by *W. Tweedie*, 1773–4. – MONU-
MENTS. Several good slate plates, for example Perran Hoskyn
† 1675, by the same hand as the Lawrence plate at Cubert.
– Nicely lettered inscription plate to the subscribers for the
building of the church, by *Isbell* of Truro.

PHILLACK   5030

The parish church of Hayle, a C15 building but rebuilt in 1856
by *William White*. Only the W tower remains, of regular
granite blocks, three stages, with buttresses to the second stage
set back from the angles. – FONT. If it is at all medieval, it has
been so thoroughly re-tooled that nothing worth having
survives. Square bowl with sloping sides and motifs of rosette,
cross, etc., in medallions (cf. Gwithian). – PULPIT. Made up
from panels of a rood screen with the same vertical foliage
serpentines as at Gwinear. – Linenfold PANELLING in
sanctuary and organ case. – STONE WITH XP MONOGRAM in
the gable of the S porch; probably C6 or C7.
INSCRIBED STONE, in the churchyard. The inscription runs
CLOTVALI MOBRATTI. The date (cf. the Hiberno-Saxon letters)
may be anything between C7 and C10.
COPED STONE, in the churchyard. Only half of it preserved.
One of four surviving examples (cf. Lanivet, St Buryan,
St Tudy).
CROSS, in the churchyard. Wheel type, with Crucifixion and
poorly executed plait-work decoration of Hiberno-Saxon style.

PHILLEIGH   8030

ST FILIUS. W tower of two and a half storeys; buttresses only
to the S and W and on the lower storey. N transept and S aisle,
the aisle arcade of seven bays, white granite on circular piers
with four attached shafts, with four rather low capitals. The
entrance arches to tower and transept unmoulded. – FONT.
Octagonal, C13, with two flat blank niches with pointed heads
on each side. – PLATE. Chalice and Paten by *Jons* of Exeter,
Elizabethan; pretty, ornate Sweetmeat Dish of *c.*1660–70.
GLEBE HOUSE. A lovely Georgian front of five bays, all slate-

hung. Behind it and opposite the churchyard a slate-roofed white COTTAGE with two rounded bays, a porch between them, and Gothic windows: very much like the round houses of Veryan near by.

PILLATON

ST ODULPH. Architecturally not specially interesting. The usual W tower of regular granite blocks, three stages, with the buttresses set back from the angles, the usual transept on one side – left over in plan, if not in elevation, from an earlier church – and the usual late S aisle also of regular granite blocks and with an arcade of six bays. The piers are very slim, of the same profile as at Callington and in its neighbourhood, that is square with four attached demi-shafts. An exceptionally large squint, at the same time entrance to the rood-loft staircase, connects transept and chancel (cf. Quethiock). Old wagon roofs in S porch, aisle, and S transept. – MONUMENT to James Tillie † 1772, very good, in the best London style of the moment; no figures.

CLAPPER BRIDGE, 1¼ m. NW. Late C15, of three round arches, granite.

PLUSHA BRIDGE see LINKINHORNE

POLEYS BRIDGE see BLISLAND

POLKINGHORNE FARM see GWINEAR

POLPERRO

6b (Polperro was left out of the first edition entirely because it has no individual building of special merit, but, as a whole, it is certainly worth visiting. This is what John Betjeman has to say about it in the *Shell Guide* (second edition): 'Polperro is picturesque in the extreme; there are some simple Georgian houses round the harbour, and the streets are narrow and higgledy-piggledy, and from almost every cottage window orange curtains can be seen to flutter, betokening the artistic inhabitants within. There are plenty of teashops and places for buying Cornish ware, not always manufactured in Cornwall. Despite its air of sophistication, Polperro is well worth seeing.')

(St John the Baptist. Built in 1838 as a chapel of ease to Lansallos; well sited. In the porch a small bowl, square, with stars and rosettes. Is it Norman? G. W. Copeland)

POLRUAN CASTLE
Across the estuary from Fowey

1050

(A square harbour-fort, ruined at the top. Massive; originally of two storeys. c16 doorways, fireplace, etc. G. W. Copeland)

POLTESCO
2½ m. NNE of Lizard Town

7010

(Millhouse. 1785. The small and primitive Crucifixion figure inside, facing the door, may come from a local holy well.)

POLWHELE
N of Truro

8040

On three sides of a courtyard. The N wing was probably the old house, the W wing for farm purposes (the large S window is early c19). The E wing is difficult to date, as it was thoroughly overhauled and also added to after 1870; its S part and the whole E front are of that date. The architect was *Scott*.

POOL

6040

Trevenson Chapel, a chapel of ease to Illogan. 1806–9. In the mining district, but away from the workmen's houses and shopping streets. A thin castellated W tower and a rectangular building with pointed windows of granite. The dainty tracery of the windows, geometrical in intention, is cast iron.

PORT ELIOT

3050

The house of the Earls of St Germans was originally the Priory 60 of St Germans. Of this an undercroft with c13 lancet windows still exists. The refectory also is preserved, converted into the hall of the house. Most of what is visible now is the work of *Sir John Soane*, 1802–6, especially the castellated and sash-windowed E front and the symmetrical, also castellated, S porch. The W part with the projecting office wing and the porch were added by *H. Harrison* in 1825–9. Inside, the most prominent rooms are the drawing room (originally library), the circular NE drawing room, and the surprisingly simple staircase. A few rooms go back to *c*.1730. The grounds were laid out by *Repton*, who was consulted in 1792–3. The projected connexion between church and house was not carried out.

PORTHCURNO
3020

Close to the village are scanty fragments of an early oratory of the type of St Piran's and St Gwithian's oratories in the sands.

PORTHILLY
9070

ST MICHAEL. Close to the estuary, small, humble, long neglected, and then in 1865–7 restored and much rebuilt. The tower not at the W but over the S transept (rebuilt), of two stages with gabled top. The S transept has a narrow E.E. lancet window, but is in its main structure Norman. The foundations of a corresponding N transept have been ascertained. Small S chancel chapel added in the C15. – FONT. Simple, Norman. – ROOD SCREEN. Only the framework survives. – PULPIT. With linenfold panelling; early C16. – CROSS HEAD in the churchyard, from St Minver. Of wheel type, with plait-work on the remains of the shaft.

PORTHLEVEN
6020

(HARBOUR HOTEL and HARBOUR HOUSE are C18; WEST WHARF is an early C19 three-storeyed warehouse (MHLG). The church of ST BARTHOLOMEW is of 1841, with Lady Chapel by *C. R. Corfield*, 1934.)

PORTHPEAN
0050

ST LEVAN. PLATE. Very pretty Chalice with strapwork ornament, 1570s.

PORT ISAAC
9080

ST PETER. PLATE. French Chalice and Paten by *A. Chetier* (cf. Delabole).

PORTREATH

The pier, the cottages of the harbour staff, and the curious inclined plane up the hill are connected with Francis Basset's interest in Cornish industry. Coal was to be brought to Portreath (near his house at Tehidy) to help the mining of tin. The pier was begun in 1760.

The church of ST MARY, by *Wightwick*, 1841, is rather depressing, with pointed windows and a bellcote.

PORTWRINKLE

WHITESANDS BAY HOTEL. The re-erected Thancke's House from Torpoint, built by Lord Graves, in a rather dull neo-Elizabethan style, with a symmetrical façade, presumably *c*.1860.

POUGHILL

ST OLAF. A Danish dedication. Nave of four bays. S aisle with arcades of Cornish granite standard section. N aisle and E bay of S aisle with thicker sandstone piers, shorter than usual, of a section inserting a keeled projection l. and r. of each of the standard hollows (cf. St Veep); quatrefoil decoration of the abaci. E window with good C14 tracery. W tower of three stages, with buttresses leaving the corners free. – FONT. Of Purbeck table-top type, but with two tiers of blank arcades (cf. Poundstock, St Tudy). The heads of the arches are pointed. – BENCH ENDS with abbreviated representations of the Instruments of Christ's Passion (*see* Kilkhampton and Launcells – same workshop). – ROYAL ARMS. *Temp.* Charles II, yet still with strapwork decoration (cf. Kilkhampton). – WALL PAINTINGS. Two large St Christophers, entirely repainted by *Frank Salisbury*, R.A. – PLATE. Tazza Cup and Paten, a lovely piece of a shape rare in Cornwall, and with rich band decoration; Elizabethan; mark *M*.

POUNDSTOCK

ST NEOT. Beautifully situated in a little hollow, surrounded by trees. Below the church on the S and at right angles to it a C14 GUILDHALL, two-storeyed, buttressed, with wooden four-light casements: a very pretty group with the church (tactfully

restored by *Sedding*). Unbuttressed w tower. Nave, s transept
and n aisle, that is probably the ghost of a Norman cruciform
plan, its n arm incorporated with the aisle. The aisle is c15
built in two stages, the e part a little later. – FONT. Square
with two tiers of blank niches with pointed heads, probably
c13 (cf. Poughill). – PULPIT. Octagonal, Jacobean. – BENCH
ENDS. A few in the chancel. – CHEST of *c*.1530–50 in the n
aisle. – ROYAL ARMS, with strapwork decoration, against the
s wall of the tower. – WALL PAINTINGS on the n wall. Very
faded, but iconographically interesting: the Tree of Deadly
Sins, the Warning to Sabbath-Breakers (*see* Introduction)
and the Weighing of Souls.

(PENFOUND MANOR. The house is built round a large medieval
hall, the roof of which has collar-beams on arched braces. A
massive chimneystack has been inserted in the n wall of the
hall, and at the sw corner a small room has been added with
solar above. The windows are Tudor. Entrance porch with
granite doorway with inscription of 1642 in the spandrels
e of this, the inner hall or buttery, which contains a c17 staircase, and then a former dairy, built in Stuart times. *See*
H. Dalton Clifford, *Country Life*, 12 February 1959.)

PRIDEAUX
Near Luxulyan

Of the manor house one wing still exists, early c16, with a porch
and three-light windows. In 1808 the Rashleigh who then
owned the manor built a new house lower down with a view
towards St Austell Bay, a square, handsome granite block of
three by three bays with a niche in the centre and tripartite
windows l. and r.; a lower wing on the l. Inside, a charming
plain curved staircase. – CROSS in the grounds. Of wheel type
(but octagonal, not round), four-holed. The shaft has plain
ornament on two sides, leaf scrolls on the others.

PRIDEAUX PLACE *see* PADSTOW

PROBUS

ST PROBUS AND ST GRACE. The glory of the church is its
tower, although its interior is also surprisingly generously
spaced. The tower, the tallest in Cornwall, is 123 ft 6 in. high,
of three stages, and lavishly decorated, though with more taste

and taste than in the Trecarrel buildings in and around Launceston. The leading squire here was John Tregian of Golden, and work was in progress in 1523. The tower has a plinth with the not unfamiliar quatrefoil decoration, and another strip of ornament above. The hoodmould of the w door is the upper moulding of this second strip conducted round. On the N and S sides the ground floor has three niches each for statues. The first stringcourse is again ornamented; so is the second; so are the buttresses, set back from the angles (with pinnacles in relief). The second stage has windows with narrowly decorated sound-holes. But on the third stage are two windows on each side, again with the same ornamentation of the sound-holes. Above them are another eight little blind windows and then the decorated battlements and the pinnacles, each with four little sub-pinnacles, a most satisfying fullness of orchestration. The ensemble is not at all Cornish; it is entirely Somerset, especially similar to North Petherton. The body of the church has two aisles of identical design, buttressed, with not specially interesting side windows, and more elaborate E windows, no transepts, but N and S porches. The arcades are tall, unifying the spatial effect of the church, which is in itself by no means tall. They are of seven bays and have the same Devonshire section of the piers as St Ives of the same date – instead of the usual hollow between the two attached shafts a wavy curve, and an exceptionally complex moulding of the arches. The tower arch also is very tall and has responds with large panelling. The church was restored by *Street* in 1851. – ALTAR SLAB with five consecration crosses. – BENCH ENDS of no unusual quality or design worked into the rood screen, N parclose screen, and tower screen. – MONUMENTS. Brass to John Wulvedon † 1514 and wife, two figures with inscription beneath, as usual. – Thomas Hawkins † 1766, a very good epitaph with a seated mourning figure holding a medallion with Hawkins's portrait, a flying angel above, the whole against the usual pyramid. Sculptor not recorded. – In the churchyard monument to the Hawkins family, with four kneeling pall-bearers at the corners, as in the Villiers monument in Westminster Abbey; 1914.

VICARAGE. By *Wightwick*, 1839. Information from Mr Howard Colvin.)

PROBUS GRAMMAR SCHOOL (now disused). By *G. E. Street*, 1852–60, abutting and partly incorporating an earlier two-storey late C18 (?) workhouse. Good, characteristic work in

grey local stone. Limestone quoins, enlivened by red brick
bands and arches over square-headed sash windows; black
slate roof. All rather harsh. Large, steep, sweeping roofs with
hipped gables and bold slabs of chimneystack. Particularly
noble the N dormitory block, simply and finely scaled, with
bold dormers. Did Webb work on this? So many elements of
Red House derive from this type of Street work.*)

CHURCH SCHOOL, E of the church. By *W. White*; very simple
informal, un-Gothic and indigenous in feeling.

(TREHANE. Rebuilt in 1701–3; it remains unaltered. CPRE)

TREGASSOW. *See* p. 223.

TREWITHEN. *See* p. 231.

5020

PRUSSIA COVE
7 m. E of Penzance

(PORTH-EN-ALLS. By *Philip Tilden*, 1910–14. Only partly
executed, owing to the First World War. The house is
approached from the back nearly at roof level. Circular court
with concave-fronted lodges. The main rooms are all below.
The style is a kind of free Tudor.)

3060

QUETHIOCK

ST HUGO. A most remarkable W end, with a thin W tower rising
above the roof of the broader nave, and a staircase tower with
a saddleback roof coming up on the r. to the height of the foot
of the tower. It has battlements, but no pinnacles. The W
front is heavily buttressed at the corners. The date is probably
C13. Of the cruciform church, which is the form most Cornish
churches possessed before the later C14 and the C15 added
aisles, much can still be seen: the whole S transept with its
angle buttresses, and with a good strong arch connecting it
with the nave, and the N transept with the same buttressing
although only little of it comes out beyond the later aisle.
Inside the N transept is an early C14 funeral recess, finely
moulded but badly preserved (cf. St Ive). The N arcade is
standard Cornish C15. The old wagon roofs are remarkably
well preserved. An exceptionally large squint connects
transept and chancel. One can walk into it, for at the same
time it gives access to the rood-loft staircase (cf. Pillaton).

* I owe this contribution and the following one to Dr Royston Lambert

REREDOS. Charming C19 tiling (Commandments, etc.). – STAINED GLASS. Much of it in an appealing, if amateur and rather timid, taste, c.1880, by a local vicar. – A very little C15 glass in the top of a N aisle window. – MONUMENTS. Large brass to Roger Kyngdon † 1471, his wife and sixteen children. – Tomb-chest with slate top and back plates to Hugh Halkinow † 1599. – Brass of 1631 to Richard Chiverton and family, not good.

CROSS. Hiberno-Saxon type with wheel head, and interlace and scrollwork on the shaft. In the head trefoil openings between the arms of the cross which look curiously Gothic. Hencken believes in a C13 date and a kind of Celtic Revival (cf. Padstow).

RAME

4040

ST GERMAN. In an exposed position, built all of rough slate. The W tower with its broached spire is slender and un-buttressed. It has no W door, and the long lancets on the W side, the small dormer windows in the spire, the plain arch towards the nave inside, all make it likely that here is a part belonging to the church consecrated in 1259. The nave is wider than the tower (cf. for instance the C13 tower of Sheviock). The chancel also is C13 work: cf. its two N windows. The rest of the church is mostly C15, with the exception of a Norman tympanum decorated with three circles with four-spoked wheel, four-petalled flower, and saltire cross motifs. The S aisle of five bays has an exceptional pier profile, circular, with four demi-shafts and simple moulded capitals. A squint high up connects S transept and chancel. The aisle has a good original ceiled wagon roof. – BENCH ENDS. The old ones mostly with tracery in the Devon way, not the usual Cornish motifs of shields with initials or Instruments of the Passion. – PLATE. Chalice and Paten by *Mathew* of Barnstaple, Eliza-bethan; other pieces of 1733, 1799. – MONUMENT to Roger Ashton, Vicar of St Andrew's, Plymouth, † 1677, good, robust workmanship of its date, with a large cherub's head at the foot.

(ST MICHAEL'S CHAPEL, Rame Head. It is said to be Norman. Dr Athelstane Hill)

REDEVALLEN MANOR HOUSE *see* **MINSTER**

REDRUTH

In character more of an industrial town than any other in
Cornwall. The main street, running down a hill and up again,
is the typical shopping street of any county, made interesting
only by the WESLEYAN CHURCH of 1826 at its E end, a
proud, plain rectangle of six by eight round-headed windows,
a larger edition of the typical Cornish Methodist chapel.
Further down the street on the N side the ambitious, somewhat
cheap, but grand Italianate FREE METHODIST CHURCH of
1864 and then the CLOCK TOWER of 1828, raised c.1900,
granite, like a Cornish version of a Palazzo Vecchio tower.
There are plenty of dignified Latest Georgian and Early
Victorian granite and cement-covered fronts of smaller
houses. (Old COUNCIL OFFICES. Of c.1830. WORKHOUSE.
1838 by *George Gilbert Scott*; Elizabethan (P. Laws).) The
CHAPEL OF EASE, now disused, of 1828 by *C. Hutchins*, is a
granite version of the typical Commissioners' church with
pinnacles on NW, SW, NE, and SE corners, lean lancet windows,
and a little W turret, similar to St Day. The QUAKER MEET-
ING HOUSE is of 1833, a plain solid rectangle, much like
St Austell and Truro.

ST EUNY, the parish church, lies right outside the present
town, in a little dip, between trees. It is of 1756, granite, with
nave and aisles and a Venetian E window. Inside it has white
columns up to the ceiling and no galleries. The W tower is C15,
also of granite, with buttresses set back from the angles, and a
fine tower arch into the nave. The jambs are panelled. Against
the N wall of the tower is a primitively carved demi-figure
from a Norman corbel table, a reminder of the original Norman
church, the plan of which (with an apse) has been excavated.
The churchyard entrance is C18 Gothic, battlemented. –
PLATE. Flagon by *Pearson*, 1716–17, tankard shape. – MONU-
MENTS of the eighteen-twenties and thirties, for example by
Chantrey, *Theakston* of Pimlico (W. Davey † 1827: medallion
and tablet), and *Pearce* of Truro.

The view from the churchyard is towards Norman keeps and
obelisks all in ruin. They are in fact the remains of Cornish
tin-mining in a more prosperous era, every one now appearing
a folly of follies. (The house of William Murdoch, whom the
tin-mining industry brought to Cornwall, is in Cross Street.
Originally it was the chapel of St Rumon, later a prison.
Here Murdoch made his first model steam locomotive in 1784,
and invented gas-lighting and used it in the house in 1792.)

(CORNWALL TECHNICAL COLLEGE (Catering and Engineering Blocks). 1962 by *F. K. Hicklin*, County Architect.)
(CURNOW TRAINING CENTRE FOR THE MENTALLY HANDICAPPED, Drump Road. 1962 by the County Architect's Department (*F. K. Hicklin*).)
GWENNAP PIT. *See* Gwennap.

RESPRYN BRIDGE *see* LANHYDROCK

RESTORMEL   *1060*

By far the most perfect example of military architecture in 46 Cornwall, and in its plan one of the most consummate of England. The base court was to the W, but nothing survives of it. There only could the castle be easily approached. On the other sides the hill slopes down steeply, especially towards the river Fowey on the E. The natural hilltop has been artificially scarped, and a circular moat dug, about 60 ft wide and 30 ft deep. Inside this is the keep, a shell keep, as at Launceston, Trematon, and Totnes (Devon). The whole inner face of the wall was later covered by the various necessary domestic buildings, with partition walls radiating from the centre of the ward. The size of the castle is 110 ft diameter within; the original height was 27½ ft. Outside there is sheer wall all the way round, except for the gate to the W, and the chapel tower nearly opposite (to the NE), projecting a little into the moat. The plan has the somewhat artificial but highly impressive symmetry of the classic moment of the Middle Ages. Its British parallel is the polygonal chapter houses of cathedrals, its Continental parallel Castel del Monte in Apulia. Its parallel in town planning is the new towns of Edward I in England (Winchelsea) and their opposite numbers in France. The dates tally with this stylistic placing of the plan.
The castle belonged to the Cardinhams in the C12. Of that date (*c*.1100) only the inner part of the gate survives. The curtain wall seems to be C12 or early C13, the rest is all late C13, if not *c*.1300. Andrew de Cardinham's daughter married Thomas de Tracey, in whose possession the castle appears in 1264. It then went to Simon de Montfort and to Henry III's brother, Richard of Cornwall (cf. Lostwithiel). Richard died in 1271, his son Edmund in 1300. A further indication that Edmund may have been the one to whom we owe this classic reconstruction of Restormel is a fragment found on the site

and now kept in the little Castle Museum (or rather cupboard). It has beautifully carved realistic, if a little flat, foliage, typical of *c.*1275.

From the gatehouse the domestic quarters follow each other anti-clockwise, looking down into them from the battle-mented rampart walk: the kitchen, the great hall on the upper floor, the solar, the antechamber to the chapel, and two more apartments of which the first may have been the bedchamber and the second the guardroom. Windows opened towards the courtyard on the ground floor, the moat on the upper floors.

RESTORMEL HOUSE. Below the castle, further E and close to the river. Pretty, early Gothic Revival house of the 1760s, battlemented and with white 'Gothick' sash windows (cf. Tregenna Castle). It incorporates C16 and C17 bits.

8060   RIALTON

51 The farmhouse is the main wing of a late C15 monastic manor, of great charm inside and out. The hall, now divided into two storeys, still possesses its old decorated wagon roof and three three-light windows on the first floor. Added to it is an ex-tension in the centre of the front with a tunnel-vaulted porch on the ground floor. The vault, owing to the close transverse arches, looks like a wagon roof in stone. On the first floor are the study and bedchamber of Prior Vivian of Bodmin (*see* Bodmin), who liked to spend his time at Rialton. In the court-yard a little free-standing HOLY WELL and beyond it a wall probably once forming the front of an outbuilding.

INSCRIBED STONE in the wall of a farm building: BONE MIMORI ILLI (FILI ?) TRIBUNI, in Roman capitals; C5 or C6.

RILLATON *see* LINKINHORNE

9060   ROCHE

So called from the fantastic outcrop of jagged schorl to the SE of the village, a phenomenon as impressive now in industrial surroundings as it must have been in the rural solitude of the Middle Ages. The commanding feature of the present-day scenery are the cones of the china clay workings. In their midst rises the cliff, as improbable as if it were some C19 Victorian play of fantasy in a public park.

3b Perched on top of the cliff is ST MICHAEL'S CHAPEL, licensed in 1409. It consists of a lower room for a chaplain (or an anchorite) and the chapel proper above. The whole is of granite, and as below the lower floor a substructure was necessary, the whole looks architecturally very much like a Cornish granite tower of three stages with the usual stringcourses between. The carrying up of the granite blocks remains a feat to be wondered at. No ornamental detail of importance is preserved.

ST GONAND. Rebuilt in 1822, and again (S arcade and aisle) in 1890 (by *J. D. Sedding*).* W tower original, tall, of three stages, granite, with buttresses set back from the angles. – FONT. Norman, almost exactly like Bodmin, circular bowl, with 26b angels' heads at the corners, and between them interlaced snakes (and on the W side a curious motif like an oblong envelope). Below them stylized lilies. – PLATE. Lovely Flagon by *Grundy*, 1773 (cf. Lostwithiel); Elizabethan Chalice, no marks. – CROSS in the churchyard; very primitive head and decoration, many irregular little holes and some serpentine lines incised. (There are three more CROSSES in the parish. First a wheel-cross in Glebe Field (between rectory and church). This is probably its original site. In the rectory grounds a small Latin cross. Is it the original finial from the gable of the nave? At Cross Hand, on the N boundary of the parish, a very roughly carved cross in a lonely moorland setting.)‡

(HOLY WELL, ½ m. NW of the railway station. Arched, C14 granite superstructure.)‡

ROSCARROCK *see* ST ENDELLION

ROSECADGEHILL HOUSE *see* PENZANCE

RUAN LANIHORNE 8040

ST RUMONUS. A low W tower of slate, with buttresses only at the foot and meeting at the corners, N aisle, S transept, and S porch. The aisle has an arcade of six bays with standard Cornish granite piers with four capitals and bands of decoration between capital and abacus. The arches are four-centred.

* The main walls and the S porch 'practically untouched' by both restorations. The S arcade was re-erected on its old foundations. It is of polyphant (H. M. Creswell Payne).
‡ These notes are from H. M. Creswell Payne, *The Story of the Parish of Roche*, 1946.

The tower arch is low and unmoulded. Tower dated 1675, aisle C15, parts of the S masonry probably Norman. – FONT. Square, with quatrefoil and ogee arch decoration; C14? The cover is made up of wall plates from the old roof. – PULPIT. Made up of bench ends of c.1530 (Renaissance shell motifs). – COMMANDMENT TABLES and CREED painted in a *Volkskunst* manner; probably early C19. – MONUMENT. Priest with hands in prayer, under a trefoil arch, badly preserved, but no doubt C13.

(RECTORY (now Old Rectory Guest House). By *William White*, c.1850. 'One might almost mistake the perspective we have seen of it for an old building; it is so irregular and picturesque. We have some fears that this might, in reality, appear exaggerated.' This was the comment of *The Ecclesiologist* in February 1851.*)

RUAN MAJOR

7010

ST RUMON. A deserted church among trees, with only a few farm buildings near it, so little visited that at the time of writing a white owl was nesting in the timbers of the S porch roof. The W tower of granite and serpentine is of two stages and unbuttressed, like the neighbouring towers of Grade, Mullion, and Landewednack. S porch with panelled jambs (cf. Mullion, Cury, etc.). Inside both aisles were removed in the restoration of 1867, the arcades being built into the N and S containing walls. Portions of the ROOD SCREEN are still in position, not of high quality. Note the masons' tools in some of the panels. – PLATE. Chalice, Elizabethan, perhaps by the same hand as Stithians; Paten of 1722–3.

RUAN MINOR

7010

ST RUAN. A tiny church, with a tower of only one stage,‡ creeper-clad (a welcome exception in Cornwall). The position is exposed, and the monkey puzzle in front of the church, much higher than the tower, looks ragged and unhappy. The nave is very low, the N aisle of only four bays, of standard Cornish design, the arches no more than 10 ft high, the detailing of minimum elaboration. The S side is older than the aisle. – FONT. Norman, small, with a simple zigzag motif.

* I am grateful to Mr S. Muthesius for drawing my attention to this passage.

‡ C15, built of great blocks of serpentine. The earliest parts of the church are C13 (MHLG).

THE RUMPS see ST MINVER

RUTHERNBRIDGE see WITHIEL

ST AGNES
NW of Truro

7050

ST AGNES. 1848 by *Piers St Aubyn*, in the Cornish tradition. –
FONT. C15, octagonal, of Catacleuse stone, with quatrefoil
motifs. – (POOR BOX held up by the figure of a hungry man.
G. Grigson) – PLATE. A good set. Paten of *c.*1570–3, belong-
ing perhaps to the Chalice at Perranzabuloe; Tazza of 1579–80,
perhaps by *Newton*, richly ornamented on base and stem (*see*
Mabe); several C18 pieces.
(OUR LADY STAR OF THE SEA (R.C.). 1882 by *Cowell, Drewitt
& Wheatly* of Truro.)

ST AGNES see SCILLY ISLES

ST ALLEN

8050

ST ALLEYNE. A tall W tower of regular granite blocks below and
of slate above, in three stages, with buttresses set back from
the angles. An exceptionally tall stair-turret with a circular
spirelet (re-done in the C19). The N side has a remarkable
C13 doorway with remains of colonnettes of one order. The r.
capital belongs to the lively kind of stiff-leaf as it is familiar
at Wells. On the N side of the chancel also is an E.E. lancet
window. The church has no transept. The S side has an aisle
and a porch. The arcade is Cornish granite standard with
four-centred arches. Sedding regarded the W doorway of the
tower as E.E. too. – Three CROSSES in the churchyard.
TRUTHAN. See p. 236.

ST ANTHONY-IN-MENEAGE

7020

ST DUNSTAN. The church lies apart from the village with only
a few houses around, quite close to the little creek of Gillan
Harbour. The oldest motif is an E.E. window in the chancel.
Then follows the N aisle, buttressed, and with an arcade on
plain octagonal piers with plain double-chamfered arches.
The W tower* came last, of regular granite blocks, three-
storeyed, without buttresses and with the pinnacles on angel

* C15; also the roofs (MHLG).

corbels (cf. Mawgan; etc.). The s porch is attached to the s
transept, a feature also to be found at Mawgan. – FONT.
Circular, with shield-holding angels, but not as severely
hieratic as, for example, at St Ives. The inscription reads:
Ecce Karissimi De Deo Vero Baptizabuntur Spiritu Sancto.
The date is probably C15. – PLATE. Chalice and Paten by *WL*,
Elizabethan (*see* St Ives); Flagon of 1767.

8030

ST ANTHONY-IN-ROSELAND

ST ANTHONY. The view of the church is spoiled by the fact
that PLACE, the house of the Spry family, which stands on
part of the former priory buildings, lies like a screen between
it and the creek, connected immediately with its transept. The
house is of 1840, symmetrical neo-Gothic at its least attractive.
The church, on the other hand, although much restored in
1850, can still be regarded as the best example in the county
of what a parish church was like in the C12 and C13. No aisles
were added later, no porches, and no w tower. There is a
tower over the crossing instead with a timber and lead spire
and there are N and s transepts. The s doorway is Norman with
one scalloped colonnette on each side and in the voussoirs
an outer and an inner order of crescents filled in with stylized
foliage. Inside, the tower arches are genuine C13; cf. the
foliage of their capitals, E and w. In each arm of the transept is
still a trefoil-headed PISCINA. – PLATE. Chalice and Paten
by the same maker as Gerrans, dated 1605 on the foot. –
MONUMENTS. Sir Richard Spry, by *R. Westmacott*, c.1799. –
Thomas Spry, Admiral of the Red, † 1828 (wife 1835). Large
white marble, by *Hopper* of London. – Also other Spry
monuments.

TREWINCE. *See* p. 230.

0050

ST AUSTELL

The town grew out of a village during the C18 in consequence of
the development of Cornish mining. So what now appears a
prosperous town-church served at the time when it was built a
village and a large parish extending as far as (and including)
Pentewan and its quarries.

14a HOLY TRINITY. The most noteworthy feature of the tower
is its enrichment on all four faces by figure sculpture in
niches. On N, E, and s are four apostles each, on the w is a

pyramidal group of the Trinity at the top, Annunciation below, with the lily as an isolated motif between the two kneeling figures, and the risen Christ between two saints at the foot. The style is that familiar from C15 alabaster work, rather hard and stocky. The top of the tower, with the usual pinnacles, has four strips of ornament of the type as found at Launceston or St Mary Truro, or Fowey.* The tower can be dated by the coat of arms of Bishop Courtenay (1478–87). It is faced with Pentewan stone. Interior of nave with five bays, chancel with two bays, N and S aisles, two-storeyed S porch. Mainly C15. Of earlier buildings the following fragments or parts can still be seen: the circular pier of the S chancel arcade, the two responds of the arches, and the double-chamfered arches themselves are early C13; the N chancel arcade is also E.E., but later, with a handsome octagonal pier with four slim attached shafts in the diagonals, a motif which comes from Dartmouth and its neighbourhood; the chancel E window and N aisle E window with intersecting tracery and pointed quatrefoils look c.1300, and it is quite probable that they and the N chancel aisle can be connected with the date c.1290, recorded for the endowment of a chantry chapel of St Michael. The nave is disappointing inside, much restored in 1872 (by *G. E. Street*. The alabaster reredos and pulpit are his). The piers are slender, of standard Cornish section, with moulded capitals and on the S side some decoration of the abaci. The aisles have wide Perp windows giving an even light. The old wagon roofs are original; they rest almost immediately on the arcades. Outside, the church is much more attractive, with battlemented aisles and a battlemented, buttressed, two-storeyed S porch with a curious doorway with openwork tracery: an ogee arch inscribed into a round one (cf. Mylor, St Just-in-Roseland; the motif really originated at Gloucester and is to be found, for example, in tomb canopies at Tewkesbury). There are also carved shield-holding angels, and shields with carved Instruments of the Passion, Resurrection, Ascension, and Christ in Glory. – FONT. Norman, of Bodmin type, with faces at the corners, 'trees of life', and dragons. – PILLAR PISCINA. Norman, and of interesting design. – BENCH ENDS. Only a 31a few are preserved; and only a small part (on the S) of the

* Mr A. L. Rowse calls this a Somerset type of tower – a class which extends in a band all the way across the West Country from Cornwall to Oxford. The elaborately carved stonework of the topmost stage is typical. (*St Austell*, H. E. Warne, 1960.)

ROOD SCREEN. – CLOCK FACE outside the W tower, with twenty-four bosses for the hours; probably C16. – OAK CHEST. 1669. – PLATE. Two similar gilt Cups, with strapwork decoration, London, 1573–4; also pieces of 1707, 1708, 1751, 1753. – MONUMENT to Joeseph Sawle † 1769, by *Isbell*. Freestanding, about 6 ft high; black urn on a square base.

(ST AUSTELL TOWN CENTRE DEVELOPMENT. A pedestrian precinct was begun in 1963, with return frontages to Trinity Street, and is as yet unfinished. It contains shops, a restaurant, a supermarket, flats, offices, and a multi-storey car park, all designed by *Alister MacDonald & Partners* in reinforced concrete construction with flat roofs and simple elevations, faced mainly in local reconstructed stone and rendered. In contrast to the narrow winding High Street, the new development provides St Austell with an open, traffic-free precinct ultimately to be enclosed on all sides and commanded by a tower building.)

TOWN HALL. 1844, in an accomplished Italian Renaissance style; it is perhaps by *Eales* ?

(ST AUSTELL MAGISTRATES' COURT, Carlyon Road. By *John Crowther*, for the County Architect's Department, 1966.)

(PUBLIC LIBRARY, Carlyon Road. By *F. K. Hicklin*, County Architect, 1961.)

(ST AUSTELL PENRICE COUNTY SECONDARY SCHOOL, Charlestown Road. By the *Architects' Co-partnership*, 1960.)

QUAKER MEETING HOUSE. 1829. Rectangle of granite with hipped roof: an honest and solid shelter for quiet worship.

WHITE HART HOTEL. Inside, an interesting panoramic wallpaper of the bay of Naples by the famous *Dufour*, c. 1800.*

HOLY WELL. Menacuddle, about 1 m. N of St Austell; specially romantically placed.

PENRICE. *See* p. 135.

ST BENET'S
Near Lanivet

Now used for commercial purposes; before that as a guesthouse; again before that as a private house. It was founded in 1411 as a lazar house or hospital, and became a Courtenay mansion in the C16. It looks essentially C19 Gothic, with the C15 windows built into a regular 1859 façade. The two niches and the little oriel window with their ogee heads are also from

---

* Now in the Victoria and Albert Museum.

the original building. Most of the tower of the original church remains at the rear of the house, its top storey altered.

ST BLAZEY

St Blaise. Built c.1440, but not much of antiquity remains after a thorough restoration by *Moffatt*, of *Scott & Moffatt*, in 1839.* The w tower is old, of regular granite blocks in three stages, without buttresses, and with short, stumpy pinnacles. The old s porch entrance was evidently re-used as the s door of the tower. On the second stage of the tower is a little ogee-headed niche with finials l. and r. The N aisle was built by Moffatt in imitation of the tall old s aisle with standard Cornish piers decorated on plain capitals and abaci with a castellated or a fleur-de-lis cresting. – PLATE. Fine goblet-shaped standing Cup on baluster stem, datable 1599–1600; also Chalice and Paten of 1576 (by the same master as Lamorran, Perranarworthal, Stithians), and Flagon of 1738–9. – MONUMENTS. Slate plate of 1701 with Father Time looking like a benevolent churchwarden. – Henry Scovell † 1727. Wall-tablet with columns l. and r. and an inscription framed by draperies. At the foot an oval relief of the Last Judgement, with the two to whom the monument is dedicated being carried up by angels. It is by *Weston* of Exeter. – Sir Thomas Carlyon of Tregrehan † 1831. Gothic triptych, with figures in the wings and a long inscription (with names, etc., in Gothic capital letters in the middle). The style aimed at is Dec. By *H. Hopper*.

A few nice houses close to the entrance of the churchyard. (Former MARKET HOUSE. Early C19, on granite columns. G. W. Copeland)

TREGREHAN. *See* p. 224.

ST BREOCK

A very pretty small village with the church of ST BREOCK at the foot of a steep valley by a tiny stream under old trees. The cottages climb up the hill towards the Georgian mansion in its grounds. The church is low and not in itself of special merit. Of the C13 the rebuilt N transept arch and traces of an original cruciform plan. Of the early C14 still the two doorways and the lower parts of the w tower, without buttresses, but with a NE

* There was another restoration in 1897.

stair-turret. The third storey of the tower is Perp, as is the rest
of the church with the exception of one nave window and the
E window of the aisle (C14). Nave of six bays, S aisle, N and
S porches, N and S transept chapels. Granite piers of the
standard Cornish design, coarsely carved capitals, four-
centred arches, and Perp windows. – FONT. C15. – HIGH
ALTAR, by *E. H. Sedding*. – MONUMENT of the C13 with
foliated cross and inscription in French (Thomas P . . . gist
ici). – Brass to a member of the Tredenick family (?) and two
wives (one lost) and several children; *c.*1510. – Slate slab to
Charles Tredenick, 1578, with strapwork and two excellent
Michelangelesque putti. – Large slate wall-monument to some
member of the Prideaux-Brune family, 1598, with kneeling
figures and plenty of heraldry.

PILLAR STONE used as a gatepost at Nanscowe Farm, about
1 m. SW of St Breock. Inscriptions in Roman capitals:
VLCAGNI FILI and SEVERI. Date probably C5 or C6.

PAWTON QUOIT, 1½ m. SW. A much damaged megalithic
chamber, roughly rectangular in plan, 7 ft 6 in. long by 3 ft
6 in. wide, set at the S end of a long barrow 70 ft long.

ST BREOCK BEACON LONGSTONE, 200 yds SW of Haycrock
Farm, on the N edge of the St Breock Downs. This standing
stone fell in 1945 and was re-erected in 1956. It has a maximum height of 16 ft. No finds were made during the excavations at this time. It is presumably of Bronze Age date.

ST BREWARD

ST BRUEREDUS. At the N end of a long straggling village which
skirts the W slopes of Bodmin Moor. It is bleak country, close
to granite quarries. Yet, in spite of the loneliness of the neighbourhood, which must have been more pronounced in the
Middle Ages, there was here an aisled Norman church of
sizable dimensions. After a drastic restoration traces of five
circular Norman piers remain (cf. Morwenstow), especially
their capitals, scalloped, and one with odd stylized tree
motifs, two to a side, like candelabra. The first three piers are
shorter than the fourth and fifth; the N transept does not
correspond exactly with them. To the S the C15 added a
granite aisle of standard design, the capitals and abaci finely
moulded, the arches almost segmental. The windows are of
four lights, similar to Egloshayle. The E window is of five
lights; the wagon roof is original. The S porch is granite too,

also with a wagon roof. The W tower is unbuttressed, of granite, with bands of long, flat slabs of granite alternating with square slabs. The third storey is later, recessed so that buttresses can be formed at the corners. – FONT. Made up of Norman fragments. – PARCLOSE SCREEN to the N chancel chapel; dilapidated. – BENCH ENDS. A few worked into the parclose screen, and more made into a reredos. – MONUMENT. Christopher Rogers, 1609, originally a tomb-chest covered with slate plates, the plates now against the W wall.

STONE CIRCLE, 2½ m. NE. The circle is 140 ft in diameter and comprises seventy-six stones. To the NE is a single outlying stone. To the E and NE are numerous HUT CIRCLES.

FERNACRE STONE CIRCLE, on Rough Tor, 4 m. NE. A large circle, 150 ft in diameter, comprising sixty-four stones, the largest 4 ft 6 in. high. Two fallen stones lie inside the setting. To the E and N are a large number of HUT CIRCLES, on the slopes of Rough Tor.

STONE CIRCLE, ¼ m. NE of Leaze Farm. The circle has a diameter of 81 ft and consists of ten standing stones and six fallen ones. There were probably twenty-two in the original setting. The tallest surviving stone projects 3 ft 6 in. above the ground.

KING ARTHUR'S HALL, ½ m. WNW. A rectangular enclosure, 159 ft by 60 ft, consisting of an earth bank up to 20 ft wide and 7 ft high revetted internally with large facing stones. The site is unexcavated and undated, although parallels exist in both Neolithic and Dark Age contexts.

STRIPPLE STONES AND TRIPPET STONES. *See* Blisland.

ST BURYAN

4020

ST BERIAN. One of the proudest churches of west Cornwall, all Perp,* all granite, in a fairly high position, its four-stage tower, 92 ft high, a landmark from far away. The village is of no significance compared with the scale of the church. The tower has a NE stair-turret rising above the pinnacles, and buttresses set back from the angles. The nave has six bays with identical N and S aisles, and there is a battlemented,

---

* In 1473 a commission recommended that the C13 church should be pulled down and rebuilt. The C14 tower was left standing and the present church built up to it in the late C15 or early C16. A number of restorations took place from the mid C18 onwards, including one by *Butterfield* in 1872, according to Dr Paul Thompson.

buttressed, pinnacled s porch. The staircase to the rood loft
projects from the s wall. Most of the windows are of three
lights, without tracery. Inside, most of the thin timbers of the
ceiled wagon roofs are new. The piers of the arcades are tall
slim, of standard section, with very finely moulded capitals.
In the N wall of the chancel are clearly visible traces of a
Norman chancel aisle, two round arches now walled up, and a
short circular pier with a scalloped capital. The reason for this
unusual lavishness of plan is the same as at Crantock: St
Berian was a collegiate church, traditionally founded by King
Athelstan. The college was refounded by Bishop Brewer of
Exeter in 1238. The glory of the church is its ROOD SCREEN,
though much of it is new (by *E. H. Sedding*). Yet what remains
of the original panels of the wainscoting, of the rood beam, and
of the tracery is enough to show that the work must have been
done by one of the best Devon workshops and not locally.
The screen runs right across nave and aisles. Each of the three
sections has a central opening and two panels l. and two r. of it.
Each panel has in the wainscoting four narrow upright motifs
with foliage arranged in undulating, zigzag, or patera fashion.
The rood beam has an upper trail of vine, and a lower trail
with birds, beasts, grotesque heads, etc., all hiding in and peep-
ing out of foliage scrolls. Traces of the original colouring
remain: blue, red, and gold. – FONT. With shield-holding angels
at three of the corners, rudely carved. Is it C14 or C15? – ALTAR
AND REREDOS. *c.* 1920, by *Pinwill* of Plymouth, designed by
E.H. Sedding. – BENCH ENDS made into a litany desk. Note the
mermaid on one of them. – MISERICORDS in the choir, with
plain shields. – PLATE. Good and characteristic plain Chalice
of 1683–4; also a Paten of 1740–1. – MONUMENT to Clarice de
Bolleit, with cross and inscription in Norman-French, coffin-
shaped, C13.

TREWOOF. *See* p. 231.

The parish is exceptionally rich in prehistoric and Celtic
remains:

COPED STONE, in the churchyard, one of four remaining in
Cornwall. Only one-third of the length survives; cf. Lanivet,
St Tudy, Phillack.

CROSS HEAD, just outside the s porch. Roughly circular, with
Crucifixus.

MERRY MAIDENS, 2 m. SE, just s of the B3315. A circle of
nineteen roughly rectangular granite blocks with a diameter of
75 ft.

STONE CIRCLE, 1 m. N. An elliptical setting of nineteen stones with an eccentrically placed upright inside the circle. The setting has a maximum diameter of 80 ft, and no stone exceeds 4 ft 7 in. in height. An excavation in the C19 produced no small finds.

TRELEW STANDING STONE. In the C19 a cremation burial was found in the hole dug to accommodate this stone.

ST CLEER

2060

ST CLARUS. An exceptionally fine W tower of regular granite blocks in three stages, with buttresses set back from the angles, and decorated with pinnacles in relief. In addition the third stage has another set of little relief pinnacles at the corners. Above these rise the big main pinnacles of the tower. The church has N and S aisles, both buttressed and both inside consisting of four bays and one lower one for the chancel. The S aisle windows have Perp tracery, the N windows are straight-headed, that is later. The N arcade on the other hand is earlier, say c.1400, with octagonal piers and a fairly simple profile of the arch. The S arcade has an unusual profile of the piers with a fillet on each side of the standard hollow (cf. Lewannick), and a very complex arch moulding. There is a squint between N aisle and chancel. Of the Norman church one doorway remains, on the N side, with one order of colonnettes and a zigzag outer voussoir, nothing very spectacular. – FONT. C13, Purbeck table-top type, with five flat pointed blank niches on each side. – PAINTINGS. Verses from the Bible with crude C18 cartouche work, probably originally in the spandrels of the arcade. – MONUMENTS. Robert Langeford † 1614. Slate, with kneeling figures, thirteen altogether. – Nicholas and Mary Connock † 1804, by *Isbell* of Stonehouse.

HOLY WELL, a little N of the churchyard. A pretty C15 building, though without any finery; square, of granite, with a steep-44b pitched roof and a pointed barrel-vault, heavy granite piers on front and sides, and a solid back wall with openings and niches in which bathers placed their valuables.*

DONIERT STONE, between St Cleer and Redgate Farm, 1 m. NW of St Cleer, by the main road to Liskeard. A cross base with Hiberno-Saxon interlacings and an inscription: DONIERT ROGAUIT PRO ANIMA (Doniert ordered this cross for the good of his soul), which may be connected with Durngarth, King

---

* Information from Mrs E. Ettlinger.

of Cornwall, † 875. By its side a taller cross shaft with a panel of interlace in the same style.

THE HURLERS, 1½ m. W of Upton Cross. Three large stone circles arranged in a row NNW–SSW. The N circle has a diameter of 110 ft and consists of seven upright and six fallen stones. The central circle is 135 ft in diameter and has ten upright and seven recumbent stones. The S circle is 105 ft in diameter and all nine of its surviving stones are recumbent. None of the stones in these circles exceeds 6 ft in height. Excavation in the N circle produced a number of flints of Early Bronze Age character, but no other finds. 200 yds W are two large standing stones, both leaning to the N – THE PIPERS.

1 TRETHEVY QUOIT. A massive, closed, megalithic chamber, 7 ft long and 9 ft high. One of the four uprights supporting the capstone has collapsed into the interior of the tomb.

8040

ST CLEMENT

7a ST CLEMENT. Far away from the village, in a corner of the parish, a lush landscape on the shore of the Tresillian river. W tower C14 (stone bearing the date 1326, of doubtful age) three stages, of slate, with the buttresses towards N and S from the NW and SW corners. The buttresses reach up only to the second stage and end in gargoyles. The top stage is later. The body of the church was largely reconstructed in 1865, but C13 work is still visible outside on the N side (lancet windows in the transept). The S aisle of six bays has an arcade of standard piers with elaborately moulded capitals and nearly semicircular arches. The N transept has an arch of the same details towards the nave. Fragments of the rood screen are made up into a tower screen. – FONT. C16, octagonal, with tracery motifs. – MONUMENTS. Samuel Thomas † 1796, signed by *Bacon* 1799. Two standing allegorical figures against the usual pyramid, whose top, however, is going curiously Gothic excellent workmanship. – Rear-Admiral Robert Carthew Reynolds † 1811, signed *Micali direxit* (direxit, not fecit! *Liburni* (that is at Leghorn), 1816. A young soldier and two women; he points to a monument with a naval battle; his portrait medallion higher up.

In the churchyard, a CROSS. The sign of the cross in a circle; on the shaft inscription: IGNIOC VITALI FILI TORRICI; also an

Ogham inscription (*see* Lewannick, St Kew) including perhaps a word in the ancient Irish language. Date any time
between the C5 and the C7.

LYCHGATE. With a slate-hung upper room and built immediately on to a cottage; early C19 Gothick windows; no
doubt a vestry room or schoolroom.

(KILLAGORDEN. Stone and slated. C17, with part of *c.*1510.
Two storeys. The wings with bay windows to full height are
C18. GMT)

PENCALENICK. *See* p. 133.

ST CLETHER 2080

ST CLEDERUS. The church was rebuilt in 1865, but keeps its
late medieval unbuttressed, unpinnacled granite tower. The
rebuilding used the capitals of three thick circular Norman
piers (cf. Morwenstow). The capitals are scalloped. – The
FONT is most elementary Norman.

HOLY WELL, $\frac{1}{4}$ m. NW of the church, in a lovely setting above
the river Inney, and below the rocks. There is no house visible
anywhere. The well building is the largest in the county. It
consists of the well proper with its steep gable and a chapel of
about 11 by 20 ft with a rude altar table. To the l. of the altar
the water enters the chapel, on the S side it flows out into a
niche in the outer S wall.

ST COLUMB MAJOR 9060

An attractive hill town with a few streets to the E and S of the
church and churchyard; the oldest house, the BISHOP'S
HOUSE, to the S, stone ground floor and modern slate-hanging
on the upper floor. There is much slate-hanging everywhere.
Of individual buildings one may have a glance at the TOWN
HALL, plain, classical, 1848; at BANK HOUSE, by *William
White*, Venetian style, in grey and yellow stone, some detail
in black marble, and two thin red brick bands, with admirable
Ruskinian ironwork and a vaulted vestibule;* at the various
Nonconformist chapels in and off Fore Street; and at the
RECTORY (now Old Rectory Guest House), 1850 by *William
White*, with an interesting, spacious staircase arrangement.‡

ST COLUMBA. In a commanding position, visible from afar, and

* Information from Dr Paul Thompson.
‡ Information from S. Muthesius.

indeed one of the major churches of Cornwall. The w tower is of four stages, that is one more than usual (cf., for example, Probus, St Ives). The ground floor is open to N and S (cf. Lostwithiel). Such passages usually indicate that there was originally no space to the W of the church for processions to pass. The buttresses set back from the angles. Inside there are nave and two aisles. The aisles are only three bays long, but their arcades are followed by one lower arcade connecting nave and N and S transepts, and then the chancel has its aisles too. The arcades have the early form with two-centred arches on square piers with four demi-shafts attached. The chancel aisles open into the transept with low 'chancel arches'. For the date of the main structure the S door is important, with ball-flower ornament in one hollow of jamb and voussoirs and two little heads as label-stops, evidently early C14. It seems, therefore, that the window tracery in the S transept (four-light lancet with three circles above) and the S chancel aisle (with cusped circles and cusped pointed quatrefoils) may be correctly renewed. The other windows are Perp. – FONT. Of c.1300, octagonal, with large crude faces on five sides in quatrefoils (four *en face*, one in profile) and tracery motifs otherwise. – BENCH ENDS. Of the usual C15 type with two shields with initials, Instruments of the Passion, etc. – PISCINAS in chancel and S chancel aisle, both early C14. – BRASSES in S chancel aisle: Sir John Arundell and family † 1545, Sir John Arundell and family, brass engraved 1633, John Arundell † 1633 (cf. the Arundell brasses at Mawgan-in-Pydar). – MONUMENT to Edmund Hearle, 1796 by *Robert Isbell* of Stonehouse.

(TREWAN HALL, ¾ m. NNW. Large, the façade with two far-projecting wings. The house was built in 1633. Of that time the three-tier frontispiece with round-arched doorway and upper columns, probably not *in situ*. Also probably of 1633 the shaped gables with their obelisk finials. The fenestration is nearly all Gothic and dates either from c.1820–30 or from the time when *William White* built the rectory of St Columb Major, or from both. Until early in the C19 the house had its great hall of c.1633–5 which had a tunnel-vaulted plaster ceiling.*)

CASTLE-AN-DINAS. *See* p. 52.

(HOLY WELL, Towan. With a gabled roof of overlapping slabs.

---

* This description and the comments are based on a postcard view and an informative letter from Mr D. K. Hill.

Well moulded doorway within a rectangular frame. Corbel within. G. W. Copeland)

ST COLUMB MINOR

Now on the verge of Newquay, with bungalows coming quite close. Yet the immediate surroundings are still rural and villagey.

ST COLUMBA. A proud w tower of granite, in four stages, with the usual buttresses set back from the angles. The interior was reconstructed by *J. D. Sedding*. It belonged to the C14 with two aisles of six bays, the piers consisting of four major and four minor shafts, the arches being two-centred (their detail similar to St Columb Major). The windows are Perp, however (in one of them glass by *Gibbs & Howard*, 1885). – FONT. Norman, of Bodmin type, very much worked over. – BENCH ENDS. Several were found in 1896, some with the usual two shields to an end, some with the later composition of only one larger motif. They had an inscription saying that they had been erected out of the poor's stock in 1525. Only two are displayed now, at the back of the church. – ROYAL ARMS. Painted plaster with strapwork decoration. – PLATE. A nice collection, though no outstanding pieces: Chalice and Paten, 1577; Paten on foot by *N. Locke*, 1710–11; Chalice, Paten, and Flagon by *T. Whipham*, 1750–1, with the Godolphin arms.

ST DAY

HOLY TRINITY. Not a usual Cornish dedication, and a church refreshingly negligent of Cornish traditions. Its date, 1828, accounts for that. The architect was *C. Hutchins*. Though built of granite, the style is entirely that of Commissioners' churches all over England. All the motifs are thin – even the granite appears like paper. The windows are lancets, there are no buttresses, pinnacles appear duly at the NW, SW, NE, and SE corners. A lean w tower not projecting at all beyond the fronts of the aisles. Inside, thin tall piers right up to the slightly coved ceilings. There once were galleries; now there are only beams at gallery height connecting the shafts with each other and with the wall.

The church looks over a landscape of deserted tin mines, with their chimneys like so many monuments to the passing of human achievement, more deeply moving than the artificial picturesque mementos in c18 gardens.

ST DENNIS

9050

As the vantage point from which the craziest scenery of Cornwall can best be viewed, this CHURCH about 700 ft up should be visited. The land around is bare, with cyclopic granite walls separating road from field, with bleak slate-roofed workmen's cottages lower down, and with the cones of the china clay workings all around. The church lies inside an Iron Age hillfort (*see* below). The dedication may have originated in the Cornish word for fort: *dinas*. The tower is two-staged, of granite, with external stair-turret; the church was rebuilt in 1847 (not very correctly, as the odd window shapes show). – PLATE. Chalice and Paten by the master *IW* (*see* Bodmin and Merther).

HILLFORT. The hilltop on which the church stands was originally defended by two roughly circular ramparts. The line of the inner rampart is now followed by the churchyard wall, and scant traces of the outer defences can still be detected 60 ft NNW of the churchyard.

ST DOMINIC

4060

ST DOMINICA. A strange W tower of the c13 with corbelled-out top stage, somewhat domestic-looking. The top stage retreats again some distance below the parapet, and in the space so formed, on each side, are three sunk panels each containing a curious little figure.* The buttresses are diagonal, as usual in early Cornish towers, and a broad, flat stair-turret rises on the SE side, ending like a buttress. Of the two aisles, that on the S side is earlier. This comes out in the design of the piers: square with four attached demi-piers, whereas the N side has the later Cornish standard shape. Also the arches on the S side are simply double-chamfered, on the N side four hollows instead of the chamfers. Some good roof timbers. – PLATE. Chalice by *More* of Exeter, Elizabethan; also Paten by *T. Jenkins*, 1705–6. – MONUMENTS. To Sir Anthony Rous † 1622 and his son † 1620, the two men side by side, in armour, recumbent on a tomb-chest. The canopy of thirteen marble columns has gone, and the whole is in a shocking state. – John Clarke, 1749 by *J. R. Veale*.

* Information from G. W. Copeland.

ST ENDELLION
9070

ST ENDELLIENTA. A beautifully kept church by a main road. The three-stage tower of regular granite slabs is unbuttressed, with quatrefoil decoration on the plinth. The nave is low and wide, with two aisles of five bays, both with arcades of the same Cornish standard granite design with four-centred arches. Some capitals have the kind of decoration with large horizontal leaves which is standard in Devonshire. The aisle windows are of three lights, of standard Cornish Perp design. The E window of the chancel is of five lights, those of the aisles of four lights. The wagon roofs have angels against the wall plates at the foot of the principals.* The S doorway has fleurons in jambs and voussoirs. – FONT. Norman, very plain. – BENCH ENDS in the nave, of standard Perp Cornish type. – MONUMENT. Tomb-chest in the S aisle, c. 1400, of Catacleuse 36b stone, superb quality. It has three deep niches on each of the long sides, and one on each of the short ones. The niches have ogee arches on colonnettes and inside beautifully designed little vaults. The detail, such as the cusping, is as delicate as if it were of cast iron. The sculptor, that is the 'Master of St Endellion', made the STOUP inside the S door too, also of Catacleuse stone, and also excellent. It has coats of arms and some acorn motifs. For other works by the same master, see Padstow, St Issey, and St Merryn. – PLATE. Chalice and Paten by More of Exeter, Elizabethan; the chalice on a later stem.

CROSS SHAFT, at the cross-roads between St Endellion and Port Quin. Inscription: XP and BROCAGNI HIC IACIT NADOTTI FILIUS. Date probably C6 or C7; lettering transitional between Roman and Hiberno-Saxon.

ROSCARROCK. Among the outbuildings of the present house, along the SW side of the court, part of the medieval house survives; in particular an upper room with a four-light oriel window, and a fine timber roof with trusses of the arched collar type, but with the principals curved at the foot, making a kind of upper cruck, as at Tintagel Old Post Office. A carved wooden cornice reproduces on a small scale the castellation on the courtyard wall. V. M. and F. J. Chesher)

* The angels against the wall plates were nearly all carved by local villagers just before the Second World War, when the roof was taken down and re-erected. A principal medieval rafter was found with the date 1675, in a position suggesting that the roof was taken down and repaired at that date also. (Information from Mr Cecil Farthing.)

(TRESUNGERS. Late C16 farmhouse, L-shaped, with a gable
wing. Mullioned windows, including one of eight lights.
Embattled three-storeyed entrance tower dated 1660. Fragments of earlier work in farm buildings. GMT)

ST ENODER

ST ENODER. The most remarkable feature is the W tower, rebuilt in 1711 after a collapse in 1684, entirely of Cornish type,
though with corner buttresses. The real date is visible only by
the Baroque scrolls instead of set-offs and by the odd tracery
of the ground-floor window. The date appears in the battlements of the S aisle, which had been damaged by the fall of the
tower. The battlemented S porch, also granite, like the whole
aisle, however, is original C15, with quatrefoils decorating its
plinths, and very decayed demi-figures of angels in the doorway. The S and N windows and some of the others are of four
lights, the same Perp design. Inside, the S arcade of four bays
is C14, with octagonal piers and two-centred arches. The
arcade of four bays and N transept are C15 of standard design.
The same design appears in the lower three arcades of the
chancel aisle. Both aisles and the N transept have their old
wagon roofs. – FONT. Norman, circular, with four crude
corner faces and an upper border of carved criss-cross between
them all around. – BENCH ENDS, partly with two, partly with
one shield for an end. – STAINED GLASS. Just one C15 head
in the tracery of the SE window. – MONUMENT. Very infantile
slate plate to Dorothy Tanner † 1634, with kneeling figures.

ST ENODOC

The chapel was buried in the sands and only dug out and restored
in 1863. It is now in the midst of a golf links, in a dip, so that
one can only occasionally see its little C13 spire. The existence
of a spire is unusual in Cornwall. The nearest parallel is S
Minver. The small church is essentially Norman: nave, E
wall, N transept, and ground storey of the N tower (with a E
window and arch into the transept). The position of the tower
also is an exception, but cf. Blisland not too far away. There is
no aisle to the nave, but a S chancel aisle of three bays, low,
small, and of Cornish standard granite design. – (MONU-
MENT. In the churchyard, tomb with incised slab having crude
figures of John Mably and daughter, 1687; the latest incised
slab with effigies so far known in England. Information from
F. A. Greenhill.)

ST ERME

T HERMES. Rebuilt in 1819–20 by *John Foulston*, except for the W tower of broad proportions. Regular granite blocks, three stages, buttresses leaving the corners free. The old church had a N aisle, and the arcade of this (six bays) apparently survives, standard Cornish granite design, with four plain capitals to each pier, and heavy semicircular arches. Old roof timbers are re-used everywhere. – FONT. Norman, circular, with a large foliage scroll along the top of the bowl and four motifs of trees of life below. – BRASS of 1596 to R. Trencreek and family, not in its original form and setting.

ST ERNEY

T TERNINUS. A low, two-stage W tower of slate, with thick buttresses and no W door. In the C15 a N aisle was added of four bays with Cornish granite standard piers. – FONT. C13 (?) (Sedding suggests *c.*1080). Thick circular foot and square bowl. The top half has a section with three plates and two hollows, the lower half the most elementary line decoration.

ST ERTH

T ERCUS. A small church among trees, much restored and re-built.* The W tower is of three stages, unbuttressed, and has below the battlements grotesque heads (cf. Ludgvan). The S porch is buttressed and the jambs of its entrance panelled. It still possesses its old wagon roof. The S aisle has six bays of standard Cornish granite design, with plain capitals. The N arcade starts in the same way at the W, but is continued with taller piers with moulded capitals and leaf decoration round the abaci. In 1874 two dormer windows were put into the roofs to give more light, and they look very pretty now. – FONT. Norman, square, of unusual design, each side with two saltire crosses. – ROYAL ARMS. Painted. – PLATE. A good collection: Chalice, Elizabethan, by *IS*; Paten on three feet by *J. Mortimer* of Exeter, late C17; Chalice and Paten by *E. York*, 1718–19; two Flagons by *E. Pearce*, *c.*1704; Paten on three feet by *Rugg*, 1767–8.

* The church is C14, according to the MHLG, and the restoration was in 1874.

ROCK CLOSE TERRACE: cottages of 1791; TREBARTHA
PLACE: Nos. 1–12, curved row of cottages of 1831.

CROSSES. Cross head in the churchyard with very crude figures
of the Crucifixus; cross shaft in the churchyard with Hiberno-
Saxon interlacings and remains of a Crucifixus; cross in the
centre of the village on tall, plain shaft, rude lantern-head
with Crucifixus, probably late medieval.

BRIDGE. Of four round, low arches, called by Leland, that is in
1538, two hundred years old. But much mended in the C17
and widened in 1816.

INSCRIBED STONE, near the W end of the Hayle railway
viaduct. Unusually long inscription: HIC ? ? REQUIEVIT . .
CUNAIDE HIC . . . TUMULO IACIT VIXIT ANNOS XXXIII. Roman
capitals; probably C5 or C6.

BOSENCE. Rectangular earthwork 150 by 135 ft on which
Roman remains have been found.

(TRELOWETH FARM. Two-storeyed, with porch on Tuscan
columns; C18. – TREWINNARD MANOR. C17, with early
C18 additions, for example the shell-hooded front door. –
LANUTHNOE COTTAGE, Carnabargus. C18, T-shaped with
rounded corners, cob and rubble. MHLG)

8070

ST ERVAN

The village can never have been prosperous, or else the church
would have been enlarged at some later time, as most other
Cornish churches have.

ST HERMES. The W tower was rebuilt of reinforced concrete in
1955, incorporating the original W window, restored with
polyphant. The body of the church is of nave, N and S transepts, and chancel, all probably C13 (cf. the N door). The slate
plates were never banished to the outside walls. Ten remain in
the church. – PLATE. A pretty set. Paten by *More* of Exeter
Elizabethan; silver-gilt Paten and a Chalice, inscribed 1604
Italian; Chalice by *MV* (*see* St Wenn); Paten by *J. Elston*
1730–1; C18 Beaker.

8060

ST EVAL

ST UVELUS. The church lies all on its own on a high plateau
nearly surrounded now by Air Force establishments. Its tower
is so prominent at a long distance that in 1724–7 Bristol
merchants rebuilt it (in the old style) to use it as a landmark

The interior is low, with a Norman N wall and a (rebuilt) N transept. A Norman window in the nave wall. The s aisle was added in the C15: six bays. Of these the first four belong to the nave, then, at the stage of the former rood screen, follows a low arch, and then the sixth high again. The arcade is of Cornish standard design (not granite) with stylized leaf decoration of the abaci. The wagon roofs are original. Arches on the N side similar to the s, and a triangular space for the staircase of the rood screen, E of the N transept. – FONT. The plainest Norman cup design. – PULPIT. Elizabethan. – ROOD SCREEN. Only the base of the screen across the s aisle is preserved. – BENCH ENDS. C15, of the usual design with initials, Instruments of the Passion, etc., two shields with symbols to each end. Some parts of bench backs with arcading also remain. – PLATE. Chalice and Paten, C18, by *B*, on a rich baluster stem; Flagon by *J. Elston* of Exeter, 1716–17, good; Paten on four feet by *Jennings*, 1735–6, nicely shaped.

ST EWE   9040

ALL SAINTS. Earlier than most of the greater Cornish churches. In its most striking parts, that is tower and s aisle, C14. The w tower has broad diagonal buttresses and an octagonal spire with small broaches, and small windows at its foot and a band of quatrefoil decoration half-way up (cf. Gerrans). The s aisle belongs to the end of the C14. The arcade of six bays has piers consisting of four major and four minor shafts, capitals decorated with small stylized flowers, and castellated abaci. The arches are four-centred. The N side, as usual, is older, the arch to the N transept C13. – FONT. Norman, on five supports, with a plain bowl with four badly carved corner faces. – ROOD SCREEN. The most important object in the church. It goes across the nave only, with three sections on each side of the opening. Each section has two panels of blank tracery, then the real tracery of four lights, and above the coving an elaborate cornice with beasts, birds, a naked boy, etc., all scrambling through foliage (cf. St Buryan). – More MONUMENTS than usual, above all William Mohun † 1737, excellent London work, with a life-size bust worthy of *Rysbrack*, above a broken pediment and below a broken pediment. The fruit and flower decoration also is first-rate. – William Williams † 1785. Urn, etc., by *Isbell* of Stonehouse. – John Hope † 1813 (of Amsterdam and Trevorrick), and his son (drowned while at Eton), inscription and classical frame only, by *Bedford* of 256 Oxford Street, 1821.

HELIGAN. *See* p. 80.

ST GENNYS

1090

ST GENESIUS. A sturdy short W tower facing the sea; its two lower stages are Norman, with small windows deeply splayed inside. The upper stage is early C20 of C15 type, by *E. Sedding*, with buttresses of the type which leave the angles free. The tops of the buttresses at the second stage have pinnacles applied in relief. The chancel masonry (of Tintagel greenstone) is Norman too, and so is the tower arch to the nave, with pointed arch over simple imposts. The nave is of four bays, low, with low arcades. The S arcade is on octagonal granite piers with double-chamfered, four-centred arches (cf. Towednack, etc.). On the N side the first bay is the same, but the other three are of polyphant, Cornish standard piers with capitals, and abaci with flat, stylized flower motifs, and manifold mouldings to the arches. This later type of arch sits incongruously on the one octagonal N pier. – FONT. Square, C12, of Purbeck table-top type, with six (in the W seven) blank niches with pointed heads. – BENCH ENDS. A few fragments made into a litany desk. – PLATE. Chalice by *Mathew* of Barnstaple, Elizabethan, with Paten by *IW* (*see* Bodmin and St Dennis); other pieces of 1715 and 1776. – (In the churchyard a Delabole slate HEADSTONE to Percy Walter White † 1938, inscribed by *Eric Gill*, 1939.)

ST GERMANS

3050

St Germans with the adjoining Port Eliot is of outstanding interest in its architectural, historical, and picturesque aspects. The visitor to the church can appreciate only the first two of them; to appreciate the third would mean access to the private grounds of Port Eliot. The house stands on part of the site of the priory, separated from and further N than the church; in the Middle Ages the whole was one group. For the house, *see* Port Eliot.

ST GERMANUS. The church was the cathedral of Cornwall in Anglo-Saxon times. Bishops are known between 931 and *c.*1040, but no architectural fragments remain. In 1050 the bishopric, with that of Crediton, was merged in a new diocese,

with its see at Exeter. Between 1161 and 1184 Bishop Bartholomew reorganized St Germans as a priory of Augustinian
canons. Of this building, finally consecrated only in 1261, so
much is still in existence that no other church in Cornwall can
vie with it as an example of Norman planning. The Norman
building had two w towers, a nave of 102 ft, two narrow aisles
with lean-to roofs, and probably a chancel, but no transept and
no crossing tower. Of the e part nothing is left. The w front,
however, stands complete up to roof height. The aisle width
and height can be read from traces against the e walls of the s
tower inside and the n tower outside. Of the nave the first two
s bays survive. It had a clerestory with windows in line with
the spandrels, not, as usual, with the apexes of the arches (cf.
the upper n wall of the s aisle), a motif which such Gothic
churches as Fowey, Lostwithiel, and Callington in Cornwall,
and North Petherwin in Devon took up.

The w front is uncommonly plain and powerful for its date.
With the wide flat buttresses of the two towers it is more
reminiscent of Franco-Norman work of a hundred years
earlier (say St Étienne at Caen) than of the livelier Transitional
which more central parts of England practised towards the end
of the c12. Between the towers is on the ground floor a porch
under a gable (with the rare feature of a cross), and on the
upper floor three round-headed windows with the centre one
higher than the others. These windows are provided with
nook-shafts. Higher up the s tower has four small Norman
windows towards w and e and otherwise Perp work. The n
tower turns into octagonal shape on the second storey (cf.
Jumièges) and ends in a c13 octagon. The w portal under the
gable is unrivalled in Cornwall. It is of seven orders, built of 21
elvan from Tartan Down near Landrake. Three of the orders
and voussoirs have uncommonly vivid zigzag; whether the
innermost order possessed different ornaments cannot now be
said, as the material has weathered very badly. The hoodmould
of the outer arch exhibits foliage decoration.

Inside, the ground floors of the towers were open to nave
and aisles by transitional pointed arches of simplest design:
two steps with an inserted roll moulding (cf. Morwenstow).
The capitals of the clustered wall-shafts are mostly scalloped,
but some also of a very primitive 'Ionic' kind. On the first
floor the towers were connected by a gallery, as indicated by
the two remaining doors. The staircase of the s tower is the
only Cornish staircase of Norman date. In the nave, the two

bays which are preserved have thick, short, circular piers, with square scalloped capitals and pointed arches of plain two-step moulding. The clerestory windows, which were discovered in 1904, have rich zigzag ornament.

With no more than these bays (and what has been re-used of Norman fragments in the other s bays after the collapse of the chancel in 1592) belonging to the original building of the C12 and C13, the interior of St Germans is now more interesting than inspiring. It is dominated by the late Middle Ages and the C19. The proportions, with the aisle 6 ft wider than the nave, are unhappy, the C13 chancel (consecrated 1261) went 55 ft beyond the present E wall, and the C19 roofs are disappointing. The N transept was built in 1803 for the Port Eliot pew. (But the transept arch has re-used Norman fragments.)

The s aisle is a mixture of four styles: the Norman of the first bays, the interesting imitation-Norman of probably after 1592, the Dec of the E end, and the early C15 Perp of the rest. The E end must originally have been an E chapel attached to the narrow Norman aisle. It is of high aesthetic quality, derived in style from Exeter Cathedral. To get an impression of its pristine finesse of detail St Ive near Liskeard, consecrated in 1338, may be compared. It seems difficult therefore to connect the chapel with the transfer of relics of St German in 1358. The E wall of the chapel has two three-light windows with a niche for an image between (cf. the niches of St Ive). In the s wall are one original window and a recess with an ogee canopy. The s aisle itself can be dated by the arms of Bishop Lacy (1420–50) amongst the shields on the hoodmoulds of one of the windows. There are four such windows, all of four lights, three clearly Perp, the fourth (on the w) still reticulated, that is Dec. The aisle is battlemented outside (like the s tower) and has a handsome and original s porch with two entrance arches close to each other to w and s and a depressed tunnel-vault with a grid of thick granite ribs. Perp also the five-light chancel E window, which must have been put into the present E wall when the chancel was taken down. – FONT. Of Purbeck marble, c.1200; badly preserved. – WOODWORK. Only minor remains: one choir stall (misericord with a man called Dando, punished for hunting on Sunday), c.1375–1400; fragment of the rood screen; figure of St Anthony, indifferent, c.1500, brought over from Port Eliot. – STAINED GLASS. E window by *Burne Jones*, 1896. To see such work executed by *Morris and Co.* after the

many other Victorian windows in Cornish churches brings
home most forcibly the value of William Morris's reform.
Here are clear outlines, pleasing patterns, and simple colours
in sufficiently large expanses to be taken in individually. No
overcrowding, no competing with the art of painting, and yet a
sentiment that is wholly of the C19. – Coloured wooden
STATUE of St Nicholas. – MONUMENTS. John Moyle † 1661.
Large tomb-chest (in the vestry) with a heraldic device in bas-
relief on a black marble slab (G. W. Copeland). – Edward
Eliot, 1722 by *Rysbrack*, reclining on a sarcophagus, in Roman 42
costume, with an allegorical figure on his l., mourning. Short
pyramid in relief and putti in the background: a first-rate
example of Rysbrack's art and the most ambitious C18 monument in Cornwall. – First Earl of St Germans † 1823, by *R.
Westmacott*, a sad maiden seated by a tall pillar with an urn.
ALMSHOUSES. Down in the village, W of the church. An un- 53b
usually picturesque composition. Six houses with six gables
and miniature separate ground-floor and upper-floor flats. The
gables project and are supported on plain, tall stone piers. The
space thus gained in front of the wall is used as a loggia on the
ground floor and as a balcony on the upper floor. The balcony
is reached by outer stairs. The almshouses seem to belong to
the C17
(RAILWAY VIADUCT, across the Tiddy. Thirteen arches. Dr
Athelstane Hill)

ST GLUVIAS   7030

ST GLUVIACUS. The parish church of Penryn to this day, and
indeed on the doorstep of the town. The present church, by
J. P. St Aubyn, dates from 1883, but it has its old W tower of
regular granite blocks, with buttresses meeting at the corners
and a NW stair-turret, and a few interesting MONUMENTS.
Brass to Thomas Kyllygrewe, c.1485, with his wives, already
of the arrangement of figures and inscriptions which remained
typical right through the C16. – Wall-monuments to Samuel
Pendarves † 1693 and his wife, and to William Pendarves
† 1671 and wife. These two were originally of the current type
with two kneeling figures facing each other and columns l. and
r., and the only remarkable thing was that even after 1670 this
old convention was still preserved. Now, however, they are
strangely arranged against the E wall of the S aisle so that two
of the four figures kneel in the window jambs round the corner

from their respective husband or wife (cf. Harris monument, Plymstock, Devon). – J. Kempe † 1711, bust with wig under drapery; rather scrappy.

ST HELEN'S *see* SCILLY ISLES

5030

ST HILARY

ST HILARY. The church is of 1854 by *William White*, an interesting design, with the transepts intersecting the usual three roofs and odd effects of this arrangement on the lighting. The tower above is old, C13, with a broached spire, one of the few in Cornwall. It has buttresses on the ground floor only, and a very noticeable batter. Along the top cornice are very primitive carved faces. – INSCRIBED STONES. One has an inscription which refers to Constantine the Great and, according to the titles used, 306–8; the stone was probably a milestone. The other (in the churchyard) reads NOTI. NOTI (the monument to Notus, son of Notus) and should from its lettering be C6–7. – PAINTING. Christ blessing, Flemish, c.1500. – Modern decoration of chancel stalls and pulpit: several modern paintings (for example Pietà by *E. Procter*). – PLATE. Chalice and Paten by *WL* (*see* St Ives), Elizabethan, of very pretty shape; also a nice Paten by *PT* and a Flagon of 1710–11 by *Elston* of Exeter.

9070

ST ISSEY

ST IDA. Rebuilt in 1891. The interior has nave and two aisles. The N aisle of three bays has piers with four major and four minor demi-shafts (cf. St Columb Minor, St Wenn, etc.), and two-centred arches: typical Cornish C14. The S aisle of three bays plus two lower bays for the chancel (cf. Bodmin) is Cornish C15 standard, with horizontal leaves along the abacus of each shaft and four-centred arches. The aisles have lean-to roofs. – FONT. Plain, circular bowl on five supports with four motifs on flat decoration: cross, star, candelabra, etc. – REREDOS. Late C14 by the 'Master of St Endellion'. The five panels of Catacleuse stone with deep niches and little figures standing in pairs in each spandrel, twenty altogether, were not originally a reredos. No doubt they belonged to a tomb-chest such as that at St Endellion, and the panel with a small Pietà and two saints in the spandrels which is now on the altar of

the s aisle may have formed part of the same monument.
Henderson has drawn attention to an indulgence granted in
1399 to all those who would visit the tomb of Lady Matilda
Chyverston in St Issey church. The date is convincing. –
PLATE. Chalice and Paten probably by *IW* (*see* Bodmin),
dated 1576; also Paten on foot by *Elston* of Exeter, 1703–4.

ST IVE   *3060*

ST IVO. Essentially a C14 church, a sister church in style of
    South Hill, though more elaborate in detail. The consecration
    of 1338 refers to most of what is to be seen now. The building
    was probably cruciform. The N transept and the W tower with
    bold set-back buttresses belong to the early C14. The majority
    of the windows also of the Dec style, simple, with pointed
    trefoils and quatrefoils in the tracery. The E window of five
    lights is one of the best of its date in Cornwall. Inside it has
    on its sides graceful niches with nodding ogee arches placed
    diagonally. The arches are richly crocketed. The tracery has
    pointed trefoils and pointed 'daggers' connected by straight
    bars so as to form star shapes (cf. St Germans). The origin of
    all this is clearly Exeter Cathedral. In the N wall of the N
    transept behind the organ a funerary recess (cf. Quethiock). In
    the s wall a PISCINA and triple SEDILIA. The whole chancel is a
    very complete and satisfying example of early C14 style. The C15
    or early C16 added the s aisle and s porch and the top of the W
    tower, with twelve instead of the usual four pinnacles. The
    arcade has piers of standard Cornish pattern with carved
    capitals and four-centred arches. The wagon roofs of nave,
    aisle, and s porch are original – PULPIT. Dated 1700, yet
    entirely in the Tudor or Jacobean tradition. – ROYAL ARMS.
    1660, yet still with strapwork ornament, of a design often to
    be found in north Cornwall (cf., for example, Launcells,
    Kilkhampton). – SCULPTURE. Fragment of a St Christopher[37b]
    of excellent quality, perhaps from one of the chancel niches. –
    MONUMENT. J. Lyne † 1791, large, by *Isbell*. – The Wrey
    monument was transferred to Tawstock in 1924.

ST IVES   *5040*

The flourishing port was ecclesiastically dependent on Lelant.
There was not even a chapel of ease. Then in 1408 the town
applied for a Papal Bull for a church of their own. They did not

succeed, but a chapel of ease was erected from 1410 to 1434 which is one of the major church buildings of Cornwall. St Ives became a separate parish only in 1826.

12b ST IA. For the architectural historian one important thing about this church is that its dates are so safely established. The features we see here are all certain to belong to the first third of the C15; for the continuity of building is clearly visible. It is remarkable enough to find a W tower of four stages, over 80 ft high (of rough granite blocks, with buttresses set back from the angles and the unusual feature of pinnacles projected on corbels), and a nave of seven bays with identical aisles l. and r., as a mere chapel of ease (though the case is not unique; cf. for example, St Nicholas, King's Lynn, in Norfolk). The piers of the arcade, of sandstone, are tallish, though the church is rather low for its size, and not of Cornish but of Devon standard; they have four demi-shafts, connected at the diagonals by a concave-convex-concave undulation. The arches are four-centred. S of the E parts of the S aisle an outer S aisle was added by the Trenwith family c.1500 with a rich decora-

25a tion of vine leaves and grapes on the capitals. (Now the Lady Chapel; Madonna and Child by *Barbara Hepworth*.) Outside this aisle there are heads in the corbel table. The best view of the church is from the water, where its four gabled ends

29a spread out proudly.* – FONT. Circular base with attached corner bases of supports, decorated by lions *passant gardant* (cf. Crowan). The circular bowl has severely stylized angels in the corners, holding shields. The material, granite, imposed so much restraint on detail that the work looks as if it were of today. It is probably C15. – BENCH ENDS. Mostly of the standard design with two shields to an end, but in the chancel two complete benches with large single motifs to each panel and at the ends figures of saints with angelic shield-bearers as 'poppyheads'. Renaissance ornament is hardly apparent here, except for certain profile portraits to which Mr Cecil Farthing has drawn my attention. – PULPIT. Each side consists of a panel from a bench end with one motif and a quatrefoil below. – STAINED GLASS. Window above the W door by *Powell & Sons*, 1862, 'from designs of Mr *Poynter*'. – PLATE. Chalice and Paten by *WL* (*see* St Anthony-in-Meneage, St Hilary, St Levan, Sancreed), Elizabethan, uncommonly pretty. Also an equally handsome Chalice and Paten of 1641. A comparison

* (The baptistery of 1956 was designed by *Stephen Dykes-Bower* and built by local craftsmen.)

between the two shapes is illuminating. Also pieces of 1705, 1713, 1743 (Collecting Plate, Exeter, *John Babbage*), 1776 (Knife and Fork). – MONUMENTS. Brass to a member of the Trenwith family, kneeling, with a smaller figure of St Michael on the l.; 1463. – Slate slab to the Sise family near by; 1642. – Hitchens family monument, 1815 by *Garland & Fieldwick*. – LANTERN CROSS in the churchyard, on an octagonal shaft. Late medieval. Height 10½ ft.

(SACRED HEART and ST IA (R.C.), Tregenna Hill. 1909 by *A. J. C. Scoles*.)

CHAPEL OF ST NICHOLAS, Church Place. Rebuilt in 1909, possibly by *E. Sedding Jun.*, from the old materials; a plain little rectangle. Now the New Gallery.

On a hill further s is the KNILL MONUMENT, erected in the form of a pyramid, like a church steeple, by John Knill, mayor (and smuggler, it is said) in 1782. It was probably intended for his own mausoleum, and he stipulated that every five years ten little girls under ten years should dance around it to the sounds of a fiddle for a quarter of an hour.

The town has some picturesque streets round the harbour, and the usual C19 NONCONFORMIST CHAPELS, for example the Congregational of 1800 in Salubrious Place, off Fore Street, a typical name of its date, and the Methodist in Fore Street, 1831. Higher up the valley is the more ambitious group of Methodist schools and church, granite with round-headed windows, 1845.

The PIER was built by *Smeaton* (of Eddystone fame) in 1767–70. It has since been lengthened. The pretty octagonal lookout with its cupola belongs to Smeaton's design.

TREGENNA CASTLE on the hill, now a hotel, still has its front with five bays and two storeys, castellated and symmetrical, as it was built in 1774 for John Stephens. The architect was, it seems, the younger *Wood* of Bath. The builder was called *Daniel Freeman* of Penryn. The house has however been extended out of recognition on the sides, and there is little left of the original interior work.

(ST IVES INFANTS' SCHOOL, The Burrows. 1966 by *A. J. Groves*, County Architect.)

(BARNALOFT, facing on to the Porthmeor beach behind Back Street. By *H. C. Gilbert*, Town Architect, 1964. Flats, cottages, and residential studios. The construction includes 7 ft monolithic granite piers.)

(MANOR HOUSE, Ayr. C17, recently restored. – CULVER

HOUSE, Bussow. A medieval dovecote, circular and squat, with conical stone roof; isolated in a field. MHLG)

ST JOHN

ST JOHN. Norman w tower of two low stages, unbuttressed, the upper storey recessed. The N and S windows are clearly Norman: deep inner splay, slight outer chamfer. The tower has a pyramidal roof. The arch towards the nave is low and narrow. Nothing else of architectural interest in the little church. – Fragments of old STAINED GLASS in a N window.

ST JULIOT

ST JULITTA. In an isolated position, below the lane which passes it. It has an unbuttressed, three-stage tower, nave and granite S aisle, one bay longer to the E than the nave, and a vaulted granite S porch (the vault with a transverse arch). The arcade and the Perp tracery of the aisle windows are Cornish standard. The church was drawn in 1870 by the young architect *Thomas Hardy* (the novelist), whose wife's sister was married to the rector. In 1871–2 Hardy conducted the restoration. Some drawings of his are framed in the church. – FONT. C15, square, of granite. – BRONZE RELIEF. Deposition of Christ, by a C16 Italian Mannerist, *c.*9 in. high. – PLATE. Chalice and Paten 'by me *Nicholas* myself', 1570s, Exeter style, much re-tooled.

Two Cornish CROSSES in the churchyard, one with cross-arms consisting of four triangles especially well preserved.

ST JUST-IN-PENWITH

A little town, not a village. The church lies back from the square in which the WELLINGTON HOTEL of *c.*1813 faces a second square. Into this three short streets converge, as though they were planned, the centre one having the LITERARY IN-STITUTE (1842, two-storeyed, Greek Doric *in antis* below, Ionic above) on the l. and the METHODIST CHAPEL, 1833 (enlarged), at the end.

ST JUST. A large church. The walls of church and tower are all regular granite blocks, C15. The tower is of three stages, un-buttressed, the S porch is buttressed, battlemented, and pin-nacled (cf. St Buryan). Interior of six bays with identical aisle arcades, their Perp windows also identical, with two alternating designs. The shafts of limestone are like those of St Ives, deviating from the Cornish standard. The capitals are decorated with large horizontal leaves and fruit (by the same masons no doubt who did the Trenwith Aisle at St Ives). The E windows of the aisle have tracery of flamboyant 'palm-tree' 23a pattern. – STONE with Chi-Rho monogram and inscription SELUS IC IACIT (probably C5–C6) in the N aisle. It was found in the wall of the old chancel in 1834. – CROSS SHAFT with Hiberno-Saxon interlace walled into the N wall of the N aisle. – FONT. New. The date C14 cannot be accepted. – WALL PAINTINGS. The church walls now expose their random rubble, but were originally meant to be covered by plaster. Two wall paintings remain against the N wall of the aisle, both very restored: a St George and a warning to Sabbath-Breakers (surrounded by tools; cf. Lanivet, etc.). – Set of four CANDELABRA, given in 1746. – PLATE. Chalice and Cover, 1666; Paten, 1669; Flagon, 1747.

CROSS HEADS. One in the Vicarage garden; one with a figure of the Crucifixus near the W gate.

(PLAN-AN-GWARRY, Bank Square. A shallow amphitheatre of about 50 yds diameter, surrounded by stone and earth banks. MHLG)

BOTALLACK. *See* p. 44.

CAPE CORNWALL. *See* p. 51.

FOGOU, Lower Boscaswell. A passage 8 ft long orientated E–W and roofed with massive lintels, the whole being buried beneath an earth and stone bank. The passage at its outer end opens on to a courtyard surrounded by a thick enclosure wall, in its surviving form representing a comparatively recent structure. Iron Age B pottery was found in association with the primary phase of the structure.

PENDEEN VAU FOGOU. *See* Pendeen.

ST JUST-IN-ROSELAND   8030

ST JUST. At the very bottom of a richly wooded combe on the 11b W side of the St Mawes promontory. Even from the lychgate one looks down on the long parallel roofs of nave and aisle, and stands more or less on the same level as the tower top. A creek of an arm of Carrick Sound touches the churchyard. The W tower, of slate, in two stages, has diagonal buttresses and a stair-turret on a three-eighths plan rising above the pinnacles.

The top windows, which are preserved, are clearly C14, two lights, cusped. The N transept and the chancel have windows which may well belong to the church consecrated in 1261. In the S aisle they are all Perp, just as the S aisle arcade inside rests on Cornish standard granite piers with four plain capitals and has nearly semicircular arches. The S porch had a doorway like St Austell, but the openwork tracery on top of the arch is broken off. The jambs still show their panelling. – PISCINA (chancel). C13. – FONT. Octagonal, with uninteresting quatrefoil panels; C15. – PEWS. Coarse, vigorous carving, probably c.1840–50. – BRASS to a priest, c.1520.

ST KEVERNE

7020

ST AKEVERANUS. The church lies by a square, which gives St Keverne something of the appearance of a town rather than a village. It has several unusual features. First of all a spire, octagonal and ribbed; it was renewed as late as 1770, probably because it was useful as a landmark near the treacherous Manacles. Secondly the two aisles come forward to flank the tower and the tower opens into them (which is very rare in Cornwall, cf. Lanteglos-by-Fowey). Finally there are three rood stairs in the N wall. The tower is of two stages and unbuttressed: the Lizard custom (cf. Landewednack, Mullion, etc.). The interior is surprisingly spacious, though low: 110 ft long, with N and S aisles of seven bays. The majority of the piers must have been re-used from a previous building when the church was built in the late C15. They evidently do not fit their places. Their shape is standard Cornish, but of larger, broader, heavier section than later on. Their date may be late C13 or early C14. The outer wall of the N aisle is buttressed, also a sign of early date, and the first window from the W and the N door belong to the same period too. The rest, and especially the S aisle windows, are clearly C15, especially good on the E side. The arches connecting chancel and aisles also have a decoration of the abaci typical of a late date. The S door has a pretty doorway with two suspended shields carved at capital level. A little of the old roof timbers left. – FONT. C15, with angels at the corners holding shields and inscriptions between. – PULPIT. Jacobean, with nice ornamental panels. – BENCH ENDS. Only a few of standard Cornish type. – WALL PAINTINGS. St Christopher, surrounded by scenes from the life of the saint, very faint on the N wall.

ST KEW

A prosperous village with a tall, uncommonly large Georgian vicarage by the church.

ST JAMES. The church is large, with a w tower whose buttresses leave the angles free and a rectangular stair-turret rising above the battlements. The nave is tall, with N and S aisles of five bays, the arcades of standard Cornish granite design with four-centred arches. A few capitals are of Pentewan stone and have a decoration of large horizontal leaves. The E windows of the aisles have four and five lights, the N and S windows three. Ceiled wagon roofs with angels against the wall plates at the foot of the principals (cf. St Endellion). Wagon roof in the S porch too. – The most memorable thing about the church is its STAINED GLASS. The NE window is dated 1469 and preserved almost completely. It tells in three rows of four scenes each the story of Christ's Passion from the Entry into Jerusalem to the Harrowing of Hell. Two scenes only are missing. Between the second and third rows of the scenes is a strip of kneeling figures of donors, and on the r. a tiny scene of the Nativity. In the tracery coats of arms: Henry VI and the Beare, Kingdon, and Carminow families. – The SE window contains fragments of the Tree of Jesse: Jesse's hand gripping the vine, Solomon, David, and above the Virgin and Child; C15. – Small bits of stained glass in other windows. – FONT. Octagonal, C15, with quatrefoil panels. – PULPIT. Uncommonly good, Elizabethan, with ornamental panels. One panel with a man in a tree (a rebus?). – BENCH ENDS. A few. – PLATE. A good collection: Gilt Chalice and Paten by *AK*, 1575–6; very ornate, egg-shaped Cup of glass made probably for an ostrich egg, by *HB*, 1598–9; other pieces of 1728, 1732, 1763. – CROSS HEAD. C15, with Crucifixion; inside the church. – ROYAL ARMS. 1661, stone, with the usual strapwork decoration (*see* Kilkhampton). – SOUTH DOOR. Original. – STOCKS in the porch. – A remarkable object of antiquarian interest is an OGHAM STONE, with an additional inscription IUPTI in Latin. Such stones inscribed in Ogham, that is a script consisting of straight lines entirely, are frequent in south-west Ireland, but rare in Cornwall (cf. Lewannick, St Clement). Date probably C6 or C7.

BOKELLY. *See* p. 44.
PENGENNA. *See* p. 134.
TREGEARE ROUNDS. *See* p. 223.
TREWARNE. *See* p. 230.

ST KEYNE

2060

St Kayna. A church of little interest architecturally or in its furnishings. Three-storeyed w tower without buttresses, nave, N aisle, s porch, and s transept. The s side points to a cruciform building of the earlier Middle Ages, and the existence of part of an ornamental hoodmould with three badly carved heads, now above the s door, confirms this; but all details are Perp except for two Dec windows built (later, no doubt) into the N aisle. – FONT. Perp, octagonal, plain.

Holy Well. The most famous of English holy wells, though of no architectural interest.

ST LEONARD'S BRIDGE *see* LAUNCESTON

3020

ST LEVAN

11a St Levan. Not far from Land's End, but, in contrast to Sennen, in a sheltered position, nestling against a hillside, with the E parts half buried in it. The w tower is of only two stages, unbuttressed. The N side of the church with the N transept (note its narrow C13 window) shows earlier masonry than the granite of tower, s aisle, and s porch. The s aisle has six bays with octagonal piers and plain double-chamfered arches. At the time when the s aisle was built (C15), the N transept received two arches of the same design as the aisle arcade to screen it off against the nave. – FONT. An exceptional Norman type with a large circular bowl having a lower border of cable, an upper border of chip-carved saltire crosses, and four flat motifs of stars in circles on the sides. – ROOD SCREEN. The 31b base survives, two panels l. and two r. of the central opening. Each panel has three narrow uprights carved with a shield showing the same initials and symbols of the Passion as Cornish bench ends, and a long, narrow ornamented motif above, mainly foliage, but also two dragons standing on their tails. – BENCH ENDS. Some are old, and several of unusual, interesting designs, for example two profiles facing each other, two profiles turning away from each other, two fishes, two eagles, a St James *en face* with his pilgrim's hat, two jesters. Only one of them has Renaissance candelabra in its frame. The date is probably *c.*1535. – PULPIT. 1752, charming, solid oak panels with a little inlay work. – PLATE. Elizabethan Chalice and Paten by *WL* (*see* St Ives).

(HOLY WELL, ¼ m. S of the church, overlooking Porthchapel beach. A small, square structure, a single cell, with walls about 7 ft high is immediately adjacent to the spring. A flight of stone steps leads down to the cove. Information contributed by the Rev. P. H. Fryer.)

ST MABYN 0070

ST MABENA. A large, if not tall church, nave with two aisles both of C15 date, both of seven bays, the piers of standard Cornish granite design, the arches two-centred; their span is less in the chancel than in the nave (cf. Bodmin). The aisle windows are of three lights, of Cornish standard design. The E windows are of four lights, and that in the chancel of five. Original ceiled wagon roofs. The W tower is unbuttressed, of three stages, with a three-eighths polygonal NE stair-turret, not reaching up to the parapet. – FONT. Norman, of Purbeck table-top type, square, with eight flat blank niches with pointed heads. – STAINED GLASS. A few bits only. – PAINTING of the Bassano School: Deposition of Christ. – PLATE. A spectacular Hanap and Cover with cherub on top, 12 in. high and gorgeously decorated with leaves and incised birds. Dated 1576. – Other pieces of 1701, 1756, 1765.

COLQUITE. See p. 55.
HELLIGAN. See p. 81.
TREGARDEN. See p. 223.

ST MARTIN-BY-LOOE 2050
1 m. from East Looe

ST KEYNE AND ST MARTIN. Sufficient remains of the pre-Perp church to form some idea of its shape: Norman N door of four orders, with zigzag, etc., one narrow E.E. window uncovered towards the W end of the S wall, the walls of the transept chapels. The earliest recorded dedication is 1258. The two lower stages of the W tower are early C14 (diagonal buttresses, details of the W door), the rest of the tower with stair-turret in the SE corner is Perp, and now roughcast. The general impression of exterior and interior is Perp. Nave of three bays with S aisle and chancel of two narrower bays. Much variation in details such as piers and capital profiles. Most of the piers are Cornish standard, but with fillets between the shafts and the hollows. Some of the piers have simple decorated abaci; some have not. The ceiled wagon roofs are original. – FONT. Norman, with groups of four-petalled flowers (unusual) and a 'tree of life' on one side; considered by Henderson C15 imitation Norman. – ALTAR RAILS. First half of the C17. – Aisle PARCLOSE SCREEN. 1612, and interesting in its continuation of a basically Perp composition, with three ogee openings per section. – MONUMENTS. Tomb-chest to Phil. Maiowe † 1590, a flat slate relief of a figure in a handsome arched recess with intermittent ashlar rustication. – Walter Langdon and wife † 1667. By *Nich. Abraham*, 1678. An ambitious but a conservative work for its date. The figures face each other kneeling, with a prayer desk between. They are painted. Back wall with columns, broken pediment, and swags. – Many minor early C19 monuments.

ST MARTIN-IN-MENEAGE

ST MARTIN. A church of 1830 with the typical lancet windows of the period. The old tower (C15) was left standing: two-storeyed, unbuttressed, of rough granite, with heads projecting from the top cornice. The tower arch with its keystone is also old. – FONT. Norman, with corner shafts and rosettes in flat relief.

(TREMAYNE. Of *c.*1840, but parts C16 and even *c.*1300. Magnificent granite gatepiers, 15 ft high, capped by granite balls. GMT)

ST MARTIN'S *see* SCILLY ISLES

ST MARY'S *see* SCILLY ISLES

ST MAWES

Aesthetically the trefoil leaves of the three bastions of Henry VIII's St Mawes Castle stretching out on two levels to SW, SE, and NW from the taller circular centre give an impression of all-round symmetry and harmony of composition strikingly un-medieval and convincingly of the Renaissance. If one compares St Mawes with Pendennis, and with Deal, Walmer, and Camber in Kent and Sussex, all ingenious variations on the theme of the grouping of semicircular units, this impression is confirmed and enhanced. Yet these shapes were not devised for reasons of pleasure in geometrical play. They were considered by Henry VIII and his engineers (or *devisors*, as

they were called) the most up-to-date fortifications. The art of
defence had changed much since the Middle Ages owing to
the introduction of cannon and gunpowder. Low bastions
were now preferable to the high keeps and gatehouses of the
past. In England few monuments of the c16 exist, because
there was no warfare on land, and if Henry VIII had not, after
a ten-year truce had been concluded in 1538 between the
Emperor Charles V and the King of France, been rightly
afraid of an attack by Francis I instigated by the Pope, he
would not have set up his chain of castles along the south
coast. Their designers were probably foreigners (we know one
of them, *Stefan von Haschenperg*, from Moravia, not docu-
mentarily connected with the Cornish castles), and while their
work must have appeared wonderfully new and ingenious to
the English, it was in fact only moderately up-to-date. Round
bastions, as recommended by Dürer in his book on fortifications in 1525 and much used in Italy about and after 1500,
were just then being replaced in the most modern designs of
Francesco di Giorgio and Sammicheli by the angular bastion
to which the future belonged.

To the visitor today the lobed shape of the terraces overlooking Falmouth Bay (the middle one larger and lower than
the r. and l. ones) remains unforgettable, regardless of their
functional qualities or shortcomings. The decorative detail
also is of a high standard of craftsmanship: gargoyles, carved
coats of arms, and inscriptions. The latter were devised by
John Leland, the antiquary and chaplain to Henry VIII, and
carried out by masons familiar with the new Renaissance
fashion.

St Mawes Castle was begun in 1540 and completed in 1543.
It was approached by a drawbridge from the land side which
led into the first floor of the keep. Close to the entrance a
special staircase connected this floor with the octagonal upper
room and, higher still, the (modern) roof with a little (rebuilt)
watch-tower. From the staircase and three further, shorter
staircases the rampart walls of the bastions are reached, their
courtyards from the ground floor of the keep which was the
mess-room of the garrison (ceiling 1880). Below this in the
basement was the kitchen. The granite piers of this room as
well as some of the beams are original. The garrison, except at
moments of danger, varied from sixteen to one hundred.
Defence was by means of large cannon in the casements (with
smoke-vents) and in the courtyards of the bastions, and light

guns in socketed embrasures on the rampart walls of the
bastions (the square recesses are for keeping ammunition). In
the upper room of the keep are eight recesses for gunners, each
with an ammunition cupboard and a smoke-vent. The drawbridge could be commanded by musketry fire from cross-slits
in the NE wall of the keep.

Below the castle is a small Tudor 'blockhouse' with three
gun ports.

ST MAWGAN see MAWGAN-IN-PYDAR

₃₀₆₀
ST MELLION

ST MELLANUS. The S side clearly belongs to the C14, cf. the
(renewed) windows, Dec, just going Perp. Two PISCINAS
inside belong to the same building period. The N aisle of
regular granite blocks was added late in the C15, with piers of
Cornish granite standard with a little stylized decoration of the
abaci. The W tower of broad and short proportions is also of
regular granite blocks, in the usual three stages, with thin
corner buttresses. – PULPIT. Jacobean. – MONUMENTS. The
centre of interest of St Mellion church is the Coryton monuments, especially those to William Coryton † 1651 and wife,
and Sir William Coryton † 1711 and wife: two large, grand,
and utterly reactionary compositions. Their type, standing
solidly on the ground, with figures, life-size and kneeling
towards each other across a prayer desk, with double columns
flanking the figures, a coffer-vaulted arch above them, and
small figures and a coat of arms on the entablature and pediment, was in fashion about 1600. To find it used in Cornwall
in the 1650s may not surprise, but to find it still in 1711 goes
beyond belief. – Brass to Peter Coryton † 1551, with wife and
twenty-four children, of the usual design. – John Coryton
† 1803, with sarcophagus and urn, large and elegant. –
William Coryton, 1836 by *Thomas & Edward Gaffin*. – John
Tillie Coryton † 1843, the same composition as John Coryton.
RECTORY. Good solid early C19 with two symmetrical curved
bay windows.

₈₀₇₀
ST MERRYN

ST MERRYN. Of the early medieval church the ground floor of
the W tower (with a Norman arch into the nave), the nave, N

transept (E.E. deeply splayed E window and E.E. arch into the nave), and chancel masonry. The upper storeys of the tower later. Also C15 the S aisle, with an arcade of seven bays, the piers of Catacleuse stone but standard Cornish design and with four-centred arches. Wagon roof and standard three-light Perp tracery. – Three fragments of angel CORBELS, of Catacleuse stone, probably by the Master of St Endellion, one in the church, two by the churchyard gates. – Also by the same master the FONT, almost a copy of that at Padstow, but a little reduced in size and execution of figures. One has the impression that the master had been asked to make the same font at a lower price. – ROYAL ARMS. Plaster with strapwork decoration. – STOCKS, in the porch. – PLATE. Chalice and Paten by *W. Bartlett* of Exeter, that is first half of the C17, yet still completely Elizabethan in type; Patens by *Babbage*, 1740–1. – MONUMENT to John Michell and family † 1617, with seven kneeling figures; poor quality. – CURIOSUM. Board with a poem of instructions to bell-ringers (cf. St Minver).

HARLYN. Plain, Late Georgian stone house, restored. C18 Gothic interior. Older part on the S *c.*1400 with carving in Catacleuse stone (suggested by Sedding to come from the destroyed church of St Constantine).

TREVOSE HEAD LIGHTHOUSE. *See* p. 229.

HARLYN BAY IRON AGE CEMETERY, 1 m. NW. Five cists are now preserved on the site of a cemetery which originally consisted of over a hundred such burials. Each slate cist contained a crouched inhumation burial, in some cases two separated by a dividing slab. A number of the burials were accompanied by bronze brooches of Iberian type.

ST MEWAN   9050

ST MEWAN. The tower was intended to be tall and stately but was not continued above the second stage and finished off with battlements. It has buttresses set back from the angles and is built of regular granite blocks. The chancel has Norman windows. To the S aisle of five bays (same design as in the neighbouring St Stephen-in-Brannel) corresponds a N chancel aisle of three bays. The church was restored by *G. E. Street*, *c.*1851. – FONTS. Fragment of a Norman font, and in addition an octagonal C14 font with tracery panels, standing on the Norman base.

9040

ST MICHAEL CAERHAYS

ST MICHAEL. Of the original cruciform church some masonry on the N side, with the N transept, still exists. The N doorway has a Norman tympanum with lamb and cross (cf. Egloskerry), very minor. The S aisle is C15, the W tower of three stages, unbuttressed and unpinnacled. The S aisle is of two bays only, of standard Cornish design, with large horizontal leaves on the capitals of the responds. – FONT. Norman, circular, with large leaves in flat relief. – PISCINA, in the chancel. C14, with crocketed finials. – CORBEL, N side of the chancel: a C15 shield-holding angel. – COMMANDMENT TABLES. Of extremely pretty C19 glazed tiles. – HELMET AND SWORDS in the aisle (Trevanion Aisle); C15. – PLATE. Chalice and Paten by *Yeds* of Exeter, Elizabethan, and well shaped and decorated. – MONUMENTS. William Trevanion, 1769, with three plain urns and drapery from above. – Charlotte Trevanion, 1810, aged 27: the most interesting object in the church – Gothic, with a correct crocketed gable, *à la* Aymer de Valence in Westminster Abbey, but l. and r. of it two mourning putti of *Coade* stone, still entirely in the Baroque tradition. – Statue of Captain George Bettesworth, 1812, also by Mrs *Coade*'s firm.

62a CAERHAYES CASTLE. By *John Nash*. A very picturesque castellated mansion in a superb position, built in 1808 for J. B. Trevanion. The house overlooked a bay, with its lawns and clump of trees right to the edge of the cliff. Yet a serpentine lake was found necessary closer to the house. Its silhouette, with an asymmetrical composition of square and round towers and turrets, stands against ornamental trees and shrubs. The interior is in keeping with the exterior. Vaulted staircase at the end of a long gallery.

8040

ST MICHAEL PENKEVIL

ST MICHAEL. It is a great pity that this church was rebuilt in the C19 (by *Street*, 1863–5); for from the sadly tidied-up fragments which remain, it must have been one of the most interesting churches in Cornwall. Street's church is quite strong in itself, especially externally, but its interest *qua* C19 is very much less than that of the original church must have been *qua* C13 and C14. The following parts remain, although, it seems, only in their general form. As far as details are concerned, not a square inch of surface is not tooled up. In the N and S transepts SEPULCHRAL NICHES with SEDILIA as one composition, the sedilia with cinquefoil heads and hoodmoulds on heads as label-stops, all of noble, classical C13 proportions. In the S transept there are two seats and a PISCINA, in the N transept three seats. The architectural detail tallies perfectly with the surviving dedication stone (chancel, N side) of 1261, and is in no way provincial.* Then there are two REREDOSES of transept altars, on the S c.1300, on the N C15, with flamboyant detail. Behind them are tiny cells (to house valuables, suggested Cox). In the tower on the upper floor is another altar, a very old tradition in churches dedicated to St Michael. Why the church should have been so richly furnished is not clear. It was made into an Archpresbytery with four chaplains, that is a kind of College, in 1319. – ALTAR SLAB on the N transept altar, originally on the floor of the S transept. – MONUMENTS. Two coffin slabs with foliated crosses; C13. – Brass to John Trenowith † 1497, biggish and good. – Brass to John Trembras, M.A., parson, 1515, in academic robes. – Unimportant brasses of 1619, 1622, and 1634. – Hugh Boscawen † 1659, stiffly reclining on his elbow with a book in his hand against a background with columns. – Admiral Boscawen, signed by *Rysbrack*, 1763, designed by *Adam*; just a bust between trophies against the usual pyramid. – Edward Hugh Boscawen † 1774, by *Nollekens*; simple medallion. – The Hon. Frances Boscawen † 1774, who died 'at the Spa in Germany', also by *Nollekens*; just inscription and urn in relief. The same composition is exactly repeated for Elizabeth Ann, Viscountess Falmouth, † 1783 (by *Nollekens*), George Evelyn Boscawen † 1808 (by *Isbell* of Truro), Edward Boscawen, Earl of Falmouth, † 1841 (by *Pearce* of Truro), and two others. The family has apparently not had great confidence in monumental memorials.

ST MICHAEL'S MOUNT *5020*

The Mount is supposed to be the Ictis of the Mediterranean tin-traders and the seat of Cormoran the Giant. Tradition 47

---

* But Street dated the transepts early C14, and pointed out that their walls are not bonded with the nave walls and that the S transept arch contains a re-used part of a C13 doorway. The enlargement is perhaps connected with a petition by Sir John de Trejagu in 1319 in which he said he had repaired the church and founded four chantries in it. (On the date 1319, *see* below.) Information received from Mr W. J. C. Rickard.)

says that St Keynes and her nephew Caradoc visited it in the
c6, and the *Itinerarium* of William of Worcester records for
c.710 a vision of St Michael appearing on the summit of the
Mount, as he had done before at the Italian sanctuary of
Monte San Gargano.* A Celtic monastery is said to have
existed from the c8 to the c11. It was granted by Edward the
Confessor before 1050 to the abbey of Mont-Saint-Michel
in Normandy for a cell of Benedictine monks to be established, but this does not appear to have materialized until
c.1087–91.‡ During the intervening years a few Celtic monks
probably remained in occupation, in spite of the fact that the
Norman abbey then owned their lands. Between 1135 and
c.1150, Bernard, abbot of Mont-Saint-Michel, built a monastery for a prior and twelve Benedictine monks. Of the buildings of the c11 a rock chamber below the choir of the chapel
may survive which was found in 1720 and cannot now be
examined. The walls of the former refectory may be c12. The
community on the Mount was suppressed in 1425 as alien
and Henry VI gave the property to his favourite Brigittine
nuns, of Syon, near London. After the Reformation it
belonged to the kings, who had their appointed governors
there. In the c17 it changed hands three times, first to the
Earls of Salisbury, then to Francis Basset of Tehidy, and
finally c.1660 to the St Aubyns.

If the present appearance of the Mount is as spectacular
and picturesque as it is, this is due in equal parts to nature
and to a member of the St Aubyn family, *Piers St Aubyn*
who chose architecture as a profession and whose hand is
discernible, not always happily, in many of the old churches
of the county.

The Mount is approached by a causeway flooded at high
tide. The JETTY and PIER date from 1824 and replace older
structures. The first was built in 1427 by the chaplain
appointed by the Brigittines. The rock received its sub-
tropical planting only in the late c19; before then it was
bare. In the grounds on the w side is a CROSS of odd design
with a circular head on which is an equal-armed cross.
Below this a small Crucifixus in a circular recess, and lower
still a Latin cross in relief.

The buildings are entered from the w by a c15 archway
with the (later) St Aubyn arms above. The archway leads

* Information given to me by D. J. Valleau.
‡ The date favoured by Mr R. Neville Hadcock.

to the N terrace (CROSS HEAD with good figure sculpture and CORBEL, late medieval) extending alongside the CHAPEL. This is a much restored building of late C14 date with C15 windows and a crossing tower, on the top of which is a five-sided BEACON with transom and basin-shaped floor, known as St Michael's Chair. Behind the altar a series of small ALABASTERS, six Flemish of indifferent quality and three English (Mass of St Gregory, Head of St John, Pilate washing his hands). – ORGAN. Late C17, with Gothic Revival screen below. – CHANDELIER. Brass, C15, Flemish, of the type which so often appears in Early Flemish paintings. – PLATE. Good Chalice by *FR*, 1571–2; seven richly twisted and decorated foreign candlesticks, given at various times.

The original monastic buildings stood to the W and S of the chapel. Among them the main survival is the REFECTORY, now Chevy Chase Room, with medieval walls, a roof which may be C15, a pretty plaster frieze of 1641 (with bull-baiting, boar-hunting, hare and hounds, stag-hunting, and ostrich-hunting), and Gothick dado and doors. The latter belong to the period of Sir John St Aubyn, who died in 1744 and remodelled the Lady Chapel, an isolated structure SE of the chapel (founded in 1463 and completed before 1500), into DRAWING ROOM and BOUDOIR. Their detail is of the most charming pre-Strawberry-Hill Rococo-Gothic with stucco vaults and pretty fireplaces. Paintings by *Gainsborough*, *Zoffany*, *Opie* (a friend of the 5th Baronet), etc. Piers St Aubyn added a portion of the S court in 1850 and the SE wing in 1875–8. It contains three bedroom floors below the living room, a sight from some positions reminiscent of Mount Athos or Tibetan monasteries. The NW wing finally was erected as late as 1927.

ST MINVER

9070

ST MENEFREDA. The church has a spire, a rare thing in Cornwall. It is octagonal (rebuilt in the C19), with plain broaches at the corners and tall narrow gabled dormers in the sides between. Inside, the N arcade is early C13; short, thick, octagonal piers, with the plainest of capitals, and double-chamfered, two-centred arches. The tower arch is similar. The N aisle itself is uncommonly narrow and has a lean-to roof. The S aisle is of seven bays, Cornish granite

standard, but with two-centred arches. Wagon roof in the
s porch. – FONT. Octagonal, C15, with tracery panels. –
ROOD SCREEN. Partly preserved and set into the tower arch.
Each panel has two lights, two form one arch; the tracery is Perp.
– Many good BENCH ENDS in the nave, probably of *c.*1530–40,
all carved with secular subjects, with a strong Italian Re-
naissance flavour (G. W. Copeland). – COMMUNION RAILS.
C17, of plain balusters. – Against the w wall a NORMAN
CAPITAL found in 1927. It has three scallops, the crescents
ornamented as, for example, at St David's and in Cornwall at
St Germans and St Teath. – STAINED GLASS. E window
of the s aisle by *O'Connor*, London, 1870; very rich in the
German Renaissance way, plenty of colour, and no William
Morris restraint yet. – MONUMENTS. Brass to Roger Opy
† 1517, a small figure with a long scroll upwards from his
head. – Epitaph to John Roe † 1657, still kneeling in profile,
though with more realism and courtliness than fifty years
before. – CURIOSUM. Board with painted figures of bell-
ringers and a long rhyme for them. The board is dated 1783.
THE RUMPS PROMONTORY FORT. Three lines of ramparts
and ditches cut off a promontory of approximately 6 acres. A
single entrance occurs in the middle of the line of the defences.
A number of hut platforms are visible in the interior. Excavations so far suggest two periods of construction, one
represented by the outermost rampart, the second by the two
further banks and ditches behind it. The site has produced
wheel-turned Iron Age C pottery of the C1 B.C.

1060
ST NECTAN
w of Boconnoc

ST NECTAN. Unusual-looking in more than one way: for one
thing it has its tower at the w end of the N aisle, and secondly
that tower was damaged in the Civil War, so that now only its
ground floor is left, with buttresses set back from the angles.
Two Dec E windows and a contemporary doorway to the s
porch. The rest Perp. Entering the church, there is another
surprise. The piers are iron, dating back to the restoration of
1825. At the same time the N aisle was built, surprisingly
correctly. – FONT. The bowl seems old, but has no features to
help in dating. – PISCINA. C13, with two amazingly primitive
faces as label-stops.

ST NEOT

ST ANIETUS. The village lies at the bend of a valley and the church is consciously so designed as to show its most spectacular side to those arriving up the valley. The plan is Cornish standard, but in the exterior unusual stress is placed on the s aisle and s porch, both built of large, regular granite blocks. The porch by the addition of an upper storey becomes part of the battlemented show side, with its pinnacles on the buttresses. The oldest part of the church is the w tower, with thick diagonal buttresses and Dec windows. The rest (except for part of the chancel walls with an ogee-headed recess, perhaps an Easter Sepulchre?) is Perp, seven bays (N, because of the ogee recess, six and a half) with N and s aisles. Tall piers of standard pattern, capitals sketchily ornamented, arches four-centred. The windows are C15, all of four lights, with the exception of the s aisle E window, which has five. s aisle of *c.*1425, N aisle straight-headed, *c.*1520. The wagon roof of the s aisle is original, with shield-bearing angels along the wall plate. The s porch has a remarkable stone tunnel-vault with heavy ribs forming a purely geometrical repeating pattern; five bosses, the central one decorated with four faces. The ground floor of the tower also has a stone vault, of pointed tunnel shape with transverse arches (unique in Cornwall). Squint from the E end of the N aisle into the chancel. – FONT. C15 bowl on C13 shaft, the E side in its design still derived from the Egloshayle type. – MONUMENTS. William Bere and family, kneeling figures, 1610, slate. – The chief importance of the church, however, is its C15 and early C16 STAINED GLASS, which, although much restored and renewed *c.*1830 by *John Hedgeland*, gives an all too rare impression of the original colour character of Perp churches. One must have been inside St Neot in sunshine as well as dull weather to appreciate how the stone changes its hues as the colours of the windows are strongly or softly reflected on it. There are fifteen windows to be looked at with about half their glass old. Starting at the w end of the s aisle, the w window is by *Hedgeland*. The glass of the sixth window from the E, the one close to the s porch, was originally in the E window of the chancel. In the tracery, the Annunciation; in the four main lights St Paul, St Peter, Christ as King, St James; arms and scrolls below referring to the Tubbe and Calway families. – Fifth window from the E (Calway Window, glass originally at the E end of the N aisle): very renewed. In the tracery Resurrection; below St Lalluwy, St German, St John, St Stephen. At the bottom the Calway family and a priest, probably Robert Tubbe, vicar from 1508 to 1544, an uncle of a son-in-law of John Calway. – Fourth window from the E: four Evangelists; the inscription mentions John Mutton as donor. – Third window from the E (Martyn Window): Virgin and Child, Rood, St John and St Stephen; below the Martyn (?) family. – Second window from the E (Borlase Window): St Neot, St Leonard, St Katherine; below, Nicholas Borlase and family. – First window from the E: story of Noah, from his cutting down trees for making the Ark to his drunkenness and death; bottom part much renewed. – s aisle E window. In the tracery the Orders of Angels. Below the Story of the Creation from the beginning to God commanding the making of the Ark. – Chancel E window: Last Supper, by *Hedgeland*, after a German woodcut. – N aisle E window (Acts Window) by *Hedgeland*. – N aisle, first window from E (Redemption Window), by *Hedgeland*. – Second window from E (Harys Window), St John, St Gregory the Great, St Leonard, St Andrew; below the Harys family. – Third window from the E (Wives Window), given by the wives from the w part of the parish in 1523: St Mabena, Our Lady of Pity, Christ, St Mewbred of Cardinham. Below, twenty of the wives. – Fourth window from the E (Young Women's Window), given by the 'Sisters' in 1529. Bishops,* for example St Cleer (second), St Manacus of Lanreath (third), God with Souls in his lap. – Fifth window from the E (St Neot Window), given by the young men of the parish: Story of St Neot, iconographically interesting with its wealth of detail (cf. Canon Doble's pamphlet). – N aisle w window (the glass originally in the s aisle): Legend of St George; in especially good condition. – CROSS SHAFT in the churchyard, probably C10, Hiberno-Saxon with exceptionally elaborate interlace work.

BRIDGE. C18, with an elegant arch of 16 ft span.

CROSS on Temple Moor with interlace work, stylized leaf scrolls, and also characteristically Scandinavian scrolls of a special type usual in the early C11 in southern England (cf. Padstow).

PANTERSBRIDGE (Warleggan river), 1½ m. w. C15, granite, of two pointed arches with two rings of thin voussoirs (cf. Lostwithiel).

* The first figure on the l. is said to be St Patrick, a local saint from Plymouth.

TREVERBYN OLD BRIDGE (Fowey river). Crossing two arms
of the river. An indulgence of 1412 probably refers to it (cf.
Staverton, Devon). Two pointed arches plus a third one
now covered by a flat-topped, straight-sided arch.

LEWARNE. *See* p. 101.

ST NEWLYN EAST   *8050*

ST NEWLINA. Norman masonry of chancel and N transept
(with re-used Norman W window). Re-dedication 1259. C15
S aisle of six bays of Cornish standard design plus two lower,
two-centred ones for the chancel, as at Bodmin. The chancel
aisle must be C14, according to this arcade and the PISCINA
next to its altar. Also in the C15 the N transept was separated
from the nave by two standard arcades, and a S porch was
built. This is castellated and (cf. the staircase-turret) was
meant to have an upper chamber as at Bodmin. The N
doorway is C14. The W tower (C15) is of local stone, in three
stages, with buttresses set back from the angles and stopping
at the second stage. – FONT. Norman, of the rich Bodmin
type, with angel faces at the corners, and intertwined floriated
scrolls above stylized lilies on the four sides. – ROOD SCREEN.
A fragment has been re-used in the parclose screen between
chancel and S chancel aisle. – BENCH ENDS. Many, of Cornish
standard, eight with beasts. – ROYAL ARMS. Plaster, with
strapwork decoration. – STAINED GLASS. The E window of
the N transept by *Kempe*, 1904. – MONUMENT to Lady
Margaret Arundell † 1691; simple, but with her bust at the
top in an open segmental pediment.

(At CARGOLL, *c*.¾ m. from the church, a good C15 TITHE
BARN with one of the best timber roofs visible in Cornwall:
base-cruck principals alternating with a curious half-cruck
which supports the main, square-set, purlin. J. T. Smith)

TRERICE. *See* p. 227.

ST PETROC *see* LITTLE PETHERICK

ST PINNOCK   *2060*

ST PYNNOCHUS. A church of little importance. The best individual thing to look at is the FONT, Norman, of an un-
common type, with corner heads and arms supporting the
heavy, wide, square top. Otherwise there is a W tower of three

stages with a three-eighths NE stair-turret, S porch and S transept, and N aisle with a standard granite four-bay arcade. Old timber in the wagon roofs.

ST PIRAN'S ORATORY AND CHURCH

There is something of great historical poignancy about the little oratory of St Piran, lost in the Penhale Sands. It had to be abandoned as early as the C11, because of the movement of the dunes. It possessed a pitched roof with E and W gables, only one small window (not splayed inside) on the S, a stone seat running all round, and an altar with canopy. Its date is C6 or C7, the earliest church or chapel in the south-west of England, and a memorial to the christianization of Cornwall. St Piran is believed to have been a disciple of St Patrick, and the building technique with coarse clay instead of mortar corresponds indeed to what is found in Celtic chapels and cells in Ireland. The oratory is 29½ by 16½ by 19 ft in size, of granite, porphyry, slate, and quartz rubble, and now sheltered in a special building; thus it has none of the visual appeal of early Irish architecture.

In the C11 a new church was built further inland, but now also surrounded far and wide by the dunes. This has been excavated and shows the plan of a typical Cornish church, with N wall and N transept still in their early stage, but on the S an aisle and transept added in 1462. By the church stands now as a signpost an unornamented CROSS with a circular head. The head is of the four-holed type, but one of the holes is not pierced right through. The cross appears to be mentioned in 960. The medieval church in its turn was also engulfed by the sands, and so in 1804 a new church was built at Lambourne, taking over the ancient name of St Piran in Sabulo; *see* Perranzabuloe.

ST SAMSON *see* GOLANT

ST STEPHEN-BY-LAUNCESTON
1½ m. N of Launceston

ST STEPHEN. The mother-church of Launceston, consecrated in 1259. The date is too late to refer to the few Norman remains (traces of round-headed arches in the transepts) and too early for the nave arcade, which is of a type occurring in Cornwall between *c.*1325 and 1425 (cf. St Veep, Stoke

Climsland, Callington) with square piers to which demi-shafts are attached, and plain, double-chamfered arches. The church consists of a nave of four bays, battlemented s aisle, N transept, battlemented N chancel chapel, two-storeyed s porch, and W tower. Outer walls and tower walls of large even granite blocks. The tower (early C16; MHLG) of the type with buttresses set back from the angles. Pinnacles in relief at the top of the buttresses. The windows Perp. – FONT. Simple Norman. – Also Norman the fragmentary SCULPTURE outside the E wall: seated Saviour, and Virgin and Child probably from an Adoration of the Magi, 2 ft 3 in. and 2 ft 9 in. high. – Of the old ROOD SCREEN only one pillar left. – PLATE. Chalice and Paten by *Jons* of Exeter, 1576. – MONUMENTS. Incised slab with cross; 1528. – Two slate slabs: 1631, 1675.

ST STEPHEN-BY-SALTASH   *4050*

ST STEPHEN. Over a mile outside Saltash, yet until 1881 the parish church of Saltash, as St Martin was the parish church of Looe, and Lanteglos of Camelford. The tower stands N of the W end of the nave, forming the W end of an obviously later N aisle. It is tall, three-staged, with buttresses set back from the angles and a stair-turret on a three-eighths plan rising to the height of the pinnacles.* The exterior of the body of the church is Perp, except that at the E end joints are visible showing that the chancel was there before both aisles. The aisles are not of the same date, though both C15. The piers are both of standard section, but the capitals and the mouldings of the arches differ characteristically. They show the N arcade to be older than the s arcade. The aisle windows are large, and the interior with its present glass is rather over-lighted. The ceiled wagon roofs are preserved, also in the shallow s porch, which, with its elaborate jambs and diagonal buttresses, is quite a decorative piece. – FONT. Large, Norman, on five supports, with busts at the corners and trees of life and animals on the sides (Bodmin type). – PLATE. Gilt Chalice by *Affabel Partridge*, 1573–4; Paten on foot and Flagon of 1775–6. – MONUMENTS. Very stiffly semi-reclining woman in a flat niche, *c.*1600–20. – W. Hitchens with wife and ten children,

---

* Mr G. W. Copeland has pointed out to me that the base of the tower seems earlier than the rest, perhaps late C12, and that the pinnacles seem to be modern. Perhaps they were added by *G. Fellows Prynne*, who restored the tower and W end in 1895.

tomb-chest with large elaborate slate top, and back plates; Elizabethan. Next to it G. Wadham † 1606 and wife (Hitchens's daughter). The corner position of the two monuments is due to C19 restorations. – An *Isbell* monument of 1806 in the N tower arch. – CROSS, in the Rectory garden. Gothic, with Crucifixion and Madonna.

ST STEPHEN-IN-BRANNEL

9050

ST STEPHEN. A big church, entirely of granite outside, with two aisles of eight bays (standard piers) and a stately W tower of regular granite blocks, three-storeyed, with buttresses leaving the corners free. The date of the N aisle, 1425, is known. Good large Perp windows, especially at the E end. A Norman church preceded the present one. Its simple S door survives, after alterations. It has a very plain design with round knobs on the voussoirs. – FONT. Late Norman, on five supports with C13-looking bases, the bowl with demi-figures at the corners (two with arms, two bearded), and between them trees of life, two facing animals, etc. (Bodmin type). – COMMUNION RAIL. Early C17.

(TREVEAR. An early C17 L-shaped house built round a courtyard with an arched stone gateway. Three-light windows with mullions and hoodmoulds. Octagonal stone chimneys: rare in Cornwall. V. M. and F. J. Chesher).

ST TEATH

0080

ST TETHA VIRGIN. A large church with a wide nave and two aisles. Its Norman predecessor is still clearly recognizable. The lower part of the granite W tower with a stair-turret of three-eighths plan belongs to it, the tower arch to the nave, the beginning of the S arcade, and the first blocked bay of the N arcade. The C15 aisles are of six bays with piers of standard granite design, plain capitals, and plain four-centred arches. The aisle windows are of three lights, the E window of the S aisle of five lights. In the two easternmost windows on the N side are niches with ogee heads, probably for images. The aisles have ceiled wagon roofs. – PULPIT dated 1630. – A few bits of old GLASS in the S aisle windows, a few BENCH ENDS with shields in the aisles, Jacobean panels incorporated into the CHOIR STALLS. – Painted Jacobean ALMSBOX. – CROSS in the churchyard, 13 ft high and much restored. Little is recognizable of the original interlace ornament, but there are good leaf scrolls on the narrow sides. – MONUMENT to a priest, C14, badly preserved, with angels l. and r. of the head.

ST TUDY

ST TUDIUS. A large church with a tall three-stage, unbuttressed tower and a proud E end where the large Perp windows of nave and aisles with four and five lights appear. The S aisle accompanies nave and chancel the whole way, with six bays, the N aisle only for the three E bays. The arcades are identical, of granite standard, the windows are of three lights, mostly with standard Cornish Perp tracery. The wagon roofs are original. – FONT. Norman, of Purbeck table-top type, square, the blank niches on one side in two tiers (cf. St Mabyn, Poughill, etc.). – Also a relic of the Norman church is a primitively carved figure, probably from a corbel table. It was found in 1932. – In the porch is a pre-Norman granite COPED STONE from the churchyard, coffin- or hobgack-shaped, blind arcading on the sides, interlaced cable, and foliage scrolls on the top (cf. Lanivet, St Buryan, Phillack). These coped stones were gravestones. – STAINED GLASS. Tiny fragments in the tracery of the S aisle E window. – TILING of the altar surround by *Powell & Sons*, 1874. – PAINTING. Last Supper, late C16 Flemish. – PLATE. Chalice by *IW*, dated 1650–1, a rare date to find on church plate. Goblet shape with baluster stem. Also a pewter Flagon with arms of Jane Amydas † 1597. – MONUMENTS. Many, all of minor importance, some slate plates with kneeling figures: 1564, 1597, etc. The motif of two kneeling figures facing each other with a prayer desk between and small figures of kneeling children below is still preserved in the ambitious monument to Anthony Nicholls † 1659: the main figures are lifesize, limestone, the architecture of the monument grey marble.

TREMEER. Rebuilt in 1798. Contains a fine rough-hewn Elizabethan granite fireplace. GMT)

TINTEN. See p. 221.

ST VEEP

ST VEPUS. Of the original cruciform plan nothing remains. A dedication date is recorded (1336), and much of the present church may well refer to it. The W tower has thick angle buttresses, two stages, and no pinnacles. The tower arch towards the nave is steep, two-centred, and unmoulded. The s aisle is separated from the nave by an arcade whose piers have four demi-shafts and four sharply keeled minor shafts between (cf. Poughill). The capitals are heavily moulded, the first four arches steeply pointed. On the N side piers with four major and four minor shafts (cf. St Columb Minor, St Issey, etc.). They have the large horizontal leaf decoration of Devonshire. Contemporary the s porch, the wall plates of the wagon roofs, and most of the (renewed) windows. Squint from N chancel aisle to chancel. – FONT. C15. – ALTAR STONE. Marble, with consecration crosses. – PULPIT. Thick brackets of the second half of the C17 attached to a C19 pulpit. – BENCH ENDS. Only a few. – PLATE. Chalice and Paten of 1576; Paten by *Wilmott*, 1738–9; Flagon by *Sanders*, 1737–8. – MONUMENT. Slate plate to Nicholas Courtenay, 1589.

ST WENN

9060

ST WENNA. Two-stage (originally three-stage) w tower of granite with buttresses set back from the angles and quatrefoil decoration of the plinth. Nave and N and s aisles of three bays, the piers of four thick and four thinner attached shafts, capitals with large horizontal leaves, four-centred arches. – FONT. Norman, exactly as at Mawgan-in-Pydar and St Columb Minor (Bodmin type). – GLASS. The E window, painted grisaille, with the Good Shepherd in the centre, 1873 by *Powell & Sons*. – By the same firm the REREDOS of tile and mosaic.

ST WINNOW

1050

ST WINNOW. Exquisitely situated, with vicarage and farm, quite on its own, under old trees by the wide river Fowey, about 3 m. s of Lostwithiel. In its architectural detail there is not much to arrest attention. The N side contains Norman remains, suggesting the usual cruciform plan. The Norman transept arch was reconstructed in the C13: cf. the window w of it. Otherwise the church is Cornish Perp standard, with nave and chancel, s aisle of six bays, s porch, w tower. The tower is also standard, with buttresses leaving the corners free, though reaching very close to them. It has no pinnacles. The piers are granite and have the usual Cornish profile and capitals with ornamental carving. The wagon roofs have old carving. c16 buildings belonging to the barton of St Winnow still form a handsome group along the N side of the church. – FONT of granite with barbaric Perp carving of angels holding hands (cf. Treslothan, St Anthony-in-Meneage, with the same inscription). – BENCH ENDS. Partly the usual Cornish Perp type, partly c.1525–35 (cf. Laneast, Davidstow, Minster, Forrabury), partly Elizabethan. Amongst the unusual motifs a man 29b drinking, a St Catherine's Wheel. – Jacobean ALTAR TABLE and later c17 PULPIT (on short bulbous legs). – STAINED GLASS in the chancel E window: Crucifixion. – More important in the S aisle E window, c15 and early c16, in the original arrangement: kneeling figures, rows of standing saints, coats of arms (for example Courtenay, Kayle of Ethy, for whom the S aisle was built as a chantry). – ROOD SCREEN (well restored in 1907 by *E. H. Sedding*). One of the few surviving in Cornwall. The nave part is essentially original, except for coving and cornice. The base has four tall narrow panels for each section, carved with individual stylized flowers or leaves above each other instead of the undulating scrolls of, for example, Morwenstow and St Buryan. – PLATE. Chalice and Paten by *Jons* of Exter, 1574, only the stem original: other pieces of 1695, 1801. – MONUMENT. Slate to William Sawle † 1651, of pretty curved shape.

SALTASH 4050

The thrill of Saltash is the excessive contrast between the small scale and the variety of small shapes of the fishing town winding along the waterside and climbing up the steep hill, and the sheer height of the granite piers supporting the two by no means elegant arches of *Brunel*'s ROYAL ALBERT BRIDGE. The bridge 5 was an engineering feat for its date: 1857–9. It is a combined suspension and arched bridge. The technical reason for the curious sausage-shaped tubular arches is that their outward thrust on to the abutments counteracts the inward drag of the chains. The oval section of the arches increases their stiffness and gives enough width for the roadway between the vertical chains hanging from the arches: not a handsome, but a safe and sound solution. The high granite shafts on the other hand, standing out from the c16 houses (one has a date 1584) down in Tamar Street and the late c17 and c18 houses up Fore Street Hill, are a superb effect in the Doré sense. The charter of Saltash goes back to the C13, but (as happened so often in Cornwall) the town possessed no parish church before the C19. The church of Saltash was St Stephen's, over a mile out, just as Egloshayle was the church of Wadebridge and St Martin's of Looe.

ST NICHOLAS. Only a chapel of ease until 1881, yet the chapel must go right back to the earliest times of the town, for the tower is Norman, unbuttressed and adjoining the former N transept, that is not placed at the W end (cf. Blisland, St Enodoc), the blocked S door is Norman, and most of the masonry of the chancel with two windows, nave, S transept (including the transept arch), and W wall is Norman too. In the early C14 a N chancel chapel was added (the arcade is simply double-chamfered, and the responds have moulded capitals). Then at the usual time, in the C15, came a N nave aisle of five bays with a Cornish standard arcade and a good wagon roof. The wagon roof of the nave dates from the same time, and also the five-light E window of the chancel. A squint connects S transept and chancel. – FONT. Probably Norman, of an unusual vague shape, with corner ribs and a centre rib on each side; possibly of domestic origin. – PLATE. A good set: Hanap with repoussé work, with York and Lancaster roses on the bowl, 1608–9; Chalice with stem of the same date and Paten belonging to it; two Flagons by *AK*, 1695–6; Paten on foot by *Pentecost Symonds*, 1715–16. – MONUMENT. John and James Drew and J. W. Drew, two Captains and one Acting Lieutenant, drowned in 1798 and 1799, with three portrait medallions against the usual pyramid and reliefs of shipwrecks.

TOWN HALL, alongside the church. Built *c.*1780, with an open ground floor on Tuscan columns; now much altered.

(STOKETON. Of *c.*1770. Gothic Revival, with pointed sash windows. Cf. Restormel House, but smaller. GMT)

(ERTH BARTON, about 4 m. SW of Saltash. Late C16 house with porch and mullioned windows. C14 chapel, now a barn, with a four-centred arch; some remains of WALL PAINTINGS. Information from G. W. Copeland and GMT.)

BURRELL HOUSE. *See* p. 48.

HATT. *See* p. 80.

TREMATON CASTLE. *See* p. 225.

SAMSON *see* SCILLY ISLES

SANCREED

ST SANCREDUS. All granite, with unbuttressed W tower of two stages and N transept with narrow windows. C15 S aisle of five bays, standard Cornish granite design. Of the same date the good five-light E window of the chancel. The N transept is screened off from the nave by two arches. Old wagon roof in the S porch. – FONT. Type of St Ives, with four angels holding shields, C15, granite. – ROOD SCREEN. Old panels of the base with specially entertaining carvings: a jester blows a trumpet, with a snake winding up it, a goat among thistles, an owl, the *signum triciput*, etc. – PLATE. Chalice by *WL* (*see* St Ives), very nice, dated 1576; other pieces by *Elston* (1725–6), *Babbage* (1737–8), *Wight* (1772–3). – Two CROSSES in the churchyard, both among the important crosses of Cornwall, both Hiberno-Saxon in style, and both with exactly the same unusual shape of the heads, and a figure of the Crucifixus on one side of the head. Otherwise one of the two has the best preserved and most interesting incised decoration amongst crosses in the county (note the unique design of a lily in a vase), the other has sumptuous interlace work including on the side a biting beast (that is, probably C10) and on another a key pattern. Beast and interlace very similar to Lanherne, Mawgan-in-Pydar. The inscription there, RUHOL, also appears at Sancreed as RUNHO. Inscription on the other Sancreed cross: INCX X and NI † FILIUS in surprisingly early-looking lettering.

SANCREED WELL and BAPTISTERY, about ⅓ m. WSW of the church. The remains of a baptistery, and an exceptionally interesting well. They stand in trees in a field near the road to Grumble. Dr Athelstane Hill)

BRANE MEGALITHIC TOMB, 2¾ m. SE of St Just. An entrance grave 7 ft 6 in. long lying within a small round barrow 15 ft in diameter and 6 ft high, revetted with a substantial kerb.

CARN EUNY IRON AGE SETTLEMENT, 1¼ m. W of Sancreed. Excavation has shown the earliest structures on this site to be a series of round timber and turf huts with which was associated a fogou. This is approached by a stone-lined passage leading to a lintelled gallery having a total length of 66 ft. Two subsidiary passages lead off from the principal chamber on the N side. The later phases of occupation on the site consist of a series of oval and circular stone-built houses some of which appear to be of courtyard type. One of these houses has produced Iron Age pottery of the C1 B.C.

SCILLY ISLES*

The islands are notable for a concentration of megalithic 'entrance graves', *c.* 2000–1000 B.C., of a culture probably derived from Brittany which has left other traces in West Cornwall and Co. Waterford in Eire. Of 250 chambered tombs in England and Wales, 50 are on these islands. Simple structures of granite walls, with traces now and then of mortar roofed with granite slabs, and enclosed originally in cairns. In contrast to this large quantity of Bronze Age remains, very little remains of the Iron Age, except for a few earthworks, and very little of the time of the Roman occupation. For the Dark Age see St Helen's, for the Middle Ages Tresco. The islands were garrisoned from the C16; hence there are good examples of military architecture on Tresco and St Mary's.

*9010
inset*

ARTHUR

CHAMBERED TOMBS. On the highest point of Great Arthur is an entrance grave 12 ft long set in a round barrow 24 ft in diameter surrounded by a double kerb. On Middle Arthur are two entrance graves, and on Little Arthur five entrance graves in a line running NW–SE.

*8010
inset*

BRYHER

ALL SAINTS. 1742, rebuilt and enlarged in 1822.
CHAMBERED TOMB, on Samson Hill. A round barrow, 20 ft in diameter, within which is an entrance grave 19 ft long.
ROUND BARROWS. On Shipman Head Down are numerous round barrows, at least three of which cover megalithic tombs of entrance grave form.

*8000
inset*

GUGH

At the N end of the island on Kittern Hill are ten ROUND BARROWS, six of which contain megalithic tombs. Two further megalithic tombs occur on the S hill of the island.

*9010
inset*

HUGH TOWN

The island capital. The long principal street contains many small houses of the late C18 and early C19, excellently built of

* Much of this description of monuments on the Scilly Isles was contributed by Geoffrey Grigson.

island granite, left plain or plastered. Their low elevation is suited to the exposure of the island. Often admirable in severe simplicity of design and in detail (bay and bow windows, iron railings, trellis work, porches, door panelling), they are miniatures with a local accent of the Cornish town architecture of their time. For the church, *see* St Mary's.

ST AGNES

8000 inset

CHURCH. Built *c.*1845. Pleasant, though plain interior with woodwork in white and fawn and black.

The well-proportioned former LIGHTHOUSE, gleaming with its maritime whitewash, was built in 1680.

ST HELEN'S

9010 inset

ST ILLID or ELIDIUS. A medieval church of which only a little walling is left. It originally had nave, chancel, and N aisle. Traces around of the cells, one circular, the others rectangular, and the boundary wall of a Celtic monastery probably of the c6.

ST MARTIN'S

9010 inset

The outstanding monument is the DAY MARK, a conical tower, banded red and white, of 1683. CHURCH of 1867–8. Dissenting CHAPEL of *c.*1845, with gallery and white, fawn, and black woodwork, as in the church on St Agnes.

At the S end of the island, on Cruthers Hill, are four ROUND BARROWS, the largest 27 ft in diameter. Three of these barrows cover megalithic chambers.

ST MARY'S

9010 inset

The OLD CHURCH is a restored fragment of the original nave divided from a side chapel by a round-headed arch.

The NEW CHURCH, Hugh Town, is a plain structure of 1835, containing above the doorway inside a wooden lion, coloured and gilded, from the flagship of Sir Cloudesley Shovel, wrecked in 1707.

CASTLE OF ENNOR (Old Town) was the chief secular residence on the islands. The scanty remains of walls belong to the c13 or c14.

STAR CASTLE above the Hugh Town isthmus was built in 1593–4 by the surveyor *Robert Adams*. It consists of a building in the shape of an eight-pointed star which housed the garrison, and a thick stone rampart, also eight-pointed, with an external batter. Beyond is a rock-cut ditch. There are original gun-embrasures in the parapet of the rampart, now blocked. Also an C18 bellcote. The inner building has a basement and two upper storeys. On the first floor a masonry pier supports the radial joists and houses the fireplaces.

HARRY'S WALLS was begun about fifty years before Star Castle. It was originally square with four angle bastions.

BUZZA HILL. A small closed chamber, 10 ft long, set at the centre of a round cairn some 48 ft in diameter.

SALAKEE DOWN, on the fringe of the airfield. A small cairn 20 ft in diameter revetted with large kerb stones. At the centre are the remains of a ruined chamber, one side slab of which survives. At the E end of the Down is a small cairn, 20 ft in diameter, with intact kerb and a simple entrance grave set at its centre.

NORMANBY DOWN. At the centre of a cairn 50 ft in diameter are the remains of a ruined chamber. The site appears to have been partially excavated, although no record of this work survives.

PORTH MELLAN TOMB. A large entrance grave, some 20 ft long, set into the hill slope and covered by soil and stones.

8010 inset

SAMSON

On North Hill are twelve megalithic tombs beneath small ROUND BARROWS. On South Hill are four similar entrance graves.

8010 inset

TRESCO

ST NICHOLAS. 1877–9. – STAINED GLASS by *Kempe*.

In the magnificent sub-tropical gardens of the modern TRESCO ABBEY (begun to his own design by the Lord Proprietor, *Augustus Smith*, in 1831, built chiefly in 1841 etc., tower 1891)

17b stand two arches and some walling of the C13 from the church of the Benedictine PRIORY of St Nicholas. It was an aisleless building. Built into its walls an INSCRIBED STONE ('THI FILI COGUI', probably C6). In the garden, built into a wall, the fragment of a FONT, Norman, with blank arcading. On the edge of the gardens the VALHALLA, an extravaganza housing figureheads and ornamental fragments of wreckage.

KING CHARLES CASTLE. Not very eloquent debris of a building of c.1550. Semi-octagonal W end, four-centred doorway at the E end. A pentagonal fort was added in the Civil War.

CROMWELL'S CASTLE. Built in 1651 to replace King Charles 53a Castle. It consists of a 60 ft circular tower and granite platform,* placed to command the channel between Bryher and Tresco. Well preserved and finely situated. Entrance high up, to be reached by ladders. Below it the principal living room with a rib-vault. Open platform on top; six gunports in the wall.

The BLOCKHOUSE, or Dover Fort, above Old Grimsby, is a small fort erected in the late C16 or early C17.

SCONNER HOUSE see SHEVIOCK

SCORRIER   7040

SCORRIER HOUSE. CROSS in the grounds, originally by the road from Stithians to the Penryn road. Circular head with rude cross, two shoulder lugs, shaft with unusual incised zig-zag and raised lozenge shapes.

SENNEN   3020

ST SENNEN. The westernmost church of England, in an exposed position on the hill, not down in the cove, with its W tower facing the New World. The tower is unbuttressed, of three stages. The small, low church consists of nave, N transept (with a narrow C13 window), chancel, and an added S aisle of five bays. This has square piers with four attached demi-shafts and four-centred arches. The reconsecration of 1440 probably refers to this addition. – FONT. With inscription of 1441 on the pedestal. – SCULPTURE. A fragment of a figure of 37a the Virgin and Child. It appears of good quality and late C13 date. – PLATE. Exeter-made Elizabethan Chalice and Paten; Paten of 1766–7 on three feet by *Hannan* and *Crouch*.

MAEN CASTLE PROMONTORY FORT. The defences consist of a ditch and two lines of ramparts barring access to the

---

* B. H. St J. O'Neil considers that the present platform was added in the mid C18.

promontory. A single entrance occurs at the centre of the
fortifications. No hut sites are visible in the interior. Sherds
of Iron Age A pottery were found in association with the
rampart and entrance.

STONE CIST, 550 yds NE of Lands End Hotel. This is a massive
structure, 6 ft 8 in. long and orientated E–W. Nothing is
known of its original contents, nor is there any trace of a
covering mound.

₃₀₅₀   SHEVIOCK

ST PETER AND ST PAUL. While the usual Cornish village
church is entirely or almost entirely of the late Middle Ages,
Sheviock has enough of the C13 and early C14 to be remembered for these earlier features. The W tower is evidently C13,
slim (in fact narrower than the nave, whose roof appears to the
l. and r.), with long, narrow lancet windows and no W door.
The same type as for instance at Rame. It is unfortunate that
the tower is now covered with rough, dull grey plaster. The S
side in its exterior and interior is all early C14. The S transept
buttresses, the windows of three and four lights, the S and E
windows of the equally heavily buttressed chancel (the latter
of five lights), and the W window of the N aisle, no doubt re-
used when in the C15 the N transept was broken up and replaced by the usual N aisle, all have cusped lights, pointed and
cusped little quatrefoils, and as their main motif a five-pointed
star in a large circle. If one tries to forget about the N aisle and
to replace it in one's mind by a N transept like the one still
existing on the S side, one will have a good picture of a C14
church in Cornwall. The N aisle has Perp windows and an arcade of six bays with Cornish standard piers and some decoration of the abaci. But in the interior also the C14 dominates
over the C15 (cf. the S transept arch, the inner arches to all the
S windows, the fine slender shafts supporting this inner arch in
the case of the chancel E window, the diagonally placed ogee-
headed niche on the l. of this window (cf. St Issey), and especially the twin FUNERAL RECESSES at its S end). In them on
plain tomb-chests with quatrefoil decoration lie a knight and a
lady, in typical clothes of c.1375. Above the figures is a coving,
and then a strip of blank cusped arches. The figures are badly
defaced. Opposite (no doubt transferred from the N transept)
is another knight of about the same date on an identical tomb-
chest. They are supposed to be Sir Edward Courtenay † 1370

and his wife, and Sir Hugh Courtenay, Sir Edward's father. C19 SEDILIA and PISCINA in the chancel, both very plain. Original wagon roof in the N aisle. – FONT. Plain, circular, C13. – BENCH ENDS. A few with tracery decoration (not the shields with initials or Instruments of the Passion, as usual in Cornwall) and a few with Renaissance motifs. – STAINED GLASS. E window by *Wailes* to the designs of *G. E. Street*, who restored the church in 1850, rebuilding and reroofing the chancel, 'one of the most satisfactory of modern times' according to *The Ecclesiologist* (TK). – MONUMENT. Brass cross on black marble plate to Alphonse Charles de Morel † 1849.

(SCONNER HOUSE. Regency, stone-built and stuccoed. The design is attributed in part to *Repton*. Fine pillared entrance hall. GMT)

SHILLINGHAM
4050

MANOR HOUSE. Much altered; *c.*1700. The N door with pediment and Tuscan pilasters and the door and windows on the E belong to that period; the masonry is largely late medieval. The CHAPEL stands on its own a little further E, in ruins. It had three windows and a W door just like Henry Trecarrel's chapel at Trecarrel. Image brackets on each side of the E window. Walled GARDEN with a fine four-centred granite gateway within a moulded rectangular arch, with carved spandrels and a label with large square carved stops and a heraldic shield above (G. W. Copeland).

SITHNEY
6020

ST SIDINIUS. Some Norman or E.E. masonry in the N transept and chancel; otherwise C15. W tower of regular granite blocks, in three stages, unbuttressed. S porch with panelled jambs. The E window of the N aisle C14, with the inner arch decorated with quatrefoils, etc., uncommonly good, of a cusped type also to be found at Cury, Gunwalloe, Mullion. Inside, nave and aisles of six bays, both with standard Cornish granite piers, those on the S with undecorated capitals, those on the N with the familiar decoration of large horizontal leaves. The two arches between chancel and aisle on the N side are lower than the others. There are differences in the mouldings of the arches too. The arch to the N transept belongs to the type of the N arcade, that to the S transept is C16. – FONT. Norman, circular, small and indifferently decorated. – MONUMENT. Coffin-shaped slab with cross, c.1240. – In the churchyard a pillar on a pedestal to John Oliver, erected by his son, Dr Oliver of Bath, in 1741. The inscription is probably by Pope. It reads: William Oliver, from a filial sense that the blessings he now enjoys were, under the conduct of Providence, owing to the piety and tenderness of his mother and to the goodness and generosity of his father, erected this monument to their memorys.

TRUTHALL. *See* p. 236.

TRUTHALL. *See* p. 236.

3070

SOUTH HILL
Near Callington

ST SAMPSON. The mother-church of Callington. The consecration of 1333 refers to the present church, except for the upper storey of the tower (recognizable as C15 by its big granite blocks) and the S aisle with S porch. The parapet of the tower is supported by the twelve apostles. Nave, chancel, N transept, and tower have interesting Dec features. Originally there was a S transept as well. The Dec church was thus cruciform, that is in the Norman and E.E. tradition of Cornwall (cf. St Ive, a sister of South Hill, or Sheviock). Outside, the C14 parts have boldly projecting buttresses (tower, N wall, N transept, E wall). The N windows are tall and pointed; the N wall of the chancel has two ogee-arched tomb recesses, cusped. A squint from the transept cuts into the western recess. The E window has late geometrical tracery with 'daggers' and pointed trefoils and quatrefoils. By its side an ogee-arched PISCINA with crockets. On the S wall of the chancel the Dec window overlaps earlier SEDILIA, E.E.-looking. The C15 added the S aisle. The arcade has standard Cornish piers and moulded capitals. The aisle wagon roof is old and carved. – FONT. Norman, St Austell type, with corner faces, 'trees of life', and long animals in profile. – MONUMENT to John Manaton and wife, 1507; incised slab. – In the churchyard an INSCRIBED STONE with XP monogram and CUMREGNI FILI MAUCI, C6–7, with traditional lettering with Roman and Hiberno–Saxon features. Four feet of the cross are below ground.

Near the church, medieval fragments in a house and farm.

SOUTH PETHERWIN

3080

ST PATERNUS. There must have been a large aisled Norman church here. The Norman capital displayed outside the N porch is nearly 3 ft across. It belonged originally to a circular pier (cf. St Teath). The N door also is Norman, though modest in dimensions and design (one order of colonnettes and a crenellated motif on the voussoirs). The STOUP by its side is Norman too, the only one in Cornwall. Finally in 1889 the original Norman W respond of the N arcade was discovered, good granite blocks, vertically tooled, and a plain capital. The C15 church, built in place of the Norman one, has the usual W tower of three stages, not tall, with buttresses set back from the angles. The interior is rather low too, with an interesting C14 arcade. The piers are square with demi-shafts and moulded capitals, still with fairly simple heavy detail and simple double-chamfered arches (cf. St Stephen-by-Launceston). The N chancel aisle of two more bays was added later, to the same C15 designs as that of the S aisle: standard Cornish piers with a little decoration on the abaci. The N aisle windows are not very large. The three E windows have the typical four-light design of this district (cf. Launceston). There are N and S porches, both with old wagon roofs. – FONT. C13, circular, on octagonal supports, with flat pointed arches all round (a development of the square type of Egloshayle). – ROOD SCREEN. Only a few fragments, made up into a tower screen. – PULPIT. 1631, octagonal, with linenfold panels, standing on one not very thick shaft branching out into eight scrolls. – READING DESK. Made up of bits from Jacobean pews. – ROYAL ARMS of James I. – STAINED GLASS. Nothing but two shields in a S window dates from the Middle Ages.

SPERRIS QUOIT see ZENNOR

STANBURY see MORWENSTOW

STITHIANS

7030

ST STEDYANA. An all-granite church of no special interest. W tower of three stages with buttresses set back from the angles and panelled pinnacles. No S porch. The N aisle is buttressed and has (renewed) windows with geometrical tracery; so has the chancel on its E side. The N aisle inside has a C14 arcade of six bays with piers of standard Cornish design but heavy proportions. The s aisle of six bays has thin square piers with four attached shafts and less pointed arches than the N aisle. The tower arch has shafts attached to the responds as at Mawgan-in-Meneage and Constantine. – FONT. Plain, octagonal. – PULPIT. Nice plain Georgian. – PISCINA. On a Norman corbel with two animals facing each other. – PLATE. Good Chalice and Paten of 1576 by the same Cornish maker who appears at St Blazey, Lamorran, and Perranarworthal.

TREVALES. *See* p. 228.

STOKE CLIMSLAND
Near Callington

3070

CHURCH. Rather grimly restored, so that not much atmosphere is left. Nave of six bays, N and S aisles, S porch, W tower. Of the church dedicated in 1321 nothing is visible except the E responds of the arcades with typically complex profiles and capitals. The rest is C15: the nave arcades, with square piers and four attached demi-shafts as at Callington (in the S aisle polyphant stone, in the N aisle granite with polyphant capitals), and with simple double-chamfered arches, are older than the lower chancel arcades, with piers of Cornish standard profile. The W tower of regular granite blocks in three stages has the usual buttresses set back from the angles. The windows are mostly C19. Wagon roofs old. – PLATE. Chalice and Paten and Flagon by *William Cripps*, hallmarked 1756. – MONUMENTS. Slate plate to John Bagwill, 16.., with figure of Death. – Sir John Call † 1801, by *King* of Bath.

HORSE BRIDGE, 2½ m. E, on the road to Tavistock. 1437 (cf. Greystone Bridge), 200 ft long, of seven round arches, with double rings of voussoirs; roadway 12 ft wide.

WHITEFORD. *See* p. 240.

STOKETON *see* SALTASH

STOWE
3 m. w of Kilkhampton

2010

The house built by John Grenville, Earl of Bath, in 1680 was called by Borlase the noblest in the West of England. In 1739 it was pulled down. It was eleven bays wide and seven bays deep, two storeys high, with two-bay slightly projecting wings, a three-bay centre pediment, a hipped roof, dormer windows, and a cupola – the typical Charles II house. At the time of demolition the interior fixtures were scattered.* The staircase is now at Cross, nr Great Torrington, Devon. All that remains on the site is the STABLES.

STRATTON

2000

A fine church with a tall tower on top of a hill which the narrow streets of the little town climb up. Before the C19 the church was the parish church for Bude as well.

ST ANDREW. Nave and aisles, the N aisle C14 (original only the three w bays), building probably c.1348, when Sir Ranulph de Blanchminster expressed his wish in his will to be buried in the aisle. An EFFIGY of a cross-legged knight, preserved on the sill of a N window, may well represent him. The N arcade has square piers, with four attached demi-shafts, and double-chamfered pointed arches. The s arcade is Cornish standard, C15. The wagon roofs are old. The w tower with polygonal set-back buttresses seems to be of the C16, with a good w door and window above. – FONT. Plain Norman, circular. – ROOD SCREEN by *E. H. Sedding*, 1901. – BENCH ENDS in the N aisle, not as interesting as many others in the neighbourhood. – PULPIT. Plain Jacobean. – ROYAL ARMS, with strapwork decoration, by *Michael Chuke* (cf. Kilkhampton). – GLASS by *Kempe & Tower* in the w windows of tower and N aisle, 1906 and 1904. – PLATE. Chalice (1570) and Paten (1576) by *Jons* of Exeter; Paten on foot, 1691. – MONUMENT (*see* also above). Sir John Arundell of Trerice † 1561 and two wives; three brasses on a slate plate. – In the churchyard the tomb of Anca Winand van Wulfften Palthe † 1922, by *T. Rosandic*, a harping youth of bronze.

STRIPPLE STONES *see* BLISLAND

TALLAND

2050

CHURCH. The mother church of West Looe and the E half of Polperro. Of a church of apparently C13 date the w end of the nave survives, with three lancet windows with cusped heads, and three buttresses. Of the same date the E wall of the church and perhaps the lower storey of the tower. This is of three

---

* Most of the materials from Stowe are in Penstowe, the house which succeeded it. The porch is now in the town hall at South Molton, Devon (GMT).

storeys and in a very unusual position, detached from the church on the s and connected with it by a wagon-roofed late C15 or early C16 porch. The same date probably applies to the main body of the church: nave of six bays, s aisle, and N transept chapel. The piers are of granite and standard Cornish section. The capitals have coarse foliage. The arches are four-centred. The windows are Perp too. The wagon roof of the aisle is especially good. Much restoration in 1848. The church is very completely pewed. – BENCH ENDS are partly c.1525, partly c.1600. The benches at the corners of each block have angels with scroll, chalice, etc., as crowning features. – The CHOIR STALLS are made up of fragments of the Bernard Beville pew. – The seats in the N transept are Jacobean, as is the PULPIT. – MONUMENTS. Tomb-chest of John Beville † 1578, by *Peter Crocker*. Recumbent figure, inscriptions, and arms all incised in slate. – Slate slab to Joanna Mellow † 1625 and her baby.

TAMARSTONE BRIDGE *see* LAUNCELLS

⁶⁰⁴⁰
TEHIDY PARK

The house originally built for the Bassets in 1734 to designs by *Thomas Edwards* of Greenwich (but later rebuilt) was destroyed by fire shortly after the end of the First World War. But four detached angle pavilions survived and have been incorporated into the present hospital building. One of them still has its original painted ceiling. The clock tower is built from materials salvaged from the house. A number of outbuildings – stables, fire-engine house (by the lake) – remain.

¹⁰⁷⁰
TEMPLE

ST CATHERINE. Rebuilt in 1883, by *S. Trevail*; the w tower a remarkable example of how thick the language of the Middle Ages becomes in the hands of one of the more original later Victorian architects.* The battlements, their projection and proportion, should be specially noted. The church stands on the site of a house of the Templars. – FONT. Plain, circular Norman bowl (cf. Boyton).

TEMPLE MOOR *see* ST NEOT

* But the base of the tower appears to be late C12 or early C13 (G. W. Copeland).

TIDEFORD

ST LUKE. By *Wightwick*, 1845. – FONT. Norman, with long,
well-carved faces at the four corners and large rosettes in
circles. It comes from the chapel of St Luke near Bolventor in
Bodmin Moor, which was a chapel established by the priories
of Montacute and Launceston before 1340, and the font is
indeed of the same type as that of St Thomas Launceston,
which may come from the priory (Altarnun type). – PLATE.
Chalice and Paten, Flagon and Almsdish all by *I. J. Keith*,
1844–6, the earliest examples (according to Canon Mills) of
the Gothic Revival in Cornish church plate.
OLD BRIDGE. C18, but incorporating the moulded ribs of a
medieval bridge, perhaps of the C14.

TINTAGEL

ST MERTERIANA. All on its own in a very bleak position with
not a tree anywhere. The Norman church can still largely be
reconstructed, Early Norman presumably, with certain features reminiscent of the Anglo-Saxon. The S door is Norman,
of modest size, with one order of columns (scalloped capitals).
W of it is an early window. On the N side a very Saxon-looking
doorway and two tiny windows l. and r. of it. The N transept
and the (later lengthened) S transept have Norman masonry
too, and on the N side of the chancel a long, extremely narrow
window now looks on to the added chapel of St Symphorian,
which is also Norman. The chancel has a Norman S window too.
All these windows have deep inner splays and a slight cham-
fering on the outside. More Norman details appear in the
chancel arch, and the arch connecting S transept and nave. The
latter has its imposts at a curiously low level. A seat runs all
along the W and S sides of the S transept. Later additions are an
E.E. lancet light in the N transept, the late C13 E windows of the
S transept, the plain C14 N porch, and a sepulchral niche in the
chancel S wall. The W tower is not Norman, but whether it is
partly C13 or wholly C15 is doubtful. – FONT. Square and
plain, except for faces at the corners. On five feet, the four in
the corners octagonal. – ROOD SCREEN. Perp. – BENCH ENDS.
Made into a reredos. – MONUMENTS. Fine C13 slab with
head *en face* above a foliated cross. – Brass of *c.*1430. – The
DOOR HINGES of the N door are original C12 ironwork. – IN-
SCRIBED STONE. Probably a Roman milestone, MPCQ VA LIC

IIV (or LICIN). The inscription no doubt refers to the Emperor
Licinius (A.D. 308–24).

10a In the village of Tintagel the former OLD POST OFFICE, the
most famous of Cornish stone cottages, low, dark, picturesque,
with roofs like a cluster of hills, and of a slaty hue like elephant
hide. Originally probably a small manor house, or steward's
house. The central hall, open to the roof timbers, survives in this
form today; chamber and solar at one end. The domestic section
at the other end was possibly also originally two-storeyed. The
hall fireplace and the surviving round-headed single and paired
slit windows are consistent with an early C15 date. Local features are the slate walls (2 ft 6 in. to 3 ft 6 in. thick) and the low
slate roof, the windows cut out of solid pieces of local greenstone, and the roof construction: 'upper cruck' type, i.e. the
pairs of curved timbers forming the principals spring from
near the top of the walls and are linked by curved collars. The
stepped chimney by the front porch is modern and replaces a
straight stack.

CROSS, in front of the Wharncliffe Arms Hotel. Round head,
much cut off now, of a very unusual form. Long inscriptions
on both sides: Mathew–Markus–Lucas–John on the one, Aelnat ficit hanc crucem pro anima sua on the other, a remarkable
instance of the dedication of a cross. Aelnat is a Saxon, not a
Celtic name; the minuscules are Hiberno–Saxon.

45 TINTAGEL CASTLE. Architecturally not very rewarding, but as
a piece of scenery of supreme majesty: 'Black cliffs and caves
and storm and wind', Tennyson noted in his diary. The connexion with King Arthur has not found any archaeological con-
firmation. If, however, it has been said that nothing Celtic
attaches to the site before the time when Geoffrey of Monmouth (c.1140) made Tintagel King Arthur's residence, recent
excavations have proved this to be a mistake. On the island remains of small rectangular stone huts have been found, evidently belonging to a Celtic monastery. The medieval chapel
stood close to the place of the oldest of these cells, and as the
chapel was dedicated to St Julitta (or St Juliot) it can be assumed that this cell was the saint's own hut, later preserved
as a sanctuary. Its date would then be c.500. Of the date c.1145,
when the medieval chapel was built on the island for Reginald,
Earl of Cornwall, Henry I's son (W porch and E end added
C13), there also survive remains of the great hall, closer to the
isthmus. This isthmus must in the Middle Ages have been
wider than it is now. Under Richard, Earl of Cornwall, Henry

III's brother, a spacious lower and upper ward were built on the mainland and connected by a bridge with the inner ward with which Richard surrounded the C12 hall. He also built the Iron Gate by the cove below the sea wall (*c.*1235–40). The hall was rebuilt twice in the C14, both times smaller than originally. The outer walls standing up to about 10 ft are those of the C12, with C13 buttresses.

TRETHEVY, 1½ m. E of Tintagel. INSCRIBED STONE, no doubt a milestone, like the one at Tintagel. The Roman inscription here refers to the Emperors Gallus and Volusianus, that is to 251–3 (C DOMIN GALLO ET VOLUS).

TINTEN   *0070*
Near St Tudy

The chapel of the old manor house is still recognizable, with a three-light C15 window; now a barn.

TONACOMBE   *2010*

MANOR HOUSE, 1 m. SW of Morwenstow church. A friendly, modest Tudor house.

CROSS. Round-headed, discovered *c.*1920, 'of primitive design' (Henderson), the northernmost of all the Celtic crosses of Cornwall.

TORPOINT   *4050*

ST JAMES. 1819, chancel 1885. Plain, with lancet windows whose elaborate wooden tracery survives in only one window. W gallery nicely curved back in the centre, on iron columns.

(METHODIST CHURCH. 1795, with later enlargements. A.S.B. New)

Facing the W front of the church is TOR HOUSE, Georgian, block-shaped, and now rather gloomy-looking, the house which stood in that spot before Torpoint grew around it. The town has little to attract the eye. GRAVES END is of the early C19, with a mock-medieval circular tower, built by Lord Graves whose main house, Thancke's, was pulled down and re-erected at Portwrinkle (*q.v.*).

TOWAN *see* ST COLUMB MAJOR

TOWEDNACK

St Tewennochus. A chapel until 1902. Low, two-stage granite tower without buttresses or pinnacles. c13 nave and chancel (cf. the N wall). Nave and chancel are connected by a
double-chamfered chancel arch, a feature unique so far W in
Cornwall. A S aisle was added in the c15, the arcade with
octagonal piers and four-centred arches. All the windows are
renewed. The intersecting tracery of the E window and its
cusping point to the end of the c13 (cf. Zennor). – FONT.
Granite, octagonal, with faces at the corners, dated 1720. Its
base is the inverted bowl of a Norman font. – BENCH ENDS.
With the profiles of James Trevella and Matthew Trenwith. –
The ALTAR SLAB with consecration crosses, and a long stone
with incised cross used as a bench in the S porch, show the
early existence of a church in this place. – PLATE. Elizabethan
Chalice, and another dated 1830–1 but also of Elizabethan
type (unusual at its date).

TREATHAGUE
Near Stithians

Nice, plain, two-storeyed Early Georgian granite house.

TREBURSYE
1½ m. SW of Launceston

(House said to be by *Wyatville*.)

TREBYAN QUOIT *see* LANHYDROCK

TRECARREL

Henry Trecarrel, who built the church of Launceston, was a
proud patron of architecture on his own estate too. The HALL
of his manor house, now shamefully the barn of a farm, is still
one of the most spectacular domestic buildings of the Middle
Ages in Cornwall. On the S wall, one large four-light window
of two storeys height with a transom across and tracery of the
same design as at Launceston, two three-light windows, and a
(later ?) four-light window below one of them. In this wall is
an entrance too. Another is now the doorway into the cottage.
The N wall of the hall has only two three-light windows. Excellent roof, with the remains of carved decoration between

the rafters. The CHAPEL is a detached little building, also still structurally intact, with one three-light Perp window on the S, N, and E.

TREEN *see* ZENNOR

TREFFRY VIADUCT *see* LUXULYAN

TREGARDEN
Near St Mabyn

0070

An excellent Stuart manor house, dated 1631 on the doorway into the front garden. The house has the familiar E plan with central porch and symmetrical gabled wings. The windows are small and mullioned.

TREGASSOW
Near Probus

8040

Parts of a late medieval manor house survive.

TREGEARE ROUNDS
2 m. NNE of St Kew

0080

This Iron Age fort is defended by two slight banks and ditches enclosing an area 500 ft in diameter. The ramparts run down the slope of the hill towards the valley bottom and the site is overlooked by higher ground to the NW – both features strategically unsound. There is a simple gap in both ramparts on the SE. This belongs to a series of hill-slope forts which appear to have served primarily as cattle enclosures rather than defensive sites.

TREGENNA CASTLE *see* ST IVES

TREGONING HILL *see* GERMOE

TREGONY

9040

ALMSHOUSES. 1696 (rebuilt in 1895), with a gallery of six short, thick, uncarved granite piers below and a wooden gallery above.

A substantial Georgian HOUSE just NE of the Market House.

(COUNTY SECONDARY SCHOOL. 1962 by *F. K. Hicklin*, County Architect.)

8040
TREGOTHNAN

61 The splendid mansion of the Earls Falmouth, i.e. the Boscawen
family. Of their mid C17 house two rooms survive, the Corner
Parlour with a broad-banded plaster ceiling and a wooden
chimneypiece with caryatids, and the room above it with a
plaster ceiling looking somewhat earlier and a chimneypiece
looking somewhat later, i.e. typical 1650–60. Compact fruit-
bundles, thick volutes, very pronounced lugs. The C17 house
was encased and enlarged by *William Wilkins* in 1816–18 for
the fourth Viscount and again in 1845–8 for the second Earl by
Vulliamy. The C19 work is in an elaborate East Anglian Tudor
with polygonal angle turrets and large mullioned and trans-
somed windows. In the picturesquely irregular s front there is
more Vulliamy than Wilkins. On the entrance side Vulliamy
added the prominent tower at the r. corner. By Wilkins, however, the square tower over the large staircase with its Gothic
iron handrail. Other interiors are classical.

0050
TREGREHAN
Near St Blazey

A pretty little lodge with lancet windows. The house itself is
Late Georgian, by *Wightwick*, of granite, seven bays with
lower projecting wings and a one-storeyed colonnade of piers
of Ionic columns across five bays of the front.

TREHANE see PROBUS

TREHANE BARTON see TREVALGA

2050
TRELAWNE
Near Pelynt

The general appearance of the house is late C16, grey stone. It
belongs to the time of Sir Jonathan Trelawny, who bought the
house from Queen Elizabeth. On the E is a staircase turret of
late C13 date, and the SE building of *c.*1750 has party walls
belonging to the same medieval structure (Champernowne,
originally Bodrugan family). N of the turret wall, porch and
chapel (now C19) of a building of *c.*1450 (Bonville family).

TRELEW see ST BURYAN

TRELISSICK
8030

The severest neo-Greek mansion in Cornwall. Centre with six- 62b
column giant Ionic portico after that of the Erechtheion at
Athens. Built by *P. F. Robinson, c.*1825.

TRELOWARREN
7020
Near Mawgan-in-Meneage

Historically much more complex than it appears at first. Of the 56a
main building of *c.*1450 much of the E wing remains, with
four-, five-, and six-light windows on two storeys, and also the
chapel windows (that is the windows of the s wing). A polygonal bay window on the s side is dated 1662 (and yet still not
classical). The stables with their cupola are 1698 (W of the
main building). In *c.*1750 Sir Richard Vyvyan extended the
chapel* to the W and redecorated it inside in a pretty Rococo 57b
Gothic. He probably also added the battlements to the E
front. Finally the N wing and the N end of the E wing belong
to the C19. In spite of that the low, evenly spread-out building
appears a happy unity on its large lawn.

The HALLIGYE FOGOU is the largest in Cornwall and excellently preserved. It is 90 ft long and 6 ft high. The entrance is
modern.

TRELOWETH FARM *see* ST ERTH

TREMAINE
2080

ST WINWALLO. An isolated chapel on a hill, unaisled, with
two-staged unbuttressed tower. The N wall is Norman with a
little blocked doorway, the tympanum, alas, hacked away. The
Norman N windows are altered, the s windows are square-
headed C16. A curious feature is the narrow visible steps in the
N wall which lead to the rood loft. – FONT. Circular with cable
moulding, like Egloskerry.

TREMATON CASTLE
4050
1 m. SW of Saltash

One of the most extensive castles in Cornwall, more impressive
than Launceston, if not as perfect as Restormel. The position

---

* The MHLG dates the chapel C17, lengthened in the C19.

is superb, with wide views towards the Hamoaze and the Sound. The castle is mentioned in Domesday. It went to the Duchy of Cornwall in the C14 and still belongs to it. The main surviving structures are the tall walls of the inner bailey, the C13 gatehouse, 'one of the most beautiful and untouched examples of its period' (S. Toy), with two main rooms above each other, each with a fireplace flanked by C13 columns with excellent stiff-leaf capitals, and the shell keep on the mount of the same type as Launceston, Restormel, and Totnes. The keep at Trematon is vaguely oval, 57 by 71½ ft and 27 ft high to the rampart. The parapet is complete with the merlons solid, except for one. The hall was somewhere in the inner bailey. It was built 'de plaustro' by Edmund Duke of Cornwall in the C14 and has entirely disappeared. Instead there is now a castellated dwelling house with regularly disposed Georgian windows, erected in 1808. It was built for the then Surveyor-General to the Duchy, *Benjamin Tucker*, and was perhaps designed by him. Part of the bailey wall was pulled down to obtain for the house a view of the sea.

TREMAYNE see ST MARTIN-IN-MENEAGE

TREMEER see ST TUDY

7030
TREMOUGH
Near Penryn

A five-bay centre of 1712 and slightly projecting wings with tripartite windows of uncertain date.

2080
TRENEGLOS

St Gregory. Tower perhaps medieval; otherwise built in 1858, but with an interesting Norman tympanum: two lions facing each other, with a tree standing between them: the composition not specially Cornish. The workshop may have been the same which made the tympana for the neighbouring Egloskerry. Old wagon roof in the porch. – FONT. Small circular bowl on one shaft, with faces at the corners of the base. – STOCKS preserved. – PLATE. Chalice and Paten, 1684 by *R.A.*; flagon by *J. Strong*, 1733–4.

TRENETHICK see WENDRON

TRENETHICK BARTON *see* HELSTON

TRENOWTH
Near Grampound

9050

Below the neo-Georgian house of 1928 the remains of a chapel mentioned in 1405.

TREREIFE

4020

MANOR HOUSE. An c18 block, undecorated but of good proportions, seven by five bays, two storeys, with a simple door with pediment on carved brackets. Hipped roof with dormer windows.

BURYAS BRIDGE, ½ m. SW. Built in 1774.

TRERICE
Near St Newlyn East

8050

Excellent Elizabethan house of the Arundells. Largely built of elvan. Symmetrical front with two-storey porch and slightly projecting wings. These have scrolly gables which alternate with gables of a different shape. The hall goes through both floors with a vast lattice window of four plus four lights and two transoms. The S wing has a plain E gable, and to the N are oriel windows. Ceilings with good plasterwork, with thin ribs and pendants in hall and drawing room. The fireplaces of these two rooms are dated 1572 and 1573. (Trerice is now a guest house.)

52

TRERITHICK
Near Altarnun

2080

The farmhouse has the date 1585 over the door Its original E-shape can still be traced but has been much altered. The gables also are not in their original state. Extensive outbuildings.

TRESCO *see* SCILLY ISLES

TRESILLIAN
3 m. NE of Truro

8040

CHURCH. 1878 by *Edmund Sedding*, with prominent bellcote. – FONT from Merther. Medieval, with corner projections of the Bodmin type, but without faces. – PULPIT. Jacobean. G. W. Copeland)

6030

TRESLOTHAN

ST JOHN. The chapel to Pendarves House,* small, with a bell-cote, 1841 by *Wightwick*. – FONT from Camborne church, C15, granite, with four angels holding shields and an ornamental band connecting them. So summary and bold in the treatment of the hard material that it looks decidedly modern (cf. St Ives). – SCULPTURE. In the vestry a late C14 or C15 alabaster panel (Professor Charles Thomas). – In the churchyard the rather sad-looking Gothic Pendarves MAUSOLEUM.

THE GIANT'S QUOIT, in Pendarves Park, Carwynnen. The present structure of three uprights and a capstone represents the reconstruction of an original megalithic tomb which collapsed in the C19.

2080

TRESMEER

ST NICHOLAS. 1880, but a two-stage unbuttressed C15 W tower, and a few E.E. three-light lancet windows, that at the E end as a triplet. – The FONT is circular, with one cable moulding close to the top. – PLATE. Chalice and Paten by *Coton* of Barnstaple; Elizabethan.

TRESUNGERS *see* ST ENDELLION

TRETHEVY *see* ST CLEER *and* TINTAGEL

7030

TREVALES
Near Stithians

Built *c*.1800, library and several other rooms added *c*.1900.

0090

TREVALGA

ST PETROCK. Far out towards the sea, the unbuttressed, un-pinnacled W tower faces the ocean. It is supposed to be as old as the C13. The interior gives the impression of an outpost chapel, low, without an added aisle. The N transept seems to be E.E. too (see its small two-light windows). It is connected with the chancel by a squint. Old roofs in chancel and transept. – FONT. Plain, circular. – REREDOS. Carved triptych, Flemish C16, of indifferent quality. – PLATE. Chalice and

---

* A Georgian house demolished in 1955.

Paten by *Jons* of Exeter, very pretty, *c*.1576; also a Paten on
foot by *J. Strang*, 1728–9.

TREHANE BARTON, simple, rebuilt 1743, but mentioned as
early as the C14.

TREVASSACK MANOR *see* HAYLE

TREVEAR *see* ST STEPHEN-IN-BRANNEL

TREVEASE FARM *see* CONSTANTINE

TREVELGUE HEAD   *8060*

TREVELGUE HEAD PROMONTORY FORT, 2 m. NE of Newquay. The headland is defended by a complex of seven lines of
banks and ditches in addition to a natural cleft in the rock
which separates the fortifications into two groups. Within the
defences are a series of hut circles whose finds suggest occupation from the Iron Age to the Dark Ages. The site overlooks an
excellent natural harbour with a flat beach.

ROUND BARROWS. *See* Newquay.

TREVENSON *see* POOL

TREVERBYN   *0050*

(ST PETER. 1848–50 by *G. E. Street*, the second church he designed in his own name (the first is at Par). *The Builder* called
it 'plain but good'. It is indeed good early Street: local
materials, strong design (specially good the great barn-like
roof), simplification of detail to achieve bold internal scale,
subtle use of levels and lighting to give prominence to the
altar. The vocabulary is simple. Early Dec, but the virtues not
decorative but purely architectural. Dr R. Lambert)

TREVERBYN OLD BRIDGE *see* ST NEOT

TREVOSE HEAD   *8070*
2¼ m. NW of St Merryn

(LIGHTHOUSE. 1847. Circular tower of white-painted masonry,
69 ft high. Lobby round the lower part, leading to two single-
storey dwelling blocks.)

TREWAN HALL *see* ST COLUMB MAJOR

1070
TREWARDLA
Near Blisland

Plain two-storeyed house of eleven bays; it was built in 1773 and enlarged in 1839.

TREWARDREVA *see* CONSTANTINE

0070
TREWARNE
Near St Kew

One of the most perfect Cornish mid C17 manor houses (*c*.1645), with garden, garden wall, and contemporary entrance. The house has mullioned and transomed windows on the ground floor and smaller windows above, a hipped roof and no gables. Doorway and garden doorway still have four-centred heads. Some fine plaster overmantels inside, in particular a figural one in a bedroom.

9040
TREWARTHENICK

A plain house with a front of seven bays in two storeys with a pediment over the three central bays. 1686, remodelled in 1831 by *Henry Harrison* of London. The wings which he added have since been demolished.

2080
TREWEN

ST MICHAEL. Small chapel and no W tower, only a bellcote. N aisle only, arcade on four low piers of Cornish standard, entirely plain. The aisle windows are straight-headed; that at the E end is of three lights with Cornish standard tracery. – FONT. Norman, completely plain, square, with chamfered corners. – PLATE. Elizabethan Chalice and Paten by *Mathew* of Barnstaple, very plain.

TREWERN *see* MADRON

TREWHITTEN *see* MINSTER

8030
TREWINCE
Near St Anthony-in-Roseland

A very pleasant house of five bays, two-storeyed, with quoins and a door with an alternatingly rusticated (i.e. Gibbs) surround: 1750.

TREWINNARD MANOR *see* ST ERTH

TREWITHEN
Near Probus

9040

A plain and stately house of 1715–40, rendered, nine bays wide, with a recessed five-bay centre and an arched doorway. Detached wings are placed at r. angles. To the s a different, though probably contemporary façade, of ashlar,* with raised window surrounds. The architect of these parts was probably *Thomas Edwards* of Greenwich. The E front is evidently later, say mid-century, though probably of before 1758. It is of silvery Pentewan stone and has a canted bay window in the middle. Splendid mid C18 dining room with stucco decoration on the walls and screens of columns to E and w. The architect to the house in 1764 was *Sir Robert Taylor*. Panelled sitting room of *c.*1730 with fluted pilasters to full height. Staircase with glazed dome.‡

TREWOOF
Near St Buryan

4020

(Farmhouse, mainly C17, but with an early C16 doorway, and several later additions. Near by an C18 clapper cornmill with cottage. MHLG)

TREWORGEY
Near Liskeard

2060

Plain Georgian house, though much restored after a fire (information from Lady Mander). Seven bays and two storeys, with an open Tuscan porch and a Venetian window above. (C16 parts survive. MHLG) Garden with huge yews, an unusual display of topiary. In the garden a clock tower, weatherboarded, with a Chinese roof. Is it C18?

TRIPPET STONES *see* BLISLAND

TRURO

8040

Of medieval Truro little can be said. Of the CASTLE not a wall survives; it was on Castle Hill. Of the town itself there is only

---

* The predominantly pink shade of the garden front is due to the profuse growth of a very smooth lichen (Alec Clifton-Taylor).

‡ In the house is a sand PAINTING of *c.* 1800, representing Caius College, Cambridge, and especially the Gate of Honour.

the one aisle of St Mary's which Pearson and Bishop Benson decided to save when they started building the cathedral. The pattern of the central streets is still visible, and some cottages in the back streets. The ALMSHOUSES of 1631 in Pydar Street have their inscription still, but the old buildings are now unrecognizable. The RED LION HOTEL,* terribly treated by *Sylvanus Trevail*, still had its lower storeys of 1671, with pediments to all windows (just going classical), and its staircase. At BOSCAWEN HOUSE in Princes Street also the mid-C17 staircase can be seen, and some other C17 features.

But essentially Truro is a Georgian, or rather a Later Georgian town. It had much of the county town, although it was not the county town. The ASSEMBLY ROOMS‡ of 1772 (of which now only the S façade remains) was the best individual building, a charming front of Bath stone with the medallions of Handel and Shakespeare, good enough in detail to be at Bristol or Dublin. In 1797 the Truro Philharmonic Society was founded. In 1799 the INFIRMARY was built in Calenick Street, remarkably stately, though plain. In 1794 the building of BOSCAWEN STREET in the centre of the town and of LEMON STREET up the hill to the S started. The W side of Lemon Street is exceptionally well preserved, having three-storeyed, stone-fronted houses of uniform character. Then there are such individual buildings as, for example, the MANSION HOUSE in Prince's Street (built by Ralph Allen Daniell of Bath stone, the gift of Ralph Allen of Bath), PRINCE'S HOUSE, also in Prince's Street (with a good interior), and one or two others.§ Both the Mansion House (1751) and Prince's House (1737) are by *Thomas Edwards* of Greenwich. Noteworthy also the ROYAL HOTEL in Lemon Street, TREHAVERNE HOUSE in Kenwyn Road (early C18, of five bays), THE PARADE in Malpas Road, eighteen houses of the early C19, each of three bays, and most of them with first-floor verandas, and BENSON HOUSE, up Moresk Road, early C18, with a one-bay central pediment. In Pydar Street are several more nice houses, and STRANGWAYS TERRACE has an early C19 group of four-bay blocks with the entrances recessed between the blocks.

At the upper end of Lemon Street in 1835 a Doric column was erected to commemorate Lander, the explorer, who was born

---

* Recently demolished.
‡ Now Cathedral Garage, High Cross.
§ In particular, BLACKFORD'S, with wide Venetian windows (MHLG).

at Truro,* and terraces of houses with stuccoed Tudor fronts of typical 1840 character followed. A contemporary development, also quite unspoilt, is at the far end of RIVER STREET. In the town a CITY HALL was erected in 1846 to the designs of *Christopher Eales*: very up-to-date, that is in the Italian Renaissance style. Truro's character did not change much with the later Victorian decades, until the cathedral arrived.

CATHEDRAL. Designed by *John Loughborough Pearson* in 1880, the E parts built before his death, the nave and central tower between 1898 and 1903, and the W towers between 1903 and 1910, all by *F. L. Pearson*, Pearson's son, to the father's design. The building is in the E.E. style, with the exception of the spires, which are Normandy Gothic (cf. Coutances). It is strange that so sensitive an architect should have chosen this craggy sharpness for a county of whose churches nothing is more characteristic than the absence of spires and the long lowness of naves and aisles. Once one has got over the shock of this compressed, upward-pointing, and yet somehow neat silhouette, however, the merits of the design can be appreciated. The interior is in many ways a *beau idéal* of the E.E. style, perfected as against the proportions of, say, Salisbury, and purged of the many lovable irregularities of the others. The cathedral is vaulted throughout. Pearson knew better than any other architect of his generation how necessary stone vaults are to Gothic perfection. In the nave, oddly enough, he has chosen sexpartite vaults, a French rather than an English tradition. Otherwise English characteristics are evident everywhere: the gallery (which France in the C13 had given up), the straight E end with its lancets, the double transepts, the moulded capitals. The E parts have more decoration; the nave is almost bare. Architectural sculpture, wherever it appears inside and outside, is of a regrettably dull quality. Specially successful architectural motifs are the tall W tower halls opened towards the nave, the niches in which the aisle windows are placed, and the circular BAPTISTERY, E.E. at its richest and most compact.

Recently a MEMORIAL HALL has been added to the cathedral on its NE side. Below the hall is the CHAPTER HOUSE, and there are cloakrooms etc. as well. The hall itself is cruciform. The building is of concrete with surfaces of grit-blasted granite aggregate. The heaviness of the horizontal concrete members is in total contrast to the verticalism of the cathedral, and the

* His statue, on top of the column, is by *Nevil Northey Burnard*, 1853.

tiny round arches of the vertical slit windows cut into the top slab – a fashionable motif initially derived from Le Corbusier's Maisons Jaoul – have no more convincing relation to the pointed arches of Pearson's building. Not that imitations of Pearson's C13 style would have been preferable, but modern forms, more consistent in vertical emphasis, might have been chosen. The architect is *John Taylor*, and the building was completed in 1967.

Of the parish church of Truro, ST MARY, Pearson allowed the s aisle to remain, while the rest (with a spire of 128 ft, rebuilt in 1768) was pulled down. The aisle, of 1504–18, is indeed one of the most ornate Gothic structures in Cornwall, probably by the same masons as Probus tower. It has the same decoration of the plinth in two tiers, the same use of niches for statuary, the same decorating of the buttresses. The window spandrels have tracery, and the battlements also are adorned with quatrefoils. The s windows are large, of four lights, the E window of five. The interior had its arcade with piers of standard Cornish design with plain capitals and arches nearly semicircular. Some of the roof timbers are still to be seen, and a few bits of old glass.

The new FURNISHINGS of the cathedral are on the whole not fortunate. Artists of conventional tastes have been used, not those of stronger individuality. STAINED GLASS by *Clayton & Bell*, except on the s side of the old aisle, where there is good glass by *Warrington* (1840s; TK). – CHOIR STALLS and BISHOP'S THRONE designed by *Pearson* himself. – PULPIT. Of a comfortably bulgy shape and with inlay of local workmanship. – PLATE. Gilt Chalice and Paten by *FW* (*see* Holy Trinity, Hull, and Batford St Martins, Wilts.), 1619–20; two similar Flagons, 1623–4; several C18 pieces; gold Chalice and Paten designed by *Pearson*; all the rest also C19. – MONUMENTS. In the crypt two lifesize kneeling alabaster figures of *c*.1620, not well carved. – Richard Robarts † 1614 ('of his age seventy or thereabouts') and wife, a large affair with the two effigies reclining stiffly and behind each other, double columns l. and r., and on their entablatures two very good smaller figures of Father Time and Death. The carving of the larger figures is by no means good. – Some late C18 and early C19 monuments to Vyvyans, too high up to be seen.

ST JOHN. 1828 by *P. Sambell*, a plain rectangle with gallery on columns painted *à la Grecque* to resemble Doric columns. Otherwise much altered in 1893–1900.

St Paul. 1848, but a new chancel added by *J. D. Sedding*, 1882–4. In the exterior, Sedding at his best; ornate and dramatic, with his original variations on Perp tracery themes, the gabled centre with battlemented turrets l. and r., and the straight parapets to the aisles. The tower is close to the se and broad and strong and battlemented. The interior after this is disappointing.

(Convent of the Epiphany (formerly Alverton House), Tregolls Road. Early c19, but greatly extended, with main entrance, clock tower, and carving in the chapel designed by *J. H. Comper*. The chapel itself is by *E. Sedding Jun.*, 1910.)

Most of the Nonconformist places of worship are unfortunately no longer in their Late Georgian shape. The exceptions are the Quaker Meeting House of *c.*1830, a plain, dignified granite rectangle (cf. St Austell and Redruth) off the far end of Moresk Road, and the big granite front of the Methodist 16b Church in Union Place of 1830 (since enlarged).

County Hall, Treyew Road and Penwethers Lane. Outside the town, with magnificent views. Designed by the County Architect's Department (*Alan J. Groves*) and completed in 1966. The building is lavish in scale and excellent in finishes. It is a square with a spacious inner courtyard, imaginatively laid out and planted by *G. A. Jellicoe*. A future extension is to join on in the nw corner and will be another square with an inner courtyard. The site falls to the s by 10 ft; hence the courtyard steps down and the s range is placed on two-storeyed pilotis and the w range on pilotis of diminishing size. The skyline, in spite of the fall, could thus be kept even. The frontages are even too, except for the slight variation where the staircases are and the conspicuous change in the e range where the Council Chamber is. The building is of reinforced concrete frame construction and clad with pre-cast concrete members making a grid of relatively tall and narrow openings. The Council Chamber has no windows. It cantilevers forward boldly and has a sloping roof of a kind of half-hip design. Below it is the principal entrance. This leads into a large entrance hall and to the principal staircase. At the upper landing is a long gallery with access to the Council Chamber. The chamber is square, yet the seating is arranged circularly. Furnishing is taken seriously throughout and is of a high standard. – In the courtyard is a tall holed piece of sculpture by *Barbara Hepworth*.

(TREYEW INFANTS' SCHOOL, Malabar Estate. 1960 by the County Architect's Department (*F. K. Hicklin*).

POLWHELE. *See* p. 143.

6030
TRUTHALL
Near Sithney

FARMHOUSE. The r. wing is a medieval hall of small dimensions; the centre, dated 1642, has a continuous drip-course and a flat, chamfered door-head; the l. wing is modern.

8050
TRUTHAN
Near St Allen

FARMHOUSE. Five-bay granite front with Tuscan porch; earlier irregular back.

6040
TUCKINGMILL

In the mining district, along an arterial road which does not really touch the countryside anywhere between Redruth and Camborne.

ALL SAINTS. 1843–4, in the Norman style, by *J. Hayward* of Exeter; stone with granite lesenes, corbel table, and window dressings. Inside a heavy granite arcade for the N aisle. – FONT. From St Derwa's Chapel, Mendarva; *c.*1100 (Professor Charles Thomas).

0050
TYWARDREATH

Of the priory founded here by Richard Fitz-Turold, Lord of Cardinham Castle shortly after the Conquest and later in possession of much land and many livings in Cornwall, nothing remains. With Glasney College, Penryn, and the two priories of Bodmin and Launceston it was the most notable monastic foundation in the county.

ST ANDREW. Only the W tower is old* and in a reasonable state: with a SE stone turret and no pinnacles. The arcade inside the church is of Cornish standard type: rebuilt in 1880 by *R. Coad*. – FONT. Octagonal, C15, with shields in quatrefoils in

* Mid C14 (MHLG).

circles. – PULPIT. Made up of bench ends, a large figure of Christ, a smaller St Laurence; they come from the same workshop as the series at Golant. – PLATE. Chalice and Paten, 1576–7; two tankard-shaped Flagons, 1636–7; Paten on foot, by *A. Nelme*, 1711–12; two domestic Dishes on three feet, by *Lambourn*, 1783–4. – MONUMENTS. Thomas Colyns † 1534, prior, slate plate with a foliated cross. – Slate plate with good inscriptions and ornament to Jane (surname illegible) † 1636. – Jane Pole † 1795, graceful relief of a woman by an urn, by *C. Regnart* (Cleveland Street, Fitzroy Square). – Caroline Rashleigh † 1842 (interred at Kensal Green), Gothic with name, etc., in Gothic capital letters, by *Pearce* of Truro (who had learnt a lesson from Hopper of London; *see* St Blazey).

VERYAN

The position of the village amid trees is exquisite. Amongst cottages the distinguishing feature of Veryan is the ROUND HOUSES, five whitewashed thatched cottages with Gothick windows, and in one case an elaborate porch (early C19, by *Hugh Rowe* of Lostwithiel, a builder). 8

ST SYMPHONIAN. A most unusual plan. Nave, N aisle, S transept, tower to the S of the transept (cf. Mawgan-in-Pydar, Duloe), and W porch. The doorway to the W porch has the oddest of capitals, scalloped, with six heads in a row above the tops of the scallops. Remains of heads of a Norman corbel table, two in the porch, one above the apex of the porch entrance (wrongly restored). The tower of slate in three stages has angle buttresses (not diagonal) and Early Dec windows on its top stage. The aisle arcade is eight bays long (an unusual length), white granite, of standard Cornish profile, with limestone capitals and large horizontal leaves, etc., to decorate the abaci. – FONT. Square, with corner faces and odd ornament between (the local reactionary continuation of Norman conventions, or a self-conscious late medieval copy?). – ROOD SCREEN. Two sections of the base, each with two panels; undistinguished carving. – PLATE. Chalice by *Jones* of Exeter, c.1574, very different from his usual patterns; Chalice, 1666–7; Flagon by *Micon Melun*, 1741–2; two similar Patens, Exeter-made, 1763–4.

(HOMEYARD HOMES. By *Dawber, Fox & Robinson*, completed 1956.)

WADEBRIDGE

The only structure of importance is the magnificent BRIDGE across the river Camel, one of the best medieval bridges in England. It was built *c*.1468 at the expense of John Lovebond, Vicar of Egloshayle, the mother-church of Wadebridge. The bridge, 320 ft long, is the longest in Cornwall. It has seventeen arches, of which one is now walled up, and was widened in 1847 and again in 1962–3. The piers are said by Leland to have been sunk on a foundation of packs of wool. There is a similar bridge at Bideford, Devon.

The MOLESWORTH ARMS HOTEL in the High Street is a longish, low, early C19 building with an asymmetrically placed Tuscan porch.

(GONVENA. 1780. Three storeys, five bays, in a fine position overlooking the river Camel. Pleasant contemporary interiors. GMT)

(COUNTY SECONDARY SCHOOL, Gonvena. 1958 by *F. K. Hicklin*, County Architect.)

WARBSTOW

ST WERBURGH. A plain, humble, unbuttressed tower of two stages, and a nave with N aisle only. The arcade of granite, low, with Cornish standard piers and four-centred arches. The aisle windows with standard three-light Perp tracery. – FONT. Altarnun and St Thomas Launceston type, with faces at the four corners and stylized six-petalled flowers in niches on the four sides.

WARLEGGAN

ST BARTHOLOMEW. In the loneliest village on Bodmin Moor, close to some old trees. Originally the church had a spire which, however, fell in 1818. The tower is of two stages with a stair-turret and no buttresses. The nave and S aisle are low, the arcade of five bays, that is not small. The date of the aisle is C15; cf. the standard granite piers. The N side is considerably older. One C13 lancet remains. Of furnishings only the ROYAL ARMS of 1664 (but still with Jacobean strapwork) deserve mention. – PLATE. Paten of the 1570s by *Jons* of Exeter, made for domestic use; Chalice of 1582–3, very handsome, of egg-cup shape, covered in strapwork, openwork stem.

WASHAWAY

St Conan. 1882. – font from Lanteglos-by-Camelford; one of the oldest in Cornwall, of the same size and indistinct vaguely circular shape as Morwenstow, but with plenty of decoration of a Celtic character, not easily distinguishable now: interlacings and probably intertwined animals too (c.1100 or earlier). – (Fine PULPIT, possibly German, with a carving of the Nativity. Information from Mrs Ettlinger.)

Croan. *See* p. 59.

Pencarrow. *See* p. 133.

WATERPIT DOWN *see* MINSTER

WEEK ST MARY

Nativity of St Mary. Unbuttressed granite tower with carved figures on the plinth and above and below each of the three stringcourses. The motifs are squares with trefoil, quatrefoil, star, etc., set in (cf. North Tamerton, Jacobstow). Nave and aisles, s aisle late c14, n aisle c15 of standard Cornish type, the s arcade with shorter, thicker, piers of polyphant stone, the n arcade slim and of granite as usual; the E bays on the s also belong to this later phase (cf. North Tamerton near by). The aisle wagon roofs still remain, though much restored. The E window is the only one with original tracery. – FONT. Octagonal, Late Gothic, with coarse carving. – STAINED GLASS. Three Martyrs, by *Kempe*, 1887.

(Much of the college or chantry founded early in the c16 by Thomasine Bonaventure survives as a farmhouse. There are good doorways, one especially with a carved tympanum of a plain shield and foliage; etc. G. W. Copeland)

WELLTOWN *see* FORRABURY

WENDRON

St Wendrons. The n aisle c14 or earlier, the rest c15,* with granite w tower with diagonal buttresses, early c15 aisle, and later buttressed and battlemented s porch. Inside there is between nave and s aisle an arcade of five bays plus two lower bays at the E end, separated by one yet lower, narrow arch,

* Canon Doble dates the chancel E.E. (cf. a lancet window in the n wall) and the n transept Dec (cf. the E window).

where the rood screen went across. The piers are all Cornish granite standard, with plain capitals. Only one of them, in front of the former rood screen, has angels holding shields, as have the capitals opposite supporting the two arches between nave and N transept. A funeral recess in the N wall of the chancel. – FONT. C14? With quatrefoils and very crude corner shafts. – MONUMENTS. Brass to W. Penhalluryk, Rector, 1535; headless. – Stone wall-tablet to Canon Doble † 1945, the great expert on Cornish hagiology. – Wall-tablet to an unknown family in the chancel; late C16. – Over the lychgate a granite-built PARISH ROOM, C17, according to Canon Doble. – CROSS SLAB with incised cross, the head encircled. Langdon regards this as the earliest of all Cornish crosses. – There is also an old Celtic CROSS HEAD near the porch.

(TRENETHICK. Late C16. Important for its delightful gatehouse with Tudor arch and heavy hoodmould. Room above with a three-light mullioned window. The gatehouse opens on to the garden court and faces the house, which is gabled, with a projecting two-storeyed porch and many fine mullioned windows. GMT)

THE NINE MAIDENS, 1½ m. SE of Troon. Two circles of standing stones, the N 50 ft in diameter the S 60 ft in diameter.

WEST LANYON see MADRON

3070

WHITEFORD
Near Stoke Climsland

Of Sir John Call's mansion of 1775 little survives. The house of the agent of the home farm close by incorporates some fragments: a Tuscan Doric porch and several tripartite windows. The appearance of the house before it was pulled down in 1912 is known from engravings. All that can still be seen *in situ* is an insignificant outbuilding now divided into cottages, the STABLES with a pretty cupola and projecting wings, a ghost of the layout of the grounds, a BRIDGE close to the main Callington road, and a neglected GARDEN TEMPLE (now a cattle byre) with figure reliefs in *Coade* stone.

WHITESANDS BAY see PORTWRINKLE

2090

WHITSTONE

ST ANNE. Not a large church; outside the village against the

hillside, shaded by trees. Unbuttressed W tower with NE stair-
turret. Interior of five bays with aisles, the piers of standard
Cornish type, with plain capitals and four-centred arches.
Rather over-restored (by *Hooper* of Hatherleigh; 1882). The s
door is very plain Norman; the later porch has an unusual
window into the s aisle. – FONT. Norman, circular, with a
simple undulating leaf frieze along the top of the bowl. –
PLATE. Chalice by *Jons* of Exeter, 1570–3. – Outside against
the s wall pretty SLATE SLAB with scrolly decoration to Thomas
Edgcumbe † 1712.

WITHIEL   9060

ST CLEMENT. Quite a large church, with a tall three-stage
tower, yet lying so deep in a combe that in approaching the
village one sees only its top. The tower has buttresses set back
from the angles, and a NE stair-turret. The nave and chancel
are older than the s aisle. The former are not of granite, the
latter and the s porch are. Both have original wagon roofs. The
small N door is C13. The N chancel aisle has an arcade contemporary with the s aisle. In its outer wall old stones must have
been used. The arcades are of Cornish standard. – FONT. C15,
with coarsely chip-carved ornamental motifs. – PLATE. Chalice, Paten, and Flagon by *B. Stephens*, 1835–6; nice, if somewhat ornate.
RUTHERNBRIDGE, 1½ m. NE. Early C15, of two pointed arches
with two rings of slate voussoirs; roadway 9½ ft wide.

WOODWAN *see* MAWGAN-IN-PYDAR

WORTHIVALE *see* MINSTER

YEOLMBRIDGE   3080
1 m. N of St Stephen-by-Launceston

BRIDGE. C14, the oldest and most ambitious Cornish bridge;
two pointed arches of dressed stone with three chamfered
ribs. The roadway widened.

ZENNOR   4030

ST SENNER. The church was given in 1150 to Tywardreath
Priory, one of the chief monastic houses of Cornwall. In 1270
it was appropriated by Bishop Bronescombe to Glasney

College, founded by him. The s side of the nave is partly Norman, with a narrow window of deep inner splay. The transept and chancel further E are later, but still earlier than the
C15 N aisle of six bays. The arcade of the N aisle and also the
arches screening off the N transept have octagonal piers and
plain double-chamfered arches. There is a squint from the s
transept into the chancel. The W tower is of three stages, unbuttressed. Some of the windows are straight-headed, but the s
window of the s transept has intersecting and cusped tracery of
c.1300 (cf. Towednack). – FONT. Octagonal on five supports,
the four outer supports corbelling out like stove-pipes to make
corner shafts of the bowl. The bowl decorated by quatrefoils
which also extend behind the corner shafts. Difficult to date;
probably rather late C13 than C14. – BENCH ENDS. Only two,
made into a chancel seat, but one of them the pretty Mermaid
of Zennor (*en face*). – PLATE. Paten by *Mathew* of Barnstaple,
Elizabethan; Chalice with baluster stem, 1671–2.

ZENNOR QUOIT. This is a massive closed megalithic chamber of
rectangular plan with two stones of a straight façade on the E.
The single large capstone has been partially displaced and now
has one end resting on the ground. The chamber was originally covered by a round barrow, 40 ft in diameter, scant traces
of which still survive. Fragments of Late Neolithic pottery
and a token cremation burial were found in the chamber.

SPERRIS QUOIT, 400 yds ENE of Zennor Quoit. A much ruined
megalithic chamber marked by two granite slabs projecting
above the turf. Excavation revealed a cremation pit adjacent
to one of the uprights. Traces of a mound 40 ft in diameter are
still discernible.

THE GIANT'S HOUSE, Pennance. An entrance grave with chamber 13 ft long enclosed in a barrow 26 ft in diameter and 6 ft
high revetted with a massive kerb.

ROUND BARROWS. ½ m. SW of the Giant's House are four
round barrows running in a line N–S. The N barrow, 25 ft in
diameter and 5 ft high, contains the remains of a ruined entrance grave. The third site from the N also contains a chamber, 12 ft 6 in. in length. No chambers are visible within the
other two barrows.

NINE MAIDENS, 1¼ m. S of Porthmeor. A circle of eleven
stones having a diameter of 70 ft. The tallest stone, on the
N, is just over 6 ft in height. A ROUND BARROW cuts the
circle on the S. A Middle Bronze Age urn was found in this
barrow in the C19.

TREEN DINAS PROMONTORY FORT, $\frac{1}{2}$ m. s of Treen. The promontory is cut off by five lines of fortifications. These occur in three distinct groups and presumably represent separate structural phases; the outer and innermost ramparts, and the central group of three lines of banks and ditches.

GLOSSARY

ABACUS: flat slab on the top of a capital (q.v.).

ABUTMENT: solid masonry placed to resist the lateral pressure of a vault.

ACANTHUS: plant with thick fleshy and scalloped leaves used as part of the decoration of a Corinthian capital (q.v.) and in some types of leaf carving.

ACHIEVEMENT OF ARMS: in heraldry, a complete display of armorial bearings.

ACROTERION: foliage-carved block on the end or top of a classical pediment.

ADDORSED: two human figures, animals, or birds, etc., placed symmetrically so that they turn their backs to each other.

AEDICULE, AEDICULA: framing of a window or door by columns and a pediment (q.v.).

AFFRONTED: two human figures, animals, or birds, etc., placed symmetrically so that they face each other.

AGGER: Latin term for the built-up foundations of Roman roads; also sometimes applied to the banks of hill-forts or other earthworks.

AMBULATORY: semicircular or polygonal aisle enclosing an apse (q.v.).

ANNULET: see Shaft-ring.

ANSE DE PANIER: see Arch, Basket.

ANTEPENDIUM: covering of the front of an altar, usually by textiles or metalwork.

ANTIS, IN: see Portico.

APSE: vaulted semicircular or polygonal end of a chancel or a chapel.

ARABESQUE: light and fanciful surface decoration using combinations of flowing lines, tendrils, etc., interspersed with vases, animals, etc.

ARCADE: range of arches supported on piers or columns, free-standing: or, BLIND ARCADE, the same attached to a wall.

ARCH: round-headed, i.e. semicircular; pointed, i.e. consisting of two curves, each drawn from one centre, and meeting in a point at the top; segmental, i.e. in the form of a segment;

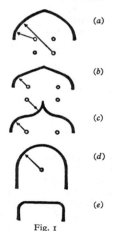

Fig. 1

pointed; four-centred (a Late Medieval form), see Fig. 1(a); Tudor (also a Late Medieval form), see Fig. 1(b); Ogee (introduced c.1300 and specially popular in the C14), see Fig. 1(c); Stilted, see Fig. 1(d); Basket, with lintel connected to the jambs by concave quadrant curves, see Fig. 1(e) for one example; Diaphragm, a transverse arch with solid spandrels carrying not a vault but a principal beam of a timber roof.

ARCHITRAVE: lowest of the three main parts of the entablature (q.v.) of an order (q.v.) (see Fig. 12).

ARCHIVOLT: under-surface of an arch (also called Soffit).

ARRIS: sharp edge at the meeting of two surfaces.

ASHLAR: masonry of large blocks wrought to even faces and square edges.

ATLANTES: male counterparts of caryatids (q.v.).

ATRIUM: inner court of a Roman house, also open court in front of a church.

ATTACHED: see Engaged.

ATTIC: topmost storey of a house, if distance from floor to ceiling is less than in the others.

AUMBRY: recess or cupboard to hold sacred vessels for Mass and Communion.

B AILEY: open space or court of a stone-built castle; see also Motte-and-Bailey.

BALDACCHINO: canopy supported on columns.

BALLFLOWER: globular flower of three petals enclosing a small ball. A decoration used in the first quarter of the C14.

BALUSTER: small pillar or column of fanciful outline.

BALUSTRADE: series of balusters supporting a handrail or coping (q.v.).

BARBICAN: outwork defending the entrance to a castle.

BARGEBOARDS: projecting decorated boards placed against the incline of the gable of a building and hiding the horizontal roof timbers.

BARROW: see Bell, Bowl, Disc, Long, and Pond Barrow.

BASILICA: in medieval architecture an aisled church with a clerestory.

BASKET ARCH: see Arch (Fig. 1e).

BASTION: projection at the angle of a fortification.

BATTER: inclined face of a wall.

BATTLEMENT: parapet with a series of indentations or embrasures with raised portions or merlons between (also called Crenellation).

BAYS: internal compartments of a building; each divided from the other not by solid walls but by divisions only marked in the side walls (columns, pilasters, etc.) or the ceiling (beams, etc.). Also external divisions of a building by fenestration.

BAY-WINDOW: angular or curved projection of a house front with ample fenestration. If curved, also called bow-window: if on an upper floor only, also called oriel or oriel window.

BEAKER FOLK: Late New Stone Age warrior invaders from the Continent who buried their dead in round barrows and introduced the first metal tools and weapons to Britain.

BEAKHEAD: Norman ornamental motif consisting of a row of bird or beast heads with beaks biting usually into a roll moulding.

BELFRY: turret on a roof to hang bells in.

BELGAE: Aristocratic warrior bands who settled in Britain in two main waves in the C I B.C. In Britain their culture is termed Iron Age C.

BELL BARROW: Early Bronze Age round barrow in which the mound is separated from its encircling ditch by a flat platform or berm (q.v.).

BELLCOTE: framework on a roof to hang bells from.

BERM: level area separating ditch from bank on a hill-fort or barrow.

BILLET FRIEZE: Norman ornamental motif made up of short raised rectangles placed at regular intervals.

BIVALLATE: Of a hill-fort: defended by two concentric banks and ditches.

BLOCK CAPITAL: Romanesque capital cut from a cube by hav-

Fig. 2

ing the lower angles rounded off to the circular shaft below (also called Cushion Capital) (Fig. 2).

BOND, ENGLISH or FLEMISH: see Brickwork.

BOSS: knob or projection usually placed to cover the intersection of ribs in a vault.

BOWL BARROW: round barrow surrounded by a quarry ditch. Introduced in Late Neolithic

times, the form continued until the Saxon period.

BOW-WINDOW: see Bay-Window.

BOX: A small country house, e.g. a shooting box. A convenient term to describe a compact minor dwelling, e.g. a rectory.

BOX PEW: pew with a high wooden enclosure.

BRACES: see Roof.

BRACKET: small supporting piece of stone, etc., to carry a projecting horizontal.

BRESSUMER: beam in a timber-framed building to support the, usually projecting, superstructure.

BRICKWORK: *Header:* brick laid so that the end only appears on the face of the wall. *Stretcher:* brick laid so that the side only appears on the face of the wall. *English Bond:* method of laying bricks so that alternate courses or layers on the face of the wall are composed of headers or stretchers only (Fig. 3a). *Flemish Bond:* method of laying

(a)

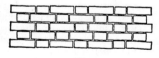

(b)

Fig. 3

bricks so that alternate headers and stretchers appear in each course on the face of the wall (Fig. 3b).

BROACH: see Spire.

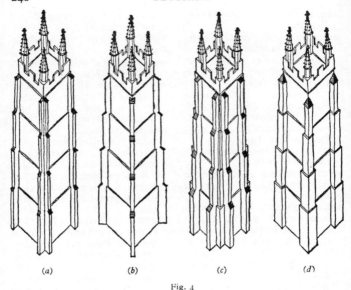

(a)   *(b)*   *(c)*   *(d)*

Fig. 4

BROKEN PEDIMENT: *see* Pediment.

BRONZE AGE: In Britain, the
period from *c*.1800 to 600 B.C.

BUCRANIUM: ox skull.

BUTTRESS: mass of brickwork or
masonry projecting from or
built against a wall to give
additional strength. *Angle Buttresses:* two meeting at an angle
of 90° at the angle of a building
(Fig. 4*a*). *Clasping Buttress:*
one which encases the angle
(Fig. 4*d*). *Diagonal Buttress:*
one placed against the right
angle formed by two walls, and
more or less equiangular with
both (Fig. 4*b*). *Flying Buttress:*
arch or half arch transmitting
the thrust of a vault or roof
from the upper part of a wall

to an outer support or buttress.
Setback Buttress: angle buttress set slightly back from the
angle (Fig. 4*c*).

CABLE MOULDING: Norman
moulding imitating a twisted
cord.

CAIRN: a mound of stones usually
covering a burial.

CAMBER: slight rise or upward
curve of an otherwise horizontal structure.

CAMPANILE: isolated bell tower.

CANOPY: projection or hood
over an altar, pulpit, niche,
statue, etc.

CAP: in a windmill the crowning
feature.

CAPITAL: head or top part of a
column.

CARTOUCHE: tablet with an ornate frame, usually enclosing an inscription.

CARYATID: whole female figure supporting an entablature or other similar member. *Termini Caryatids:* female busts or demi-figures or three-quarter figures supporting an entablature or other similar member and placed at the top of termini pilasters (q.v.). Cf. Atlantes.

CASTELLATED: decorated with battlements.

CELURE: panelled and adorned part of a wagon-roof above the rood or the altar.

CENSER: vessel for the burning of incense.

CENTERING: wooden framework used in arch and vault construction and removed when the mortar has set.

CHALICE: cup used in the Communion service or at Mass. *See also* Recusant Chalice.

CHAMBERED TOMB: burial mound of the New Stone Age having a stone-built chamber and entrance passage covered by an earthen barrow or stone cairn. The form was introduced to Britain from the Mediterranean.

CHAMFER: surface made by cutting across the square angle of a stone block, piece of wood, etc., usually at an angle of 45° to the other two surfaces.

CHANCEL: that part of the E end of a church in which the altar is placed, usually applied to the whole continuation of the nave E of the crossing.

CHANCEL ARCH: arch at the W end of the chancel.

CHANTRY CHAPEL: chapel attached to, or inside, a church, endowed for the saying of Masses for the soul of the founder or some other individual.

CHEVET: French term for the E end of a church (chancel, ambulatory, and radiating chapels).

CHEVRON: Norman moulding forming a zigzag.

CHOIR: that part of the church where divine service is sung.

CIBORIUM: a baldacchino.

CINQUEFOIL: *see* Foil.

CIST: stone-lined or slab-built grave. First appears in Late Neolithic times. It continued to be used in the Early Christian period.

CLAPPER BRIDGE: bridge made of large slabs of stone, some built up to make rough piers and other longer ones laid on top to make the roadway.

CLASSIC: here used to mean the moment of highest achievement of a style.

CLASSICAL: here used as the term for Greek and Roman architecture and any subsequent styles inspired by it.

CLERESTORY: upper storey of the nave walls of a church, pierced by windows.

COADE STONE: artificial (cast) stone made in the late C18 and the early C19 by Coade and Sealy in London.

COB: walling material made of mixed clay and straw.

COFFERING: decorating a ceiling with sunk square or polygonal ornamental panels.

COLLAR-BEAM: *see* Roof.

COLONNADE: range of columns.

COLONNETTE: small column.

COLUMNA ROSTRATA: column decorated with carved prows of ships to celebrate a naval victory.

COMPOSITE: *see* Order.

CONSOLE: bracket (q.v.) with a compound curved outline.

COPING: capping or covering to a wall.

CORBEL: block of stone projecting from a wall, supporting some feature on its horizontal top surface.

CORBEL TABLE: series of corbels, occurring just below the roof eaves externally or internally, often seen in Norman buildings.

CORINTHIAN: *see* Order.

CORNICE: in classical architecture the top section of the entablature (q.v.). Also for a projecting decorative feature along the top of a wall, arch, etc.

CORRIDOR VILLA: *see* Villa.

COUNTERSCARP BANK: small bank on the down-hill or outer side of a hill-fort ditch.

COURTYARD VILLA: *see* Villa.

COVE, COVING: concave undersurface in the nature of a hollow moulding but on a larger scale.

COVER PATEN: cover to a Communion cup, suitable for use as a paten or plate for the consecrated bread.

CRADLE ROOF: *see* Wagon roof.

CRENELLATION: *see* Battlement.

CREST, CRESTING: ornamental finish along the top of a screen, etc.

CRINKLE-CRANKLE WALL: undulating wall.

CROCKET, CROCKETING: decorative features placed on the sloping sides of spires, pinnacles, gables, etc., in Gothic architecture, carved in various leaf shapes and placed at regular intervals.

CROCKET CAPITAL: *see* Fig. 5. An Early Gothic form.

CROMLECH: word of Celtic origin still occasionally used of single free-standing stones ascribed to the Neolithic or Bronze Age periods.

Fig. 5

CROSSING: space at the intersection of nave, chancel, and transepts.

CROSS-WINDOWS: windows with one mullion and one transom.

CRUCK: big curved beam supporting both walls and roof of a cottage.

CRYPT: underground room usually below the E end of a church.

CUPOLA: small polygonal or circular domed turret crowning a roof.

CURTAIN WALL: connecting wall between the towers of a castle.

CUSHION CAPITAL: *see* Block Capital.

CUSP: projecting point between the foils in a foiled Gothic arch.

DADO: decorative covering of the lower part of a wall.

DAGGER: tracery motif of the Dec style. It is a lancet shape rounded or pointed at the head, pointed at the foot, and cusped inside (*see* Fig. 6).

Fig. 6

DAIS: raised platform at one end of a room.

DEC ('DECORATED'): historical division of English Gothic architecture covering the period from c.1290 to c.1350.

DEMI-COLUMNS: columns half sunk into a wall.

DIAPER WORK: surface decoration composed of square or lozenge-shapes.

DIAPHRAGM ARCH: see Arch.

DISC BARROW: Bronze Age round barrow with inconspicuous central mound surrounded by bank and ditch.

DOGTOOTH: typical E.E. ornament consisting of a series of four-cornered stars placed diagonally and raised pyramidally (Fig. 7).

Fig. 7

DOMICAL VAULT: see Vault.

DONJON: see Keep.

DORIC: see Order.

DORMER (WINDOW): window placed vertically in the sloping plane of a roof.

DRIPSTONE: see Hood-mould.

DRUM: circular or polygonal vertical wall of a dome or cupola.

E.E. ('EARLY ENGLISH'): historical division of English Gothic architecture roughly covering the C13.

EASTER SEPULCHRE: recess with tomb-chest, usually in the wall of a chancel, the tomb-chest to receive an effigy of Christ for Easter celebrations.

EAVES: underpart of a sloping roof overhanging a wall.

EAVES CORNICE: cornice below the eaves of a roof.

ECHINUS: Convex or projecting moulding supporting the abacus of a Greek Doric capital, sometimes bearing an egg and dart pattern.

EMBATTLED: see Battlement.

EMBRASURE: small opening in the wall or parapet of a fortified building, usually splayed on the inside.

ENCAUSTIC TILES: earthenware glazed and decorated tiles used for paving.

ENGAGED COLUMNS: columns attached to, or partly sunk into, a wall.

ENGLISH BOND: see Brickwork.

ENTABLATURE: in classical architecture the whole of the horizontal members above a column (that is architrave, frieze, and cornice) (see Fig. 12).

ENTASIS: very slight convex deviation from a straight line; used on Greek columns and sometimes on spires to prevent an optical illusion of concavity.

ENTRESOL: see Mezzanine.

EPITAPH: hanging wall monument.

ESCUTCHEON: shield for armorial bearings.

EXEDRA: the apsidal end of a room. See Apse.

FAN-VAULT: see Vault.

FERETORY: place behind the

high altar where the chief shrine of a church is kept.

FESTOON: carved garland of flowers and fruit suspended at both ends.

FILLET: narrow flat band running down a shaft or along a roll moulding.

FINIAL: top of a canopy, gable, pinnacle.

FLAGON: vessel for the wine used in the Communion service.

FLAMBOYANT: properly the latest phase of French Gothic architecture where the window tracery takes on wavy undulating lines.

FLÈCHE: slender wooden spire on the centre of a roof (also called Spirelet).

FLEMISH BOND: see Brickwork.

FLEURON: decorative carved flower or leaf.

FLUSHWORK: decorative use of flint in conjunction with dressed stone so as to form patterns: tracery, initials, etc.

FLUTING: vertical channelling in the shaft of a column.

FLYING BUTTRESS: see Buttress.

FOIL: lobe formed by the cusping (q.v.) of a circle or an arch. Trefoil, quatrefoil, cinquefoil, multifoil, express the number of leaf shapes to be seen.

FOLIATED: carved with leaf shapes.

FOSSE: ditch.

FOUR-CENTRED ARCH: see Arch.

FRATER: refectory or dining hall of a monastery.

FRESCO: wall painting on wet plaster.

FRIEZE: middle division of a classical entablature (q.v.) (see Fig. 12).

FRONTAL: covering for the front of an altar.

GABLE: *Dutch gable:* A gable with curved sides crowned by a pediment, characteristic of *c.*1630–50 (Fig. 8*a*). *Shaped gable:* A gable with multi-curved sides characteristic of *c.*1600–50 (Fig. 8*b*).

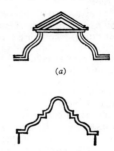

(a)

(b)

Fig. 8

GADROONED: enriched with a series of convex ridges, the opposite of fluting.

GALILEE: chapel or vestibule usually at the W end of a church enclosing the porch. Also called Narthex (q.v.).

GALLERY: in church architecture upper storey above an aisle, opened in arches to the nave. Also called Tribune and often erroneously Triforium (q.v.).

GALLERY GRAVE: chambered tomb (q.v.) in which there is little or no differentiation between the entrance passage and the actual burial chamber(s).

GARDEROBE: lavatory or privy in a medieval building.

GARGOYLE: water spout projecting from the parapet of a wall or tower; carved into a human or animal shape.

GAZEBO: lookout tower or raised

summer house in a picturesque
garden.

'GEOMETRICAL': *see* Tracery.

'GIBBS SURROUND': of a doorway or window. An C18 motif
consisting of a surround with
alternating larger and smaller
blocks of stone, quoin-wise, or
intermittent large blocks, sometimes with a narrow raised
band connecting them up the
verticals and along the face of
the arch (Fig. 9).

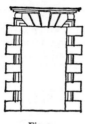

Fig. 9

GROIN: sharp edge at the meeting of two cells of a cross-vault.

GROIN-VAULT: *see* Vault.

GROTESQUE: fanciful orna-
mental decoration: *see* also
Arabesque.

HAGIOSCOPE: *see* Squint.

HALF-TIMBERING: *see* Timber-
Framing.

HALL CHURCH: church in which
nave and aisles are of equal
height or approximately so.

HAMMERBEAM: *see* Roof.

HANAP: large metal cup, generally made for domestic use,
standing on an elaborate base
and stem; with a very ornate
cover frequently crowned with
a little steeple.

HEADERS: *see* Brickwork.

HERRINGBONE WORK: brick,
stone, or tile construction
where the component blocks
are laid diagonally instead of
flat. Alternate courses lie in
opposing directions to make a
zigzag pattern up the face of
the wall.

HEXASTYLE: having six de-
tached columns.

HILL-FORT: Iron Age earthwork
enclosed by a ditch and bank
system; in the later part of the
period the defences multiplied
in size and complexity. They
vary from about an acre to
over 30 acres in area, and are
usually built with careful
regard to natural elevations or
promontories.

HIPPED ROOF: *see* Roof.

HOOD-MOULD: projecting
moulding above an arch or a
lintel to throw off water (also
called Dripstone or Label).

ICONOGRAPHY: the science of
the subject matter of works of
the visual arts.

IMPOST: bracket in a wall,
usually formed of mouldings,
on which the ends of an arch
rest.

INDENT: shape chiselled out in
a stone slab to receive a brass.

INGLENOOK: bench or seat
built in beside a fireplace,
sometimes covered by the
chimneybreast, occasionally
lit by small windows on each
side of the fire.

INTERCOLUMNIATION: the
space between columns.

IONIC: *see* Order (Fig. 12).

IRON AGE: in Britain the period
from c. 600 B.C. to the coming
of the Romans. The term is

also used for those un-Romanized native communities which survived until the Saxon incursions.

JAMB: straight side of an archway, doorway, or window.

KEEL MOULDING: moulding whose outline is in section like that of the keel of a ship.

KEEP: massive tower of a Norman castle.

KEYSTONE: middle stone in an arch or a rib-vault.

KING-POST: see Roof (Fig. 14).

KNEELER: horizontal decorative projection at the base of a gable.

KNOP: a knob-like thickening in the stem of a chalice.

LABEL: see Hood-mould.

LABEL STOP: ornamental boss at the end of a hood-mould (q.v.).

LACED WINDOWS: windows pulled visually together by strips, usually in brick of a different colour, which continue vertically the lines of the vertical parts of the window surrounds. The motif is typical of c. 1720.

LANCET WINDOW: slender pointed-arched window.

LANTERN: in architecture, a small circular or polygonal turret with windows all round crowning a roof (see Cupola) or a dome.

LANTERN CROSS: churchyard cross with lantern-shaped top usually with sculptured representations on the sides of the top.

LEAN-TO ROOF: roof with one slope only, built against a higher wall.

LESENE or PILASTER STRIP: pilaster without base or capital.

LIERNE: see Vault (Fig. 21).

LINENFOLD: Tudor panelling ornamented with a conventional representation of a piece of linen laid in vertical folds. The piece is repeated in each panel.

LINTEL: horizontal beam or stone bridging an opening.

LOGGIA: recessed colonnade (q.v.).

LONG AND SHORT WORK: Saxon quoins (q.v.) consisting of stones placed with the long sides alternately upright and horizontal.

LONG BARROW: unchambered Neolithic communal burial mound, wedge-shaped in plan, with the burial and occasional other structures massed at the broader end, from which the mound itself tapers in height; quarry ditches flank the mound.

LOUVRE: opening, often with lantern (q.v.) over, in the roof of a room to let the smoke from a central hearth escape.

LOWER PALAEOLITHIC: see Palaeolithic.

LOZENGE: diamond shape.

LUCARNE: small opening to let light in.

LUNETTE: tympanum (q.v.) or semicircular opening.

LYCH GATE: wooden gate structure with a roof and open sides placed at the entrance to a churchyard to provide space for the reception of a coffin. The word *lych* is Saxon and means a corpse.

LYNCHET: long terraced strip of soil accumulating on the downward side of prehistoric and medieval fields due to soil creep from continuous ploughing along the contours.

MACHICOLATION: projecting gallery on brackets constructed on the outside of castle towers or walls. The gallery has holes in the floor to drop missiles through.

MAJOLICA: ornamented glazed earthenware.

MANSARD: *see* Roof.

MATHEMATICAL TILES: Small facing tiles the size of brick headers, applied to timber-framed walls to make them appear brick-built.

MEGALITHIC TOMB: stone-built burial chamber of the New Stone Age covered by an earth or stone mound. The form was introduced to Britain from the Mediterranean area.

MERLON: *see* Battlement.

MESOLITHIC: 'Middle Stone' Age; the post-glacial period of hunting and fishing communities dating in Britain from *c.* 8000 B.C. to the arrival of Neolithic communities, with which they must have considerably overlapped.

METOPE: in classical architecture of the Doric order (q.v.) the space in the frieze between the triglyphs (Fig. 12).

MEZZANINE: low storey placed between two higher ones.

MISERERE: *see* Misericord.

MISERICORD: bracket placed on the underside of a hinged choir stall seat which, when turned up, provided the occupant of the seat with a support during long periods of standing (also called Miserere).

MODILLION: small bracket of which large numbers (modillion frieze) are often placed below a cornice (q.v.) in classical architecture.

MOTTE: steep mound forming the main feature of C11 and C12 castles.

MOTTE-AND-BAILEY: post-Roman and Norman defence system consisting of an earthen mound (the motte) topped with a wooden tower eccentrically placed within a bailey (q.v.), with enclosure ditch and palisade, and with the rare addition of an internal bank.

MOUCHETTE: tracery motif in curvilinear tracery, a curved dagger (q.v.), specially popular in the early C14 (Fig. 10).

Fig. 10

MULLIONS: vertical posts or uprights dividing a window into 'lights'.

MULTIVALLATE: Of a hill-fort: defended by three or more concentric banks and ditches.

MUNTIN: post as a rule moulded and part of a screen.

NAIL-HEAD: E.E. ornamental motif, consisting of small pyramids regularly repeated (Fig. 11).

Fig. 11

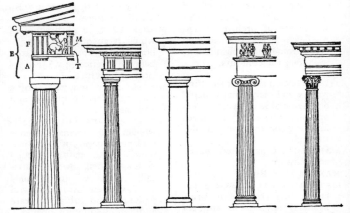

Fig. 12. Orders of Columns (Greek Doric, Roman Doric, Tuscan Doric, Ionic, Corinthian) E, Entablature; C, Cornice; F, Frieze; A, Architrave; M, Metope; T, Triglyph.

NARTHEX: enclosed vestibule or covered porch at the main entrance to a church (*see* Galilee).

NEOLITHIC: 'New Stone' Age, dating in Britain from the appearance from the Continent of the first settled farming communities c. 3500 B.C. until the introduction of the Bronze Age.

NEWEL: central post in a circular or winding staircase; also the principal post when a flight of stairs meets a landing.

NOOK-SHAFT: shaft set in the angle of a pier or respond or wall, or the angle of the jamb of a window or doorway.

NUTMEG MOULDING: consisting of a chain of tiny triangles placed obliquely.

OBELISK: lofty pillar of square section tapering at the top and ending pyramidally.

OGEE: *see* Arch (Fig. 1c).

ORATORY: small private chapel in a house.

ORDER: (1) *of a doorway or window:* series of concentric steps receding towards the opening; (2) *in classical architecture:* column with base, shaft, capital, and entablature (q.v.) according to one of the following styles: Greek Doric, Roman Doric, Tuscan Doric, Ionic, Corinthian, Composite. The established details are very elaborate, and some specialist architectural work should be consulted for further guidance (*see* Fig. 12).

ORIEL: *see* Bay-Window.

OVERHANG: projection of the upper storey of a house.

OVERSAILING COURSES: series of stone or brick courses, each one projecting beyond the one below it.

OVOLO: convex moulding.

PALAEOLITHIC: 'Old Stone' Age; the first period of human culture, commencing in the

Ice Age and immediately prior to the Mesolithic; the Lower Palaeolithic is the older phase, the Upper Palaeolithic the later.

PALIMPSEST: (1) *of a brass:* where a metal plate has been re-used by turning over and engraving on the back; (2) *of a wall painting:* where one overlaps and partly obscures an earlier one.

PALLADIAN: architecture following the ideas and principles of Andrea Palladio, 1518–80.

PANTILE: tile of curved S-shaped section.

PARAPET: low wall placed to protect any spot where there is a sudden drop, for example on a bridge, quay, hillside, housetop, etc.

PARGETTING: plaster work with patterns and ornaments either in relief or engraved on it.

PARVIS: term wrongly applied to a room over a church porch. These rooms were often used as a schoolroom or as a store room.

PATEN: plate to hold the bread at Communion or Mass.

PATERA: small flat circular or oval ornament in classical architecture.

PEDIMENT: low-pitched gable used in classical, Renaissance, and neo-classical architecture above a portico and above doors, windows, etc. It may be straight-sided or curved segmentally. *Broken Pediment:* one where the centre portion of the base is left open. *Open Pediment:* one where the centre portion of the sloping sides is left out.

PENDANT: boss (q.v.) elongated so that it seems to hang down.

PENDENTIF: concave triangular spandrel used to lead from the angle of two walls to the base of a circular dome. It is constructed as part of the hemisphere over a diameter the size of the diagonal of the basic square (Fig. 13).

Fig. 13

PERP (PERPENDICULAR): historical division of English Gothic architecture covering the period from c.1335–50 to c.1530.

PIANO NOBILE: principal storey of a house with the reception rooms; usually the first floor.

PIAZZA: open space surrounded by buildings; in C17 and C18 England sometimes used to mean a long colonnade or loggia.

PIER: strong, solid support, frequently square in section or of composite section (compound pier).

PIETRA DURA: ornamental or scenic inlay by means of thin slabs of stone.

PILASTER: shallow pier attached to a wall. *Termini Pilasters:* pilasters with sides tapering downwards.

PILLAR PISCINA: free-standing piscina on a pillar.

PINNACLE: ornamental form crowning a spire, tower, buttress, etc., usually of steep pyramidal, conical, or some similar shape.

PISCINA: basin for washing the Communion or Mass vessels, provided with a drain. Generally set in or against the wall to the S of an altar.

PLAISANCE: summer-house, pleasure house near a mansion.

PLATE TRACERY: *see* Tracery.

PLINTH: projecting base of a wall or column, generally chamfered (q.v.) or moulded at the top.

POND BARROW: rare type of Bronze Age barrow consisting of a circular depression, usually paved, and containing a number of cremation burials.

POPPYHEAD: ornament of leaf and flower type used to decorate the tops of bench- or stall-ends.

PORTCULLIS: gate constructed to rise and fall in vertical grooves; used in gateways of castles.

PORTE COCHÈRE: porch large enough to admit wheeled vehicles.

PORTICO: centre-piece of a house or a church with classical detached or attached columns and a pediment. A portico is called *prostyle* or *in antis* according to whether it projects from or recedes into a building. In a portico *in antis* the columns range with the side walls.

POSTERN: small gateway at the back of a building.

PREDELLA: in an altarpiece the horizontal strip below the main representation, often used for a number of subsidiary representations in a row.

PRESBYTERY: the part of the church lying E of the choir. It is the part where the altar is placed.

PRINCIPAL: *see* Roof (Fig. 14).

PRIORY: monastic house whose head is a prior or prioress, not an abbot or abbess.

PROSTYLE: with free-standing columns in a row.

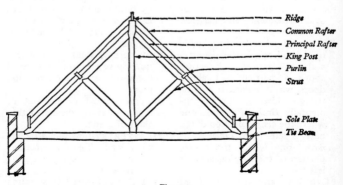

Ridge
Common Rafter
Principal Rafter
King Post
Purlin
Strut

Sole Plate
Tie Beam

Fig. 14

PULPITUM: stone screen in a major church provided to shut off the choir from the nave and also as a backing for the return choir stalls.

PULVINATED FRIEZE: frieze with a bold convex moulding.

PURLIN: see Roof (Figs. 14, 15).

PUTHOLE or PUTLOCK HOLE. putlocks are the short horizontal timbers on which during construction the boards of scaffolding rest. Putholes or putlock holes are the holes in the wall for putlocks, which often are not filled in after construction is complete.

PUTTO: small naked boy.

QUADRANGLE: inner courtyard in a large building.

QUARRY: in stained-glass work, a small diamond- or square-shaped piece of glass set diagonally.

QUATREFOIL: see Foil.

QUEEN-POSTS: see Roof (Fig. 15).

QUOINS: dressed stones at the angles of a building. Sometimes all the stones are of the same size; more often they are alternately large and small.

RADIATING CHAPELS: chapels projecting radially from an ambulatory or an apse.

RAFTER: see Roof.

RAMPART: stone wall or wall of earth surrounding a castle, fortress, or fortified city.

RAMPART-WALK: path along the inner face of a rampart.

REBATE: continuous rectangular notch cut on an edge.

REBUS: pun, a play on words. The literal translation and illustration of a name for artistic and heraldic purposes (Belton = bell, tun).

RECUSANT CHALICE: chalice made after the Reformation and before Catholic Emancipation for Roman Catholic use.

REEDING: decoration with parallel convex mouldings touching one another.

REFECTORY: dining hall; see Frater.

RENDERING: plastering of an outer wall.

REPOUSSÉ: decoration of metal work by relief designs, formed by beating the metal from the back.

REREDOS: structure behind and above an altar.

RESPOND: half-pier bonded into a wall and carrying one end of an arch.

RETABLE: altarpiece, a picture or piece of carving, standing behind and attached to an altar.

RETICULATION: see Tracery (Fig. 20e).

REVEAL: that part of a jamb (q.v.) which lies between the glass or door and the outer surface of the wall.

RIB-VAULT: see Vault.

ROCOCO: latest phase of the Baroque style, current in most Continental countries between c.1720 and c.1760.

ROLL MOULDING: moulding of semicircular or more than semicircular section.

ROMANESQUE: that style in architecture which was current in the C11 and C12 and preceded the Gothic style (in England often called Norman). (Some scholars extend the use of the term Romanesque back to the C10 or C9.)

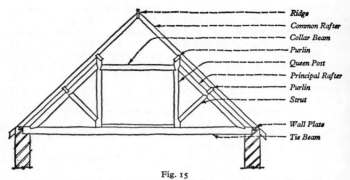

Fig. 15

ROMANO-BRITISH: A some-
what vague term applied to the
period and cultural features of
Britain affected by the Roman
occupation of the C1–5 A.D.

ROOD: cross or crucifix.

ROOD LOFT: singing gallery on
the top of the rood screen,
often supported by a coving.

ROOD SCREEN: *see* Screen.

ROOD STAIRS: stairs to give
access to the rood loft.

ROOF: *Single-framed:* if consisting entirely of transverse
members (such as rafters with
or without braces, collars, tie-
beams, king-posts or queen-
posts, etc.) not tied together
longitudinally. *Double-framed:*
if longitudinal members (such
as a ridge beam and purlins)
are employed. As a rule in such
cases the rafters are divided
into stronger principals and
weaker subsidiary rafters.
Hipped: roof with sloped instead of vertical ends. *Mansard:*
roof with a double slope, the

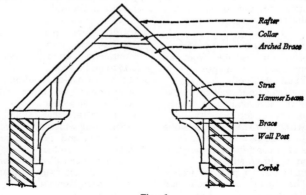

Fig. 16

lower slope being larger and steeper than the upper. *Saddleback:* tower roof shaped like an ordinary gabled timber roof. The following members have special names: *Rafter:* roof-timber sloping up from the wall plate to the ridge. *Principal:* principal rafter, usually corresponding to the main bay divisions of the nave or chancel below. *Wall Plate:* timber laid longitudinally on the top of a wall. *Purlin:* longitudinal member laid parallel with wall plate and ridge beam some way up the slope of the roof. *Tie-beam:* beam connecting the two slopes of a roof across at its foot, usually at the height of the wall plate, to prevent the roof from spreading. *Collar-beam:* tie-beam applied higher up the slope of the roof. *Strut:* upright timber connecting the tie-beam with the rafter above it. *King-post:* upright timber connecting a tie-beam and collar-beam with the ridge beam. *Queen-posts:* two struts placed symmetrically on a tie-beam or collar-beam. *Braces:* inclined timbers inserted to strengthen others. Usually braces connect a collar-beam with the rafters below or a tie-beam with the wall below. Braces can be straight or curved (also called arched). *Hammer-beam:* beam projecting at right angles, usually from the top of a wall, to carry arched braces or struts and arched braces. (*See* Figs. 14, 15, 16.)

ROSE WINDOW (or WHEEL WINDOW): circular window with patterned tracery arranged to radiate from the centre.

ROTUNDA: building circular in plan.

RUBBLE: building stones, not square or hewn, nor laid in regular courses.

RUSTICATION: *rock-faced* if the surfaces of large blocks of ashlar stone are left rough like rock; *smooth* if the ashlar blocks are smooth and separated by V-joints; *banded* if the separation by V-joints applies only to the horizontals.

Saddleback: *see* Roof.

SALTIRE CROSS: equal-limbed cross placed diagonally.

SANCTUARY: (1) area around the main altar of a church (*see* Presbytery); (2) sacred site consisting of wood or stone uprights enclosed by a circular bank and ditch. Beginning in the Neolithic, they were elaborated in the succeeding Bronze Age. The best known examples are Stonehenge and Avebury.

SARCOPHAGUS: elaborately carved coffin.

SCAGLIOLA: material composed of cement and colouring matter to imitate marble.

SCALLOPED CAPITAL: development of the block capital (q.v.) in which the single semi-circular surface is elaborated into a series of truncated cones (Fig. 17).

Fig. 17

SCARP: artificial cutting away of the ground to form a steep slope.

SCREEN: *Parclose screen:* screen separating a chapel from the rest of a church. *Rood screen:* screen below the rood (q.v.), usually at the W end of a chancel.

SCREENS PASSAGE: passage between the entrances to kitchen, buttery, etc., and the screen behind which lies the hall of a medieval house.

SEDILIA: seats for the priests (usually three) on the S side of the chancel of a church.

SEGMENTAL ARCH: see Arch.

SET-OFF: see Weathering.

SEXPARTITE: see Vault.

SGRAFFITO: pattern incised into plaster so as to expose a dark surface underneath.

SHAFT-RING: motif of the C12 and C13 consisting of a ring round a circular pier or a shaft attached to a pier.

SHEILA-NA-GIG: fertility figure, usually with legs wide open.

SILL: lower horizontal part of the frame of a window.

SLATEHANGING: the covering of walls by overlapping rows of slates, on a timber substructure.

SOFFIT: underside of an arch, lintel, etc.

SOLAR: upper living-room of a medieval house.

SOPRAPORTE: painting above the door of a room, usual in the C17 and C18.

SOUNDING BOARD: horizontal board or canopy over a pulpit. Also called Tester.

SPANDREL: triangular surface between one side of an arch, the horizontal drawn from its apex, and the vertical drawn from its springer; also the surface between two arches.

SPERE-TRUSS: roof truss on two free-standing posts to mask the division between screens passage and hall. The screen itself, where a spere-truss exists, was originally movable.

SPIRE: tall pyramidal or conical pointed erection often built on top of a tower, turret, etc. *Broach Spire:* a broach is a sloping half-pyramid of masonry or wood introduced at the base of each of the four oblique faces of a tapering octagonal spire with the object of effecting the transition from the square to the octagon. The *splayed foot spire* is a variation of the broach form found principally in the south-eastern counties. In this form the four cardinal faces are splayed out near their base, to cover the corners, while the oblique (or intermediate) faces taper away to a point. *Needle Spire:* thin spire rising from the centre of a tower roof, well inside the parapet.

SPIRELET: see Flèche.

SPLAY: chamfer, usually of the jamb of a window.

SPRINGING: level at which an arch rises from its supports.

SQUINCH: arch or system of concentric arches thrown across the angle between two walls to support a superstructure, for example a dome (Fig. 18).

SQUINT: a hole cut in a wall or through a pier to allow a view of the main altar of a church from places whence it could not otherwise be seen (also called Hagioscope).

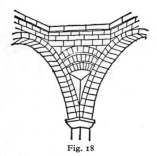

Fig. 18

STALL: carved seat, one of a row, made of wood or stone.

STAUNCHION: upright iron or steel member.

STEEPLE: the tower of a church together with a spire, cupola, etc.

STIFF-LEAF: E.E. type of foliage of many-lobed shapes (Fig. 19).

Fig. 19

STILTED: *see* Arch.

STOREY-POSTS: the principal posts of a timber-framed wall.

STOUP: vessel for the reception of holy water, usually placed near a door.

STRAINER ARCH: arch inserted across a room to prevent the walls from leaning.

STRAPWORK: C16 decoration consisting of interlaced bands, and forms similar to fretwork or cut and bent leather.

STRETCHER: *see* Brickwork.

STRING COURSE: projecting horizontal band or moulding set in the surface of a wall.

STRUT: *see* Roof.

STUCCO: plaster work.

STUDS: the subsidiary vertical timber members of a timber-framed wall.

SWAG: festoon formed by a carved piece of cloth suspended from both ends.

TABERNACLE: richly orna-mented niche or free-standing canopy. Usually contains the Holy Sacrament.

TARSIA: inlay in various woods.

TAZZA: shallow bowl on a foot.

TERMINAL FIGURES (TERMS, TERMINI): upper part of a human figure growing out of a pier, pilaster, etc., which tapers towards the base. *See also* Caryatid, Pilaster.

TERRACOTTA: burnt clay, un-glazed.

TESSELLATED PAVEMENT: mo-saic flooring, particularly Ro-man, consisting of small 'tes-serae' or cubes of glass, stone, or brick.

TESSERAE: *see* Tessellated Pave-ment.

TESTER: *see* Sounding Board.

TETRASTYLE: having four de-tached columns.

THREE-DECKER PULPIT: pulpit with Clerk's Stall below and Reading Desk below the Clerk's Stall.

TIE-BEAM: *see* Roof (Figs. 14, 15).

TIERCERON: *see* Vault (Fig. 21).

TILEHANGING: *see* Slatehanging.

TIMBER-FRAMING: method of construction where walls are built of timber framework with the spaces filled in by plaster

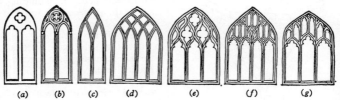

(a)   (b)   (c)   (d)   (e)   (f)   (g)

Fig. 20

or brickwork. Sometimes the timber is covered over with plaster or boarding laid horizontally.

TOMB-CHEST: chest-shaped stone coffin, the most usual medieval form of funeral monument.

TOUCH: soft black marble quarried near Tournai.

TOURELLE: turret corbelled out from the wall.

TRACERY: intersecting ribwork in the upper part of a window, or used decoratively in blank arches, on vaults, etc. *Plate tracery: see* Fig. 20(a). Early form of tracery where decoratively shaped openings are cut through the solid stone infilling in a window head. *Bar tracery:* a form introduced into England *c.*1250. Intersecting ribwork made up of slender shafts, continuing the lines of the mullions of windows up to a decorative mesh in the head of the window. *Geometrical tracery: see* Fig. 20(b). Tracery characteristic of *c.* 1250–1310 consisting chiefly of circles or foiled circles. *Y-tracery: see* Fig. 20(c). Tracery consisting of a mullion which branches into two forming a Y shape; typical of *c.* 1300. *Intersecting tracery: see* Fig. 20(d). Tracery in which each mullion of

a window branches out into two curved bars in such a way that every one of them is drawn with the same radius from a different centre. The result is that every light of the window is a lancet and every two, three, four, etc., lights together form a pointed arch. This treatment also is typical of *c.* 1300. *Reticulated tracery: see* Fig. 20(e). Tracery typical of the early C14 consisting entirely of circles drawn at top and bottom into ogee shapes so that a net-like appearance results. *Panel tracery: see* Fig. 20(f) and (g). Perp tracery, which is formed of upright straight-sided panels above lights of a window.

TRANSEPT: transverse portion of a cross-shaped church.

TRANSOM: horizontal bar across the openings of a window.

TRANSVERSE ARCH: *see* Vault.

TRIBUNE: *see* Gallery.

TRICIPUT, SIGNUM TRICIPUT: sign of the Trinity expressed by three faces belonging to one head.

TRIFORIUM: arcaded wall passage or blank arcading facing the nave at the height of the aisle roof and below the clerestory (q.v.) windows. (*See* Gallery.)

TRIGLYPHS: blocks with vertical

grooves separating the metopes (q.v.) in the Doric frieze (Fig. 12).

TROPHY: sculptured group of arms or armour, used as a memorial of victory.

TRUMEAU: stone mullion (q.v.) supporting the tympanum (q.v.) of a wide doorway.

TUMULUS: *see* Barrow.

TURRET: very small tower, round or polygonal in plan.

TUSCAN: *see* Order.

TYMPANUM: space between the lintel of a doorway and the arch above it.

UNDERCROFT: vaulted room, sometimes underground, below a church or chapel.

UNIVALLATE: of a hill-fort: defended by a single bank and ditch.

UPPER PALAEOLITHIC: *see* Palaeolithic.

VAULT: *Barrel-vault: see* Tunnel-vault. *Cross-vault: see* Groin-vault. *Domical vault:* square or polygonal dome rising direct on a square or polygonal bay, the curved surfaces separated by groins (q.v.). *Fan-vault:* late medieval vault where all ribs springing from one springer are of the same length, the same distance from the next, and the same curvature. *Groin-vault* or *Cross-vault:* vault of two tunnel-vaults of identical shape intersecting each other at r. angles. Chiefly Norman and Renaissance. *Lierne:* tertiary rib, that is, rib which does not spring either from one of the main springers or from the central

boss. Introduced in the C14, continues to the C16. *Quadripartite vault:* one wherein one bay of vaulting is divided into four parts. *Rib-vault:* vault with diagonal ribs projecting along the groins. *Ridge-rib:* rib along the longitudinal or transverse ridge of a vault. Introduced in the early C13. *Sexpartite vault:* one wherein one bay of quadripartite vaulting is divided into two parts transversely so that each bay of vaulting has six parts. *Tierceron:* secondary rib, that is, rib which issues from one of the main springers or the central boss and leads to a place on a ridge-rib. Introduced in the early C13. *Transverse arch:* arch separating one bay of a vault from the next. *Tunnel-vault* or *Barrel-vault:* vault of semicircular or pointed section. Chiefly Norman and Renaissance. (*See* Fig. 21.)

VAULTING SHAFT: vertical member leading to the springer of a vault.

VENETIAN WINDOW: window with three openings, the central one arched and wider than the outside ones. Current in England chiefly in the C17–18.

VERANDA: open gallery or balcony with a roof on light, usually metal, supports.

VESICA: oval with pointed head and foot.

VESTIBULE: anteroom or entrance hall.

VILLA: (1) according to Gwilt (1842) 'a country house for the residence of opulent persons'; (2) Romano-British country houses cum farms, to which the description given in (1)

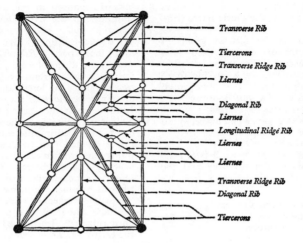

Transverse Rib

Tiercerons
Transverse Ridge Rib
Liernes

Diagonal Rib
Liernes
Longitudinal Ridge Rib
Liernes

Liernes

Transverse Ridge Rib
Diagonal Rib

Tiercerons

Fig. 21

more or less applies. They developed with the growth of urbanization. The basic type is the simple corridor pattern with rooms opening off a single passage; the next stage is the addition of wings. The courtyard villa fills a square plan with subsidiary buildings and an enclosure wall with a gate facing the main corridor block.

VITRIFIED: made similar to glass.

VITRUVIAN OPENING: A door or window which diminishes towards the top, as advocated by Vitruvius, bk. IV, chapter VI.

VOLUTE: spiral scroll, one of the component parts of an Ionic column (*see* Order).

VOUSSOIR: wedge-shaped stone used in arch construction.

WAGON ROOF: roof in which by closely set rafters with

arched braces the appearance of the inside of a canvas tilt over a wagon is achieved. Wagon roofs can be panelled or plastered (ceiled) or left uncovered.

WAINSCOT: timber lining to walls.

WALL PLATE: *see* Roof.

WATERLEAF: leaf shape used in later C12 capitals. The waterleaf is a broad, unribbed, tapering leaf curving up towards the angle of the abacus and turned in at the top (Fig. 22).

Fig. 22

WEALDEN HOUSE: timber-framed house with the hall in the centre and wings projecting only slightly and only on the jutting upper floor. The roof, however, runs through without a break between wings and hall, and the eaves of the hall part are therefore exceptionally deep. They are supported by diagonal, usually curved, braces starting from the short inner sides of the overhanging wings and rising parallel with the front wall of the hall towards the centre of the eaves.

WEATHERBOARDING: overlapping horizontal boards, covering a timber-framed wall.

WEATHERING: sloped horizontal surface on sills, buttresses, etc., to throw off water.

WEEPERS: small figures placed in niches along the sides of some medieval tombs (also called Mourners).

WHEEL WINDOW: *see* Rose Window.

INDEX OF PLATES

INDEX OF ARTISTS

INDEX OF PLACES

COMPLETE LIST OF TITLES
2001

Volumes in the new, larger hardback format are marked (NF). Corrected reprints are not listed.

London 4: North *1st ed. 1998 Bridget Cherry and Nikolaus Pevsner* (NF)

London 5: East and Docklands *1st ed. in progress*

London 6: Westminster *1st ed. in progress*

London 1: The Cities of London and Westminster *1st ed. 1957, 2nd ed. 1962, Nikolaus Pevsner, 3rd ed. 1973 revised Bridget Cherry, being revised and reissued as vols. 1 and 6 above*

London 2: Except the Cities of London and Westminster *1st ed. 1952 Nikolaus Pevsner, being revised and reissued as vols. 2–5 above*

Middlesex *1st ed. 1951 Nikolaus Pevsner, revised and reissued as vols. 3 and 4 above*

Norfolk 1: Norwich and North-East *1st ed. 1962 Nikolaus Pevsner, 2nd ed. 1997 revised Bill Wilson* (NF)

Norfolk 2: North-West and South *1st ed. 1962 Nikolaus Pevsner, 2nd ed. 1999 revised Bill Wilson* (NF)

Northamptonshire *1st ed. 1961 Nikolaus Pevsner, 2nd ed. 1973 revised Bridget Cherry*

Northumberland *1st ed. 1957 Nikolaus Pevsner with Ian A. Richmond, 2nd ed. 1992 revised John Grundy, Grace McCombie, Peter Ryder and Humphrey Welfare* (NF)

Nottinghamshire *1st ed. 1951 Nikolaus Pevsner, 2nd ed. 1979 revised Elizabeth Williamson*

Oxfordshire *1st ed. 1974 Jennifer Sherwood and Nikolaus Pevsner*

Shropshire *1st ed. 1958 Nikolaus Pevsner*

Somerset, North, and Bristol *1st ed. 1958 Nikolaus Pevsner*

Somerset, South and West *1st ed. 1958 Nikolaus Pevsner*

Staffordshire *1st ed. 1974 Nikolaus Pevsner*

Suffolk *1st ed. 1961 Nikolaus Pevsner, 2nd ed. 1974 revised Enid Radcliffe*

Surrey *1st ed. 1962 Ian Nairn and Nikolaus Pevsner, 2nd ed. 1971 revised Bridget Cherry*

Sussex *1st ed. 1965 Ian Nairn and Nikolaus Pevsner*

Warwickshire *1st ed. 1966 Nikolaus Pevsner and Alexandra Wedgwood*

Wiltshire *1st ed. 1963 Nikolaus Pevsner, 2nd ed. 1975 revised Bridget Cherry*

Worcestershire *1st ed. 1968 Nikolaus Pevsner*

Yorkshire: The North Riding *1st ed. 1966 Nikolaus Pevsner*

Yorkshire: The West Riding *1st ed. 1959 Nikolaus Pevsner, 2nd ed. 1967 revised Enid Radcliffe (being revised and reissued as two volumes)*

Yorkshire: York and the East Riding *1st ed. 1972 Nikolaus Pevsner, 2nd ed. 1995 revised David Neave* (NF)

SPECIAL PAPERBACK PUBLICATIONS

London: Docklands *1st ed. 1998, Elizabeth Williamson and Nikolaus Pevsner*

London: The City Churches *1st ed. 1998, Simon Bradley and Nikolaus Pevsner*

Manchester *1st ed. 2001, Clare Hartwell*

Looking at Buildings: the East Riding *1st ed. 1995 (with English Heritage), Hazel Moffat and David Neave*

NOTES